Sebastian Klotz, Philip V. Bohlman,
Lars-Christian Koch (eds.)

Sounding Cities

KlangKulturStudien
SoundCultureStudies

herausgegeben von / edited by

Lars-Christian Koch
und / and
Raimund Vogels

Band / volume 9

LIT

SOUNDING CITIES

Auditory Transformations
in Berlin, Chicago, and Kolkata

edited by

Sebastian Klotz, Philip V. Bohlman,
Lars-Christian Koch

LIT

Cover photos: Abhishek Adhikary, Philip V. Bohlman, and 25films

Publication of this book has been generously funded by the University of Chicago and the Trans-Atlantic Cooperation Program of the Alexander von Humboldt Foundation

Layout and typesetting: Lukas Christensen, Hohenems

This book is printed on acid-free paper.

Bibliografische Information der Deutschen Nationalbibliothek
Die Deutsche Nationalbibliothek verzeichnet diese Publikation in der Deutschen Nationalbibliografie; detaillierte bibliografische Daten sind im Internet über http://dnb.d-nb.de abrufbar.

ISBN 978-3-643-90555-0 (pb)
ISBN 978-3-643-95555-0 (PDF)

A catalogue record for this book is available from the British Library

© LIT VERLAG GmbH & Co. KG Wien,
Zweigniederlassung Zürich 2018
Klosbachstr. 107
CH-8032 Zürich
Tel. +41 (0) 44-251 75 05
E-Mail: zuerich@lit-verlag.ch   http://www.lit-verlag.ch
Distribution:
In the UK: Global Book Marketing, e-mail: mo@centralbooks.com
In North America: International Specialized Book Services, e-mail: orders@isbs.com
In Germany: LIT Verlag Fresnostr. 2, D-48159 Münster
Tel. +49 (0) 2 51-620 32 22, Fax +49 (0) 2 51-922 60 99, e-mail: vertrieb@lit-verlag.de
e-books are available at www.litwebshop.de

In memoriam
Hartmut Häussermann
(1943 – 2011)

CONTENTS

LIST OF FIGURES

ACKNOWLEDGMENTS

This book has been possible because of cooperation and collaboration that stretches across continents and connects cities globally. We gratefully acknowledge the Trans-Atlantic Cooperation Program of the Alexander von Humboldt Foundation in Bonn, which provides financial support for collaborative research when matched by a North American partner, in our case the University of Chicago. Humboldt TransCoop funding supported research in Germany, above all in Leipzig at the University of Leipzig for Sebastian Klotz and his colleagues and students, and in Berlin at the Phonogram Archive of the Ethnology Museum for Lars-Christian Koch and his colleagues and staff. TransCoop funding also enabled funding for fieldwork in Kolkata, especially at the Rabindra Bharati University in Kolkata, where Sanjoy Bandopadhyay and his students worked with us as research and musical partners on the occasion of each visit to Kolkata.

We were also fortunate to receive generous financial support from departments, divisions, centers, and research institutions across the University of Chicago. In particular, we thank the Department of Music and its Chair, Thomas Christensen, the Division of the Humanities and its Dean, Anne W. Robertson, the Committee on Southern Asian Studies and its Director, Dan Arnold, the Chicago Center for Jewish Studies and its Director, David Schloen, and the Franke Institute for the Humanities and its Director, James Chandler. Financial support from the University of Chicago took many forms, ranging from a graduate-student soundscape study of Devon Avenue to two international conferences at the Franke Institute for the Humanities ("Sound Works: Musicians and Media in South Asian Cities" and "Jewish City Music") to two visiting professorships for Lars-Christian Koch at the Franke Institute Center for Disciplinary Innovation to travel fellowships for India for faculty and students to the subvention for the present book. Many thanks to Michael Figueroa for creating the index to this book and to Ameera Nimjee for her careful attention to the page proofs. Lukas Christensen deserves very special thanks for his marvelous editorial and design work, always carried out with insight, criticism, and abundant good humor. Generous funding from the University of Chicago was only possible because it so enriched the community of collaboration in Chicago, whose members we gratefully acknowledge here: Rachel Adelstein, Tarini Bedi, Andrea F. Bohlman, Dipesh Chakrabarty, Sascha Ebeling, Michael Figueroa, Monica Mays Figueroa, Daniel Gough, Travis A. Jackson, Rehanna Kheshgi, Bertie Kibreah, Nisha Kommattam, Aiala Levy, Kaley Mason, Rochona Majumdar, Meredith Aska McBride, Ameera Nimjee, James Nye, Rumya Putcha, Martha Sprigge, Jim Sykes, and Lillian Wohl. My colleagues and I in the New Budapest Orpheum Society, ensemble-in-residence in the Division of the Humanities at the University of Chicago, are grateful for the support for performances in Chicago, as well as for those in Berlin in 2009 and 2013, made possible in part by the MusikSalon Berlin and the Berlin Ethnology Museum.

The Alexander von Humboldt Foundation was a particularly generous supporter of the research and of the book itself. The 2011 symposium that we held in Kolkata was generously supported by the Goethe Institute/Max Mueller Bhavan. Field research in Kolkata was generously coordinated with the assistance of Sanjoy Bandopadhyay, Ustad Allauddin Khan Professor of Instrumental Music at the Rabindra Bharati University, and Founder-Director of the S. M. Tagore Centre for Documentation and Research of Languishing and Obsolescent Musical Instruments (SMTC-DRLOMI). The project partners would like to thank all their research partners, artists, instrument builders, and DJs who were available for interviews. Special thanks to Reimar Volker, formerly Director of the Max Mueller Bhavan in Kolkata during the period of our research, and to Supata Ray and Somjit Das Gupta, without whose hospitality this project could not possibly have evolved the way it has.

This volume is dedicated to the late Hartmut Häussermann, the urban sociologist, independent thinker, activist, and ardent critic of gentrification processes in Berlin and elsewhere. Those who attended the 2011 Kolkata symposium to which he contributed will remember his inspiring contribution and the rich feedback that came from him. Häussermann insisted on the socializing and civilizing effects of the metropolis. Those who joined him on the "confluence of culture" tours in Kolkata will remember his bewilderment in the face of the harsh living conditions, and the creativity of local citizens who were trying to cope. In an apparent outcry of despair, he asked if the city could be organized differently, and if something could be done. We feel the loss of Hartmut Häussermann very deeply.

Berlin and Chicago
November 2017

Welcome from the Goethe Institute

In March 2011, in my capacity as director of the local German cultural institute, the Goethe Institute/Max Mueller Bhavan, which in India also carries the name of the famous German Indologist, I had the pleasure and honor of hosting the international conference "Music as a Medium for Urban Transformation" in Kolkata.

The subject matter proved to be fascinating and fitting for a cultural institute: the notion of music as a universal medium of self-expression and as a means to define identities. This is an important component in the work of an institution active in cultural exchange. In the case of the Goethe Institute, which promotes the idea of mutual dialogue, however, utilizing music as a medium is not confined to the mere presentation of music—of whatever style—from Germany. The Goethe Institute's presence also necessitates actively promoting local scenes, serving as a catalyst, and facilitating exchange and interaction, thus broadening horizons and deepening an understanding of different cultures.

In a sense, musical expression is dependent upon the sites of its practice and performance. These sites enable the coming into being of music and infuse the sites themselves with a unique history and musical biography. This dependence makes these very sites precious both for the history of an institution and to the musical scenes and topographies within which these sites are placed. Throughout its history, the Goethe Institute has demonstrated many examples not only of presenting music, but also of encouraging exchange, especially in an urban context.

I have been fortunate to have worked at Goethe Institutes that have been the focus and breeding ground for musical trends and that have established themselves as spaces for creativity, often over the span of many decades, proving that in a globalized, de-localized world, physical spaces for "real-time" encounters—musical or otherwise—are even more important, especially if they can tap into a rich history.

Having left India in 2011 to serve as the Program Director for East Asia in Seoul, I am now in Istanbul, and I can further attest to the role of the Goethe Institute in interacting with and enriching local urban cultural scenes. In Seoul the local Goethe Institute has played an important role in establishing the first-ever festival of contemporary music, as well as promoting the emergence of SamulNori, a style of Korean dance and drumming that combines the traditional with the modern, now achieving global impact. In Korea, there is a rich musical history and identity drawing from traditional East Asian music, as well as relatively recent influences from the West. The more contemporary scope of music ranges from a tradition of protest music that fueled a democratic revolution in the 1980s to the current concept of "cultural engineering" and "nation branding," which, quite successfully, has led to the spread of a specific brand of popular music, K-pop, into the countries of East Asia and beyond. In this context, music as a medium for self-expression and transformation specifically calls into question the notion of cultural boundaries and identities, for music cannot be confined to national or cultural boundaries. Such musical transformations further underscore the importance of research in music and urban studies.

The conference in Kolkata, which provided the first stage for many of the chapters in this book, provided some fascinating insights into the musical topographies of cities as different and geographically far apart as Berlin, Chicago, and Kolkata. The conference also served to underline the inter-connectivity and common denominators in areas as diverse as club culture, traditional music, heavy metal, experimental and improvised music, and diasporic musical traditions.

I am sure that this book will further the case of research into the fascinating issue of musical expression in an urban context. It already provides new methodological tools, not only to grasp the phenomenon, but also to sharpen the senses and invite a closer look at—deeper appreciation of—the fascinating musical tapestry enveloping us in the cities of the world, as diverse as they are and as far apart they may seem.

Reimar Volker

Preface

You can be so beautifully awful.
—Peter Fox, "Schwarz zu Blau"

Come and show me another city with lifted head
singing so proud to be alive
and coarse and strong and cunning.
—Carl Sandburg, "Chicago"

A city!
I want to go too; take me with you;
to a city.
—Amitav Ghosh, *Sea of Poppies*

Cities sound themselves noisily. They resound with the voices of those who dwell along their streets, speaking in countless languages and singing in disharmonious harmonies. The sounds of the city arise from the consonant tempo of the everyday and from the dissonant rhythm of labor-calibrated lives. The voices of the multitude re-sound the modern Babylon. Their bodies breach the ramparts of the modern Laṅkā. Sounding modernity echoes plaintively and symphonically in the machines that ply the arteries of the city, their din flooding the soundscapes swollen no less by the migrants arriving yesterday and tomorrow. Silence and cacophony sound the city, ironically and melodiously. And the city in turn sounds with a mellifluous counterpoint that defiantly refuses to be silenced.

The many meanings of "sounding" lie at the heart of this book. A city sounds, and it is sounded. At once sounding with active voice and passive voice, the city is never really one or the other. The sounds of the city may be subject or object, but usually they collapse the very boundaries that comfortably shore up one or the other. "Sound" can be a noun, a verb, or an adjective. It can represent a discrete sense—the sound that breaks the silence—or it can serve collectively to overwhelm our senses. Grammatically, sounding can do just about anything we ask of it. In the title of this book, *Sounding Cities*, it derives from active and passive, transitive and intransitive, verb forms. It slides with semantic slipperiness into a space between present participle and gerund. It functions as metaphor and simile, again signaling the spaces of in-betweenness in which one thing "sounds like" another. With so much potential to do so many things, sounding becomes transformative the moment of its coming-into-being, the ontological sounding of its origins. At the moment of sounding, auditory transformation begins.

Cities continuously sound in new ways, their own transformations unleashed from the multiplying moments they sound and that sound them. It is the confluence of these moments in transformations both similar and different that provides the common focus for the essays that fill the present volume. Just as cities sound in new ways, they engender new ways of listening. Sounding and listening are inevitably—we might say, phenomenologically—linked, each a precondition of the other. The linkage between sounding and listening is nowhere denser and more complex than in the city. It is in the city, nonetheless, that the linkage is least isolated, for its capacity to connect collectively is the greatest. It is in search for this greater collectivity that the contributors to this book seek to hear it in three cities, at once different and common, sounding noisily and mellifluously.

Throughout this volume, in ways both similar and different, the contributors combine sounding and listening as a single process, conjoined by the active process in both. The city itself does sound, and it does so as the human collective that occupies the city. The human collective, those who live in the city, do listen, engaging directly with an actively sounding city. The more sounding and listening are linked, the more intensively they activate auditory transformations. Each act of sounding and listening transforms the city. Such are the acts of auditory transformation that form the connective tissue of the essays that follow.

Sounding the city transforms the city. Sounding the city, as the contributors to this book demonstrate, remaps it as a place in which listening takes place. The sounding city transforms urban spaces into an auditory palimpsest of shifting tonotopes (from the Greek, τόνος/τόπος—sound/places). Temporally and historically, sounding and listening move across and among the shifting spaces of the palimpsest, transforming the links that revitalize the past in the present. Rituals return in cycles, sounding the old in the moment of the new. The city is the place of the urban tonotope. Its streets are noisy; the paths between the rural and the urban serve as arteries for the material exchange of sounding objects; the city's sounds transform history into an aural archeology of colony, empire, and nation; the sounding bodies of worker and worshiper chart the place of the everyday.

The urban sounding of space has critically transformed the ways in which we sonically map the three cities in this volume. The sounding spaces modulate as different geographies in the four sections in the main body of the book's chapters. The *musical metropolis* metaphorically forms the theoretical foundation for the book, with theory connecting the various levels of the auditory palimpsest. In the second section the expansive focus of theory turns to the local, the neighborhood, whose sounds are intimate, personal, and familiar, yet powerful because of the connectivity between class, generation, and religion, and noisy when cohabiting *topographies of the neighborhood*. The transformations of sounding cities are auditory also because they are tangible and material. The *interventions and experience of urban space* amplify when sounded in ways that join listening with all other senses. When first made audible, the *trajectories beyond the global city* may seem paradoxical, for they decenter the city as a place. They expose poverty and prejudice, and they sound the city as a place of danger.

The destabilization of the global notwithstanding, the city refuses to be silenced, for it sounds ever more noisily in the common spaces of the collective, among them the streets—MG Road in Kolkata and Devon Avenue in Chicago—the photo essays that so noisily frame this volume, and with which we seek to listen to and capture the soundings that make Berlin, Chicago, and Kolkata audible.

Philip V. Bohlman, Sebastian Klotz, and Lars-Christian Koch

Introduction: Music and Urban Transformation

Sebastian Klotz

Sounding Cities gathers methodological excursions into urban spaces and into musical conjunctivities in comparative perspective. The editors and contributors have adopted a comparative perspective in order to stimulate questions. The approaches we have taken to the sounding city result from our response to the absence of a sufficient database and the difficulties that arise when seeking to generate one. The field research that does exist has hitherto been specific and hard to generalize for comparative study. To respond to this situation, we encouraged the experimental methodologies in the present volume, which take into account the openness and connectivity of urban social processes. Our key hypothesis, according to which music is a catalyst and driving force that constituently models urban spaces and experiences, has proved to be productive to the extent that it opened research vistas that usually were less commonly explored in the traditional perspectives applied to studying *music and the city*.

It has been our intention to range across musical genres, generations, styles, and scenes. Over the course of the Alexander von Humboldt Foundation TransCoop project that supported our research and during the years of collaboration with the contributors to *Sounding Cities*, we encountered the dynamics of Chicago's neighborhoods, the rural/metropolitan commerce in Kolkata and West Bengal, and Berlin's re-metropolization. We engaged with three global cities in periods of transition: Kolkata, thus far, has been saved from global investments, and has accordingly been able to foster its own version of a musically alert metropolis. Berlin continues to cultivate a sense of subculture that is currently seeking balance with the rising tide of investments from the real-estate market. Although Berlin's responses lead to localized gentrification, investors pride themselves in Berlin and its subcultural creativity. The referendum about the future use of the former ground of the inner-city airport Tempelhof, the proliferation of guerrilla gardening, and the popularity of car-sharing signal new forms of participation and non-conformist behavior requiring negotiation with new options offered by the service industries.

In recent years Chicago has been experiencing rapid change, also manifest in the dynamics of urban development and investments in the city's cultural life (e.g., several expansions of the famous Art Institute of Chicago and the planned construction of the Obama Presidential Library and Museum). Chicago has never questioned its own image as a powerful metropolitan city dedicated to growth. In a recent development, the sustainable support of the arts (corporate, foundation, and government supporters) has been ranked high on the city's agenda, while the wide range of internationally renowned music and film festivals that seek close contact with its immigrant, ethnic, and cultural communities. The sustainability of niche cultures and the balance of non-profit and for-profit arts organizations are important challenges that Chicago and Berlin will have to meet in the next decades. On a smaller scale, in terms of financial turnover, not in terms of social and cultural urgency, sustainability also affects Kolkata, as Patrick Ghose's chapter on the Metal Pally scene in the present volume makes evident.

Music can flesh out lifestyle, nostalgia, and diaspora identity. Music making and music consumption are ways of *making the city*. They co-constitute and transcend the city simultaneously. Music is perhaps the most compelling form of expression and social adaptation in the urban arena. Due to the complexity and, at times, impossibility of isolating musical processes from other urban processes, the catalytic function of music cannot be proven in every case. More important, the potential of music and musical practice to open up almost every aspect of urban life and its transformation is illustrated by the diverse, yet intersecting, case studies in the chapters that follow. Place and local tradition matter to a remarkable extent, despite the mediation of high technology, and places, therefore, retain their anchoring function. Music connects cultural scenes and the urban imagination across city limits, and it does so in a highly selective manner, adapted to specific needs, interests, and motivations. Music can simultaneously generate an abstract expression of the local, while enhancing all that expands the local to the soundscape of the city.

* * *

The chapters in this book are organized under four thematic sections, with additional complementary materials. **Bruno Nettl**, one of the founders of the discipline of urban ethnomusicology, opens the first section ("The Musical Metropolis") by recalling the role of ethnomusicology in the exploration of the metropolis. He points to the fact that the urbaneness of immigrant music communities had historically been overlooked because such communities were regarded as isolated entities that were different from the world surrounding them, understood by earlier scholars as the "authentic norm." Only relatively recently did immigrant communities and their effects on a city's musical life move into focus. By addressing ethnomusicology's shift of focus from an almost exclusively rural setting in early fieldwork to the urban, Nettl touches upon a theme that runs through many of the chapters: the interplay of the rural and the urban, which gains new urgency under trans-urban and trans-cultural conditions. Voicing the conviction that music has become emblematic of the interrelations among cultures in an urban context, Nettl confirms an important hypothesis of the TransCoop project in this volume, characterizing the ways in which the city has become a critical cultural norm for ethnomusicology today.

The normativity of the city is equally relevant to the urban sociologist, **Rolf Lindner**, who further intensifies this notion by paraphrasing the metropolis as a total cultural fact. The constructedness of the metropolis is intimately tied to the imagination that fleshes out the construct. Various metropolitan cities may mobilize different narratives, but the fact that the narratives emerge from the metropolis renders them similar. The transformation that Lindner observes represents an important anchor that needs to be interpreted both as a part of a symbolic narrative and as a material and social process. The metropolis is imagined, and indeed functions, as a space of possibilities. Although the extent to which cities manage to realize these possibilities may differ, the narrative is shared across metropolitan areas worldwide. Lindner's critical recognition of the extent to which the metropolis is the most important cultural medium of society again highlights the methodological challenge in addressing the metropolis. Far beyond the visible institutions, traditions, and communication media in the city, the metropolis is the site for the mediations that, in their totality, we call culture.

In **Sebastian Klotz**'s chapter the concept of musical conjunctivity is discussed against the backdrop of trans-metropolitan musical agency. Klotz attempts to articulate a musical phenomenology, albeit rudimentary, of trans-cultural situations that place particular emphasis on musically driven imagined, moral, and real geographies, ranging from Kolkata to Berlin and beyond.

In the second section of the book ("Topographies of the Neighborhood") the contributors shift their focus to the urban confluence of the local and the global. No other recent popular-music practice has dominated the city narratives of Chicago and Berlin more than house music and techno, electronic dance music (EDM) in its many forms. In her account of a makeshift club on Berlin's Spree River, Bar25, **Sonja Rippert** draws our attention to the remarkable fact that, for the first time since World War II, a cultural emblem was coined in the sonic and auditory cultures of Berlin with the promise of better working conditions (post-1945 West German labor immigration campaigns had employed other cultural and political tropes). While a growing number of mobile and global club-goers, referred to by Tobias Rapp as "Easyjetsetters" (2009), have come to represent a growing share of Berlin's tourism industry since the mid-1990s, the club scene itself, with its laid-back atmosphere, lives for the moment and establishes an escapist temporal frame separated from the daily routine of the city. With its provisional sociality Bar25 expresses the visions of cosmopolitan youths who prefer to keep things in limbo and resist conformist behavior. Club-goers sport a feeling of negligence, while fully acknowledging the impossibility of extending the experience.[1] The provisional na-

---

1 Sabine Vogt (2005) studied the club-related lived-in worlds of Berlin's urban youth from the late 1990s to early 2000s, identifying the emergence of different ideals af-

ture of the attitude struck home when Bar25 lost its license, and the owner terminated the contract. Such problems have a familiar ring in Kolkata's heavy metal music scene (see Ghose in the present volume). These phenomena raise the question of how to manage inner-city areas and maintain the integrity of the sites in which urban musical practice takes place.

Narratives of musical globalization tend to level individual differences in concrete situations of appropriation. Heavy metal music, due to its stereotyped gender profile, robust *habitus*, and would-be poetic lyrics seems an unlikely candidate for committed glocalization. In his chapter the Kolkata music activist and journalist, **Patrick S. L. Ghose**, explores a scene located at the outskirts of Kolkata, but immediately connected in the city's imaginary landscape to Bengali heavy metal music. Ghose focuses on a post-2000 development (as in the case of Bar25 in Rippert's chapter), with political, social, and biographical aspects playing into the formation of a scene struggling for acceptance. In contrast to Bar25, which provides a site to those who see a space where professional prospects play no role, the Naktala scene is the product of frustration among Kolkata's youth. The struggle for recognition of their musical expertise, held in high esteem in Hindustani classical tradition, rarely receives respect in the popular and independent music sectors. For those moving within the urban music scene of Kolkata, the musicians of subcultural Metal Pally become part of a metal-related imaginary that embraces all branches of the visible metal retailers and hawkers, ranging from full-length tram tracks to miniature nails, all on display and ready to be sold in the metal area of the city. The simultaneous familiarity with and alienation from the city that marks Metal Pally is emblematic of the contested projections and actual social experiences that lie behind such attributions.

In the third section of *Sounding Cities* ("Interventions and the Experience of Urban Space") the contributors discuss artistic projects that carry trans-metropolitan relevance and pinpoint the productive irritations

---

ter 2005, when it became clear the real-estate investment would threaten affordable housing and club life in the city center. She investigated the ways in which individual consumer hedonism, propelled by social media, would increasingly dominate other social and cultural ideals.

among otherwise smooth and accepted cultural gestures. The forms of intervention and experience examined in the third section unfold primarily after they have appeared in the surprising situations and contexts explored in the section's chapters.

Giving material expression to the emphasis on situatedness that runs through this volume, the urbanologist and improvisational musician **Christopher Dell** took to the streets of Kolkata to perform his music. For his situated improvisation Dell uses the only available vibraphone in Kolkata, which had survived the heyday of jazz in the West Bengal capital. In his physical and auditory intervention, he mimics the improvised strategy of street hawkers by setting up his vibraphone at various focal points of Kolkata, musically testing the viability of an informal economy in music making and improvised public listening. The project surpasses the pop-up and flash-mob events so fashionable in Western cities, employing instead critical self-reflection on what constitutes the musical materiality of urban spaces. Borne by sympathy with the ecology of illegal urban hawking, Dell performs as a self-authorized artist, actively seeking responses from bystanders. By inviting all sorts of interaction, he strengthens the co-evolutionary process of music making rather than assuming the usual presentational format.[2] Fully aware that symmetry could not be achieved, Dell approaches the city and its citizens with respect, allowing himself to be taken by surprise in this "metropolis of non-determinacy."[3] Through improvisatory ethnography, Dell temporarily alters various urban spaces, adding a new perceptual and, perhaps, political layer to the dense public intercourse in the metropolis.[4]

Political momentum plays an equally important role in the chapter by the theater, dance, and performance historian **Patrick Primavesi**. He analyzes the deployment of parallel cities, that is, the synchronization of large

---

2   The project has been documented on the DVD *Kolkata Monodosis: Interventions in Temporary Public Spaces*, funded by the Goethe Institute/Max Mueller Bhavan in Kolkata (Dell n.d.).

3   The statement was made in passing by the philosopher-pianist Slava Senyshyn during his 2013 visit to Kolkata (Senyshyn 2013).

4   For an ethnographic intervention of a different kind, using ethnomusicological fieldwork with street musicians in Berlin, see Nowakowski 2016.

cities, outside the realm of commerce and the traffic of goods and capital that have been driving forces for the increasing interaction within large, networked cities. Instead, he follows artistic projects that turn to sound-based socialities and to auditory perceptions running counter to the paths of global capital and experience. Instead, through unexpected participatory forms and interventionist practices, the projects intervene to counteract regimes of control in the era of call centers, surveillance technologies, and corporate sonic branding. It is remarkable how prominent the audio sphere features in these projects, which seek to apply sensitivity, despite the costs of globalization, by coupling global cities in innovative contexts. The mediating role of Kolkata, furthermore, is highlighted and confirmed by one of the projects Primavesi describes, Rimini Protokoll's *Call Cutta in a Box*,[5] which also featured Berlin in a series of international performances. Music resonates across the theater of parallel cities. To engage the hidden audio-governmentality that global players engender, however, we need participatory interventions that offer alternative motivations and experiences, necessary if parallel cities are to come into being.

The soundscapes of trans-national musics and the rural-urban continuum provide the themes connecting the chapters of the fourth section ("Trajectories beyond the Global City"). The interdependence of diasporic cultures is the subject of **Philip V. Bohlman**'s chapter, which seeks an integrative view of Jewish music and South Asian music in urban settings where they are often not considered. Similar to Rolf Lindner's conviction about the city as cultural norm and to Bruno Nettl's view of music cultures becoming emblematic of a city's culture, Bohlman couples the diasporic narrative with processes of professionalization that lend musicians, singers, and instrument makers credibility and agency so they might be amalgamated into the new, larger collective of the entire metropolis. Musical traditions thus make up the urban self-image, thereby constituting the city. Whereas legal negotiations rarely become tangible, music in public and semi-public display, in private and collective worship, represents a shared aspect of expressing culture. Bohlman argues, moreover,

---

5 Protokoll was invited to Kolkata by the Goethe Institute/Max Mueller Bhavan in 2004 which also supported the TransCoop project from which the present volume grew.

that Jewish music throughout the world becomes a medium of diasporic negotiation vis-à-vis so-called host cultures (a survey of Kolkata's various religious and ethnic communities can be found in Banerjee, Gupta, and Mukherjee 2009). The carefully reconstructed, intersecting historical trajectories betray the one-dimensional narratives of origins that some believe serve diasporic cultures trying to stabilize themselves. These cultures unfold as a dynamic that not only includes intercourse with the majority culture, but also that stretches toward other urban communities in the diaspora. These interconnections transcend the municipal powers of a single metropolis. Faith and diasporic identity made tangible via music thus function as pluralizing agents within a city and across city networks.

The connectivity of music and musical practices can be accessed not only in trans-global music scenes, but also in the seemingly neat and isolated space of a music shop. In a pioneering essay, the Berlin ethnomusicologist, museologist, and sitar player, **Lars-Christian Koch**, reconstructs the genealogy of a music shop in Kolkata, drawing the reader to the shop's close dependence on political and economic conditions. Although Koch focuses on the music instruments, their manufacture, and modification over many years, their distribution and repair provide evidence for the deep integration into Kolkata's social and cultural history, ranging from considerable patronage during the era of the Nawab to the late twentieth-century artists. These musicians built an international reputation, all the while buying their instruments from the Kanailal shop on Upper Chitpur Road, a major artery that transverses Kolkata from north to south. Koch lays the groundwork for a wider social history of musical instruments and of instrument making in Bengal. As basic parts and engravings are being manufactured in the rural areas surrounding Kolkata, their makers bring them to the city along hidden trade and supply routes for instrument builders in the twenty-first century. As a consequence, musical instruments first acquire the materiality of the rural, but then undergo transformation to a new materiality that expresses an urban imaginary.

The history of musical identity connecting Assamese in India to Assamese in diaspora is addressed by the ethnomusicologist **Rehanna Kheshgi**. An underlying thread relevant to many chapters in this book is the trajectory of music in managing uncertainties of social status, either in the rites of passage accompanying adulthood and economic independence (Bar25), in the struggle of acceptance for Kolkata's upstart heavy metal musicians, or in the negotiations of diasporic communities. By reviewing the critical role of dance and ritual performance of the spring Bihu festival in Assamese identity making, Kheshgi opens a panoramic view that stretches from Guwahati, the capital of Assam, to Kolkata, Delhi, London, and Chicago. Assamese identity becomes visible in the Bihu festival as musical practices configure inter-metropolitan relations, sometimes affirming, at other times bypassing the usual flow of commerce and migration. Bihu is surrounded by tensions that can be encountered from performances and recordings in Kolkata to the public presentation of Assamese cultural identity in Chicago. Traditional genres evoking the tea harvest and close connections with the natural habitat, therefore, travel from rural Assam to the world's big cities, stressing another version of the rural-urban exchange and a sense of diaspora.

Kaley Mason addresses empathetic musicality as a means of reaching trans-cultural audiences in his biographical study of Sandip Burman, a tabla player and teacher from Durgapur, West Bengal, and Chicago. Burman was trained in Kolkata, but has based his global performance network in Chicago for many years. Mason situates Burman's creative self-authorization within the framework of music as labor and as a form of international, highly mobile artistry. With the demise of hereditary musical brotherhood models from the past, individual musicians chart specific pathways that are marked by institutional, bureaucratic, administrative, economic, entrepreneurial, and cultural frictions. The pedagogical outreach into rural areas, on a worldwide scale, which Burman and his Chicago-based manager have developed, makes it possible to see the metropolis in a new light. It is the musicians who bring about urban transformations and who establish temporary inter-urban sites by using metropolitan spaces as hubs for their professional activities. Cosmopolitan mobility emerges as a prerequisite to secure empathetic musicality. Musicality does not emerge seamlessly out of the networks that coalesce around the diffusion of Indian music, but rather is only possible because of the high personal costs accompanying them. Empathetic musicality seems to be a viable strategy to secure individual agency in a globalized world-music market that increasingly comprises not only CDs and concerts, but also highly specialized coursework and teaching packages.

The core chapters in this book are framed by two photo essays that complement the interventionist spirit of Christopher Dell's performance in public spaces and the protocol tradition of everyday life as practiced by the Chicago School of Urban Sociology (see, e.g., the classic study, Park 1925). The essays are dedicated to two phenomena that eloquently illustrate the connectedness of urban and musical processes: the famous institution of Kolkata's wedding bands, and the remarkable confluence of cultural traditions on Chicago's Devon Avenue. Similar to the model of craft guilds, wedding bands offer their services through personal advertising, selling their services along a major Kolkata thoroughfare, and expecting to land a commission. **Abhishek Adhikary**, a local musician and graduate from Rabindra Bharati University, together with **Philip V. Bohlman**, has been observing how the largely Muslim bands from the Indian state of Bihar remake urban topography through their performances at winter Hindu weddings. Adhikary and Bohlman focus on a professional group, acting in public, selling no goods other than their musical skills. It opens paths for further research in order to understand their recruitment schemes, strategies to secure musical standards, choices of repertory, internal social structure, licenses, and privileges.

The South Asian diaspora in Chicago as it displays itself on Devon Avenue has been captured by **Lars-Christian Koch** and **Philip V. Bohlman** in the second photo essay. Smells, images, and sounds coalesce into something that is tied to Chicago as a place and at the same time transcends it. The sounds and sites of music on Devon Avenue open possibilities for diasporic enculturation, enabling South Asians in Chicago to feel at home, confirming their new Illinois identity while allowing them to transform their Asian origins.

The TransCoop project includes plans for a projected website, which would map patterns of musical activity across Kolkata from ca. 2010 to 2012.

* * *

During the course of the TransCoop project and the preparation of *Sounding Cities* the editors and contributors have returned again and again to the questions, Why Berlin, Chicago, and Kolkata? And why music? The chapters that follow examine many possible answers to those questions, answers that reveal both striking similarities and distinctive differences among the three cities. No answer, however, emerges more often as a leitmotif in the project and the book than modernity. Berlin, Chicago, and Kolkata are all modern cities, and the making of their modernity owes much to the ways in which music has sounded them. When we describe the three cities as modern, we refer to very specific historical facts. Calcutta's history as a city begins first in the final decade of the seventeenth century, when the East India Company developed the city's potential as a port; Chicago was incorporated only in the 1830s, also because of its potential as a hub for commerce; the settlements that Berlin claims as its origins are older, but it was not until the rise of the Prussian empire in the eighteenth century that Berlin truly became a city, indeed, long after most of Germany's other cities, large and small.

The rise of Berlin, Chicago, and Kolkata, above all in the nineteenth century, depended on modernity, and in many ways shaped what we how understand modernity to be. Each of the three cities, for example, has played a dominant role in the history of rail transportation. The rail network that stretches from Kolkata across India and South Asia remains the largest in the world even in the twenty-first century. The rail transportation that brings North America's natural resources to Chicago have made it "nature's metropolis" (Cronon 1991). Berlin's aggressive plan to build its *Hauptbahnhof* (main train station) on the former no man's land separating East and West Berlin uses transportation to locate the city at the epicenter of the New Europe. Modernity is surely a condition that opens the spaces of the parallel cities examined throughout this book.

Music has announced and enunciated the modernity of Berlin, Chicago, and Kolkata, metaphorically sounding them into existence. Chicago lends its name to jazz, blues, and the roots of electronic dance music (EDM), known as "house." Kolkata is writ large and small across Hindustani classical music, not only distinguishing the genealogy of musicians, the *gharānās* (also glossed as "styles" or "stylistic houses"), but also laying claim to the city as the harmonium-making capital of the world. Classical symphonic music, cabaret, hip-hop, and EDM map Berlin's history onto the city itself, in many ways becoming synonymous with the city. Cityscape and soundscape define and transform each other. As the contributors to *Sounding Cities* have discovered through the historical and ethnographic research that fills the following chapters, musicians fill the streets of all three cities. Across the cities and across the world, music enhances the claim musicians make to Berlin, Chicago, and Kolkata, transforming them into the cities sounding from the pages that follow.

Website

During the TransCoop project, a database with information on some 589 music events was collected and for the first time in urban music research covers both classical and vernacular music activity in the Kolkata metropolitan area. The database has been organized as a website that can be accessed online at https://www.musikundmedien.hu-berlin.de/de/musikwissenschaft/trans/sounding_cities.

References

Banerjee, Himadri, Nilanjana Gupta, and Sipra Mukherjee. 2009. *Calcutta Mosaic: Essays and Interviews on the Minority Communities of Calcutta.* New Delhi: Anthem Press India.

Cronon, William. 1991. *Nature's Metropolis: Chicago and the Great West.* New York: W. W. Norton.

Dell, Christopher. n.d. *Kolkata Monodosis: Interventions in Temporary Public Spaces.* Kolkata: Goethe Institute/Max Mueller Bhavan, DVD.

Nowakowski, Mark. 2016. *Straßenmusik in Berlin: Zwischen Lebenskunst und Lebenskampf. Eine musikethnologische Feldstudie.* Bielefeld: transcript.

Park, Robert E. 1925. *The City.* Chicago: University of Chicago Press.

Rapp, Tobias. 2009. *Lost and Sound: Berlin, Techno und der Easyjetset.* Frankfurt a. M.: Suhrkamp.

Senyshyn, Slava. 2013. Personal communication with the author.

Vogt, Sabine. 2005. *Clubräume—Freiräume: Musikalische Lebensentwürfe Jugendlicher in den Jugendkulturen Berlins.* Kassel: Bärenreiter.

Photo Essay: The MG Road Wedding Bands—Puja, Paradox, and Passage on a Kolkata Street

Abhishek Adhikary and Philip V. Bohlman

> It was in the Jewish Museum [of Berlin], on the second floor,
> that I understood that it was the banality of modern man that
> gave me most pleasure and most moved me. This explains,
> to a certain extent maybe, why I introduce visiting friends to
> neighbourhoods in Calcutta when they ask to see the city.
> It's here that the particular history I'm speaking of resided,
> and still persists in an afterlife.
> —Amit Chaudhuri, *Calcutta: Two Years in the City*

Saraswatī Puja is a time of new beginnings in Kolkata. Depending on the Hindu calendar, the mid-winter period of devotion to and celebration of the goddess of music, knowledge, art, and science marks the passage from the darkest month of January to the lengthening days of West Bengal's early spring in February. According to tradition, Saraswatī Puja also gives way to the wedding season in Kolkata, an extended period during which it is auspicious to marry. It is also during the Bengali wedding season that the neighborhood of north Kolkata stretching along Mahatma Gandhi Road, known locally simply as MG Road, undergoes a transformation to the central market place for the planning and performance of wedding music. A single stretch of road, with many intersecting arteries, turns into an urban musical marketplace. From the end of Saraswatī Puja until the spring Holi

Festival, couples planning to marry, together with their families, descend upon MG Road, where they meet the wedding musicians who will craft the repertories and performances of music for the complex rite of passage that accompanies a Hindu wedding. The music can be intimate and public, Bengali or Western, traditional or cosmopolitan, all somehow fitting the multiple avatars of Saraswatī, symbolized by the vīṇa she holds in one set of her many arms. The MG Road Wedding Bands remap the urban thoroughfare into a musical world unto itself, the city streets ritually sounding Kolkata's passage from past to future. It is this passage that we document through the photo essay that follows.

Colonial Pasts and Paradoxes (Figures 1–4)

First encounters with an MG Road wedding band generally create the impression that one has taken a wrong turn, not only down the city street, but also through the chapters of Kolkata's history as the long-standing capital city of the British Raj. Surely, the military look of the bands in the first group of photos would have dismayed the MG Road's namesake, who, instead, sought to forsake symbols of violence in the creation of modern India. The historical photographs we witness here are not, in fact, atavistic, and the narrative arc that stretches across the entire photo essay displays a surprising degree of unity. Musical influences from outside South Asia have historically contributed to the changing instrumentaria of musical practices from folk traditions to the classical repertories of Hindustani and Karnatak music, where harmoniums and violins have undergone thorough processes of Indianization.

The colonial and wedding bands in these photographs, however, reveal a different route toward a more variegated or truncated Indianization. On one level, the brass band itself remains suspended between a vestige and a legacy. In the twenty-first century, Suzel Reily and Katherine Brucher remind us, the brass band has become a truly global phenomenon (Reily and Brucher 2013). The question that the MG Road wedding bands raise, however, is the extent to which their musical practices actually effect a rupture with the colonial past because they have so completely made the brass band their own. MG Road itself becomes a site for ritualizing the

subaltern. The symbolic passage between the army band in the first photograph and the military trappings for the wedding band in the fourth
represents the remaking of history and a reclaiming of the past for local
use on MG Road. In twenty-first-century Kolkata, the brass bands make
their own traditions, and they do so along a street that enables them to
locate the history of the present in Kolkata.

Rites and Rights of Labor (Figures 5–8)

The musicians who play in MG Road wedding bands are not from Kolkata,
or even from West Bengal. For the most part, they come from the Indian
state of Bihar, and they themselves have no religious or family connections
to Hinduism in Kolkata. They are Muslims, and they speak a variety of
languages and dialects—Hindi, Bhojpuri, Maithili—but rarely Bangla. As
musician-laborers, they appear on MG Road as Saraswatī Puja comes to
a close and they depart for Bihar as Holi approaches. Their trade both is
and is not like that of many Kolkata residents who might receive the label
"itinerant": They depend on the city for their livelihoods, but they live
much of the year elsewhere. Amit Chaudhuri writes of the omnipresence
of laborers from Bihar in Kolkata thus:

> But what of the Bihari? On Park Street and Free School Street, and in other
> parts of the city, he is everywhere, leaning out of a taxi window, eyes glazed,
> buying gutka from a vendor (who's also, possibly, Bihari) to keep himself go-
> ing for the rest of the day; or selling chanachur masala in front of a mall;
> engaged in small trade or the perennial construction work; living apart from
> his family, then mysteriously withdrawing to his des for a month. (Chaudhuri
> 2013, 51–52)

The Biharis whose labors fill the MG Road wedding season are, therefore,
both of Kolkata and not of Kolkata. When they are in the city, they play
in wedding bands; when they return to Bihar, they play other music and
have other jobs.

The musicians in the second quartet of photographs illustrate many of
the dimensions of the labor of playing in MG Road wedding bands. Musicians sit on benches within or on chairs before the small shops lined with
instruments and uniforms. Prospective wedding parties walk along MG

Road, stopping at the shop to negotiate with the manager of a band, who gladly shows photos of past wedding performances, as well as the different types of uniforms a band could don (in figure 5, for example, Abhishek Adhikary meets with Mohammad Allauddin, owner of the well-known Star Band). When the wedding party comes to an agreement with the band, negotiation of the repertory begins. The musicians are also highly skilled laborers, capable of learning in a matter of a day or two the music provided, usually on CDs or DVDs, by the wedding party. Collectively, the band members learn through oral tradition, listening again and again to the recordings and memorizing their contents so that they suit the needs of the musical repertories and rituals requested of them.

Urban Passage (Figures 9–12)

MG Road itself plays a significant role in the urban transformation of the wedding season. The shops stretch densely along the road, minuscule but immaculate in the ways they display their wares. The signs advertising the different bands—the Mahboob Band, the Calcutta Band, the Azan Hindustan Band, the Yousuf Band, to name some of the more famous—adorn the shops, proliferating through the explosion of color that typifies urban streets in India. The shops are seldom able to contain the instruments and the musicians who will eventually perform the weddings, so many of them occupy the street itself (one can scarcely speak of sidewalks). There is a seductive tension between the ways individual shops open toward the street, drawing prospective wedding parties into them, and the musicians who must be present so that, when the contract begins to take shape, they can model uniforms or provide a taste of the music the wedding party can expect for the substantial price it will be expected to pay.

MG Road itself plays a distinctive role in the passage from the everyday to the wedding ritual. The musical and ritual wares of the shops spill into the street itself. Bands expand their territory by using the median fence separating the eastbound and westbound lanes of MG Road as a place to dry uniforms (see figure 10). Or is this a different kind of display, a means whereby the street itself becomes a zone for marking the dimensions of ritual? The density of uniforms and signs along MG Road announces itself as excess, over-abundance. Passing along the road becomes more and more difficult, forcing one to step around uniformed musicians and into the shops offering fantastically imaginative musical wares.

Ritual Performance (Figures 13–16)

The passage along MG Road during Kolkata's wedding season ineluctably leads to the ritual performance of the wedding. The road itself establishes the course of the ritual process, the rite of passage in the sacred sense. Kolkata wedding parties travel to MG Road in search of the music that will accompany them as they undertake one of the most important transitions in their lives. The decision to engage an MG Road wedding band leads the party to embark along a path in which the music they request becomes their own. Daily wages remain relatively meager—Delhi band members receive only 300 rupees daily, plus room and board (Sharma 2014)—but for the wedding season the profession of musician replaces that of manual labor. One might expect the bands to play but a dispassionate, accompany-ing role, reproducing recorded music to please those who have contracted their services. The music of the wedding bands, however, is anything but dispassionate. Like the city in which it is performed, it undergoes a process of transformation. The professionalism of the musicians is also crucial to the intimacy and ecstasy with which they invest their performance. As the rite of passage itself passes through its many liminal stages, the band joins the wedding party in such a way that they share the wedding music. It is that sharing, rendered efficacious when musicians from another place and religion momentarily make ritual happen musically, that leads the wed-ding party through the wedding ritual, completing the rite of passage that had begun days before on Mahatma Gandhi Road in north Kolkata.

References

Chaudhuri, Amit. 2013. *Calcutta: Two Years in the City*. New York: Alfred A. Knopf.
Reily, Suzel Ana, and Katherine Brucher, eds. 2013. *Brass Bands of the World: Militarism, Colonial Legacies, and Local Music Making*. Farnham, UK: Ashgate.
Sharma, Manoj. 2014. "Meet the Capital's Band Baaja Baaraat Men." *Hindustan Times*, De-cember 14, Metro Section: 4.

Figure 1. Historical photo of an army band in Kolkata.

Figure 2. Colonial Star Band.

Figure 3. Punjab Band.

Figure 4. Modern military band.

Figure 5. Mohammad Allauddin (seated left) and Abhishek Adhikary.

Figure 6. Musicians and instruments in an MG Road wedding band shop.

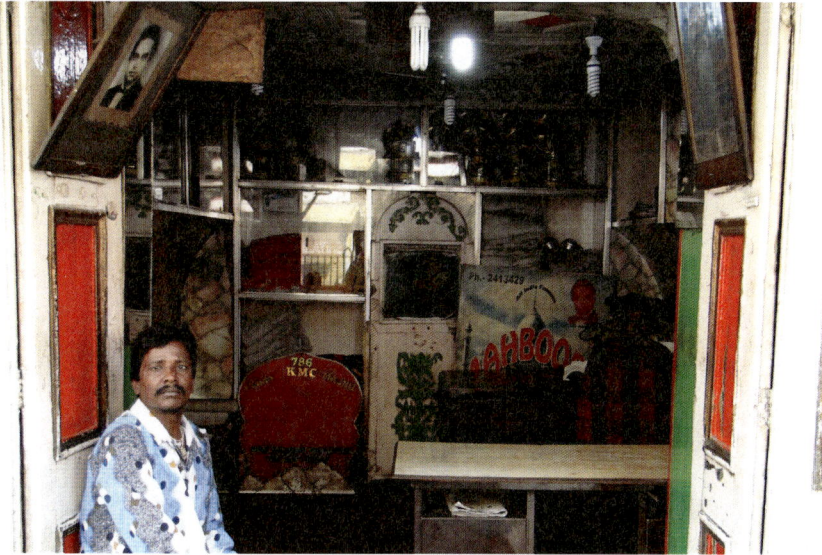

Figure 7. Shop of the Mahboob Band.

Figure 8. Members of the Azan Band.

Figure 9. Exterior of the shop of the Calcutta Band.

Figure 10. Uniforms drying on MG Road.

Figure 11. Uniformed musicians along MG Road.

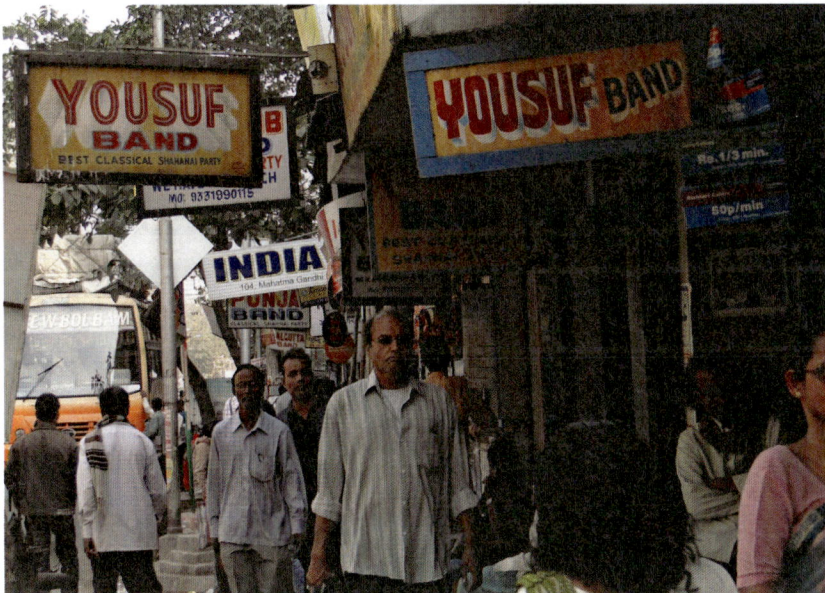

Figure 12. Exterior of the Yousuf Band shop.

Figure 13. Bagpipe band.

Figure 14. Azad Hindustan Band.

Figure 15. Napping musicians on MG Road.

Figure 16. Wedding performance.

I
The Musical Metropolis

1

Contemplating Urban Culture in Ethnomusicology: A Personal Perspective

Bruno Nettl

Having devoted over sixty years of my life to ethnomusicology, I have found it interesting to contemplate what has happened in this long period, in the field as a whole, but more particularly in my own experience. The most prominent conclusion has to be that I have had second thoughts about so many things, that I have changed my beliefs and attitudes to positions quite opposite to those I had around 1950, when I was a student. The positions of the field have been virtually reversed from those seemingly held by my main teacher, George Herzog (1901–1983), and his contemporaries, particularly those whose roots go back to the research and teachings of Erich M. von Hornbostel (1877–1935) and his students, the group of scholars sometimes loosely referred to as the "Berlin School." One area in which this is particularly the case concerns the role of cities in the history of ethnomusicology, and in my own life of study.

The gradual inclusion of studies in urban music, or rather, the urban component of music, is related to the concept of authenticity—once an important criterion for judging research—and its changing character and role in ethnomusicology. One of the questions shared, I believe, by all of the earlier comparative musicologists was, What actually is or was "the" music that belonged to a particular society? It would be assumed that a society would have both "authentic" and "inauthentic" music. Herzog must have come to his concern for authenticity from a musician he idolized, Béla Bartók, who, in collecting Hungarian and other East European folk songs, wanted to be sure that he found, and presented, the songs that were the true heritage of the villagers, not some recent import, not something concocted by urban composers, not something developed as a result of modernized contacts. This attitude, however, was prevalent not only among comparative musicologists and folk-music scholars before about 1950, but also among anthropologists and, very notably, students of folklore and oral literature. Thus, Herzog taught that one should study the authentic music of Native Americans, not what had developed in recent times as a result of contact with white people. He surely did not think one could learn anything from the ways non-Native composers used Native materials. And he did not think that ethnomusicologists should be interested in popular music, in part because of its commercial basis, but more, I suspect, because it was almost inevitably the result of cultural mixes. Such departures were seen as violations of authenticity, undesirable and unworthy of study. The term "spoiled" (*verdorben*) was often used in discussing intercultural contacts. One result may be Bartók's division of Hungarian folk music into old and new styles, both authentic—the first more so—and a third, "mixed genera," a large, heterogeneous repertory, which he largely ignored. There is some, though not absolute, correlation between "authentic" and "old" or "original."

An important basic assumption in ethnomusicology used to be that the norm of world cultures, at least in pre-modern times, was the village or the tribe, and that each of these collectives had its own, unique, and—this is important—homogeneous musical culture. It was further assumed that, fundamentally, all members of such societies knew and had access to all of the music. This was of course a totally unrealistic view, but I was taught to believe that this was, in a sense, the way things started out, and that the obvious and numerous departures from this situation were just that—departures from a norm; something had in a certain sense gone wrong. It did make sense to see this as the best way to begin learning how to analyze musical repertories and cultures.

Surely I am overstating the naïveté of our predecessors for drawing the contrast, but indeed, looking for homogeneity and for styles easily defined and described seemed to be the fundamental task of comparative musicologists. Looking at the descriptions of musics in the earliest publications of the Berlin School and of folk-song scholars, and even later ones, such as those from the 1930s, reveals this kind of approach.

It makes sense to me, therefore, to interpret ethnomusicology as orig- inally the study of the presumably unchanging music of villages and tribes, despite the fact that by the early twentieth century, the world's popula- tion had become prevailingly urban. That earlier ethnomusicology, more- over, concerned itself largely with musics unaffected by intrusions from the outside.

It is true that by 1950, a few scholars, mainly coming from anthro- pology and, importantly, motivated by their interest in African American musics, were beginning to look at the ways musics in contact interacted. Still, even among these scholars, the prevailing view involved an interest in going to the roots, looking back beyond the modern era, trying to see what a kind of imaginary culture of the folk or of isolated villagers would have been like.

The late 1950s and 1960s began to include research providing greater consideration of music in urban contexts. My own experience involved exposure, in a rather heterogeneous American city, to musical cultures of minorities, principally immigrants from Europe and Asia, and their chil- dren and grandchildren. Two things seemed primarily to be worthy of study: how some of these populations maintained and preserved forms of their music, styles, and songs that had been abandoned and changed in the old country; and the opposite, how the immigrant experience with its changes in lifestyle, largely involving urbanization and the accompa- nying multifarious intercultural contacts would produce a much changed musical culture.

To be sure, early comparative musicologists had always been con- cerned with the classical traditions of Asia, whose venues in most cases would have been urban, but they seem to me to have treated such groups of musicians and their repertories largely as isolated units in their urban contexts—in other words, somewhat as if they were isolated villages, or maybe "musical villages." For example, which folk, popular, foreign, Asian, or Western musics the performers of, say, a gamelan or Chinese opera or rāgas at the court of Tanjore might have experienced was of no concern. To be sure, my own experience studying the Persian music tradition in

Tehran followed this approach. Indeed, this was the approach expected by my teachers and consultants during fieldwork; they themselves insisted on my interpreting them essentially as an isolated network of classically-oriented musicians. They did not, for example, admire my occasional forays to visit performance venues and record shops featuring the very heterogeneous popular-music traditions in Iran, and they wondered why I would bother to take an interest in Western classical music as performed in Iran. They judged each other with reference to the concept of authenticity, not with reference to such concepts as innovation.

I found this also to be true, but perhaps in a somewhat different style, among the masters of the Karnatak tradition of South Indian classical music with whom I became acquainted in the 1970s and 1980s. The musicians of Chennai (Madras) were very much aware of the ways in which they had incorporated aspects of Western music—instruments, performance venues and practices, methods of instruction—in order, as I see it, to maintain their tradition intact, particularly the fundamental sounds of the music. Musicians seemed to see themselves as constantly interacting with and reacting to innovations suggested by modern international music culture. They nevertheless seemed to me to be a homogeneous and integrated community that did not interact personally with musicians from other cultures who happened to be around, except possibly to find ways of integrating them—as they had done with Western music—into their own musical circle. By contrast, musicians in Tehran, using a canon, the *radif*, that was actually of recent—late nineteenth-century—origin and making important changes in the sound of the music and its cultural context, had emphasized the importance of maintaining unchanged authenticity.

In the 1970s, many ethnomusicologists, myself included, seemed to come to the realization that the homogeneous village or tribe, even if conceptually transferred to an urban venue, was not a useful norm for studying the world's musics. It was, rather, the culture-bearing units of population—cities, towns, districts—that were normally heterogeneous, constantly changing, full of musics that interacted with each other and with musical and social forces from outside. In other words, while at one time ethnomusicologists wanted to identify and conceptually to separate different musics from each other, we now began to be concerned mainly with how different musics interrelate with each other.

The major distinctive characteristic of urban culture is cultural heterogeneity, and the musical culture of a city seems to me best seen not as a group of musics living side by side, but as a group of interrelationships. Urban musical culture can be defined as musics affecting each other, which seems to me to be the essence of innovation in musical traditions. So, I think that the development of an urban ethnomusicology was the result of two realizations: Musics changed when they moved from rural to urban contexts; and people changed their musics in conformance to their intercultural relationships.

For myself—and possibly for ethnomusicologists as a whole—it may have been useful, as a way of establishing certain approaches and techniques of analysis, to begin with the ideally homogeneous village or tribe, unified repertories and styles, even if artificially constructed. The change has been gradual. If, however, I compare the kind of ethnomusicology practiced by our revered forebears of the early twentieth century with our publications and our conferences in the twenty-first century, the difference is like night and day. Looking at the programs of ethnomusicology meetings today, I am struck by the emphasis on two things: popular music all over the world, meaning music that is mass-mediated; and how things have changed, what recent developments can be noted and interpreted.

Going back more recently to the town of Browning, Montana, where I tried years ago to find evidence of earlier homogeneous music from elderly Blackfoot, the Native American peoples of the region, I decided I had neglected something that was very significant, perhaps central, about the musical culture of this community of some 2,000 persons. It did have a few people who knew songs from the old times. More important, however, it was really a miniature of our urban complexes, and—if I may put it that way—the significant action was really in the relationship of the older and also the more recent tribal musics, of what people called "Blackfoot music," with that of the songs of singing groups from other Indian nations who appeared at powwows and celebration, and also of the interest of Blackfoot people in various musics they called "white"—jazz, rock, country, church music, the high school band—and their particular kind of participation in all of these. Actually, music, more perhaps than other domains of culture, was a principal emblem of the interrelationship of cultures and culture groups that characterized urban societies since the beginning of the twentieth century.

And so, one way of tracing the essential history of ethnomusicology is to see it as morphing from focus on the homogeneous to the diverse, from a field that studies musical cultures to one that studies relationships. If, at first, the "urbanness" of musical cultures was ignored in order to permit the identification of homogeneous tribal, folk, and classical styles, ethnomusicologists did well to make the changes I have been discussing here, making the city with its diversity the cultural norm, and assuming a perspective of tribe and village as miniature city.

2

The Culture of the Metropolis

Rolf Lindner

*

Metropolis is a category used with great reluctance by urban sociologists: It is too vague in terms of content, too close to marketing notions, and some only think of Fritz Lang's film *Metropolis* (1927) when they hear the word. Googling "metropolis" in Germany only confirms this view: Apart from Fritz Lang's film what comes up is the Metropolis chain of cinemas. One cannot help thinking, therefore, that perhaps the metropolis is nothing but a chimera, a utopian or dystopian fiction of urban life. The first question, then, is to ask what actually constitutes a metropolis, that is, what might distinguish it from other settlement forms. Is it sheer size, measured by population, density, area? Is it the administrative-political complex of a capital? Or is it the economic function of a headquarters of international finance in the sense of a global city? A metropolis can be all of these, as, with differing emphases, in the case of London and Paris, but it does not have to be any of them. We may be able to leave aside altogether the demography of size as a prerequisite for the necessary internal differentiation.

The metropolis is evidently an object that cannot be encompassed by an administrative definition; in fact, there is no administrative definition of the metropolis "such as has, of course, been introduced for all settlement forms from the village upwards," as Gerwin Zohlen has stressed (Zohlen 1995, 28). "Metropolis," according to Zohlen, is not a concept of a factual character, for "the word does not describe a firmly circumscribed construct, of a certain size, in a particular location" (ibid.). We can say, therefore, that objectively, as a particular form of settlement, the metropolis does not exist. What, then, is it? Is it a free product of the imagination, as Ernst Cassirer defined myth (e.g., Cassirer 1922)? This notion has turned the word into a label, attached to a city or a region with the intention of conjuring up something. This was the case, for instance, with the invention of "Metropolis Ruhr" in the context of the celebration of the European City of Culture 2010. Curiously, however, it is precisely the attempts to aspire to metropolitan status that testify to the futility of such efforts. We—whereby I mean a collective including the inhabitants themselves—evidently know all about the self-deception. "Now the year as European City of Culture is over and the Ruhr no longer has to play a part and pretend it is a metropolis," wrote a journalist in the *Süddeutsche Zeitung* at the end of the year's celebration in January (*Süddeutsche Zeitung* 2011).

What is the "more" that distinguishes a metropolis from an "ordinary" big city? In the first instance, it is not its political, economic, and cultural functions in the narrow sense that make a metropolis a metropolis, but rather a surplus of significance overriding these functions: the metropolis's role as a center of meaning production and as a projection surface. "What do Rome, New York, the Berlin of the 1920s, the Petersburg of Dostoyevsky have in common," ask Bernward Joerges, Barbara Czarniawska, and Richard Rottenburg, "if not the fact that everyone was and is talking about them, that they were and are sung about and cursed, analyzed and made the subject of novels, marketed, set to music and filmed?" (Joerges, Czarniawska, and Rottenburg 1995, 7).

The metropolis is a cultural construct that, among other things, has the capacity to generate myths. A capital is made by decree, a global city by the decisions of company boards, a metropolis because of a mythology. This mythology, which provides the feeling of being in the right place at the right time, develops a fantastic power of attraction. "Many only move to the city, in order to be part of this mythology," wrote the Hungarian writer and philosopher György Konrád (2004). Without being the subject of novels, poems, and city lore, of feature films, television serials, and pop songs—but also the subject of diverse games, including computer games—a metropolis is inconceivable; only the metropolis achieves, as Daniel Kiecol has emphasized, "a level of mythologization that could make the actual city disappear behind its symbolic power" (Kiecol 2001). Only when a city is "sung," in the literal as well as the metaphorical sense, has it acquired the aura of a metropolis.

A metropolis is a narrative space in which certain legends (of important people and events), myths (of heroes and villains), and parables (of virtues and vices) are inscribed. Urban legends, stories of the urban uncanny, have become widespread in the last couple of decades. No doubt, it has something to do with the internet, which has expanded and accelerated the possibilities of diffusion, quite apart from the suitability of urban legends as story material for blogs of the most diverse kind (e.g., place blogs and travel blogs). Even if there are certain narrative genres that turn up in all locations—animal lore, food lore—they always possess local color, which allows the story to appear plausible. Among the most famous is the (very early) urban legend of the "sewer gator," that is, the alligators in the New York sewer system. According to the story children had bought the reptiles as tiny pets, which harassed parents soon flushed away. In the sewers the beasts had thrived, growing to alarming sizes. The tale of reptiles in the city water system is certainly not restricted to New York City. A variant located in Kolkata tells of a twenty-five-foot salt-water crocodile that turned up in the suburb of Alipore.

In fact, Kolkata seems to be quite a fruitful place for urban legends, though it is noticeable that there are varieties of legends describing the ghosts of young women, "in full bridal make up," haunting, so it is said, an apartment or a house in which, whether due to natural or unnatural causes, they met their death the night before their wedding. Is the Victorian "haunted house" story here combined with the systemic importance that weddings have in India? The uncanny and the mysterious associated with the metropolis is only another way of saying that the unexpected can happen here.

In the words of Rudolf Lüscher and Michael Makropoulos, that which distinguishes the metropolis "is its characteristic mixture of the boldest constructions with unpredictable elements and activities that evade planning" (Lüscher and Makropoulos 1982). Urban legends reveal that in the big city one imagines that anything is possible, from alligators in the sewers to Dr. Jekyll and Mr. Hyde to the rags-to-riches story, the quintessential urban legend. The story of Dhirubai Ambani is a good example of the legends of unlimited potential. We become aware of how often the common denominator of these legends includes the theme of *transformation*, familiar from myths and folk tales, but as an assertion of reality only conceivable in the metropolis. Perhaps it can be said with some justification that the culture of the metropolis is condensed in the motif of transformation. The metropolis promises exactly what its critics have always held against it, that is, the dissolution of identity or the possibility of multiple identities. In the popular literature specific to the big city, in other words, in journalism, in serial novels, in comic strips, and in other formats, these forms of identity transformation come to the fore in the fundamental theme of *secret identity*. We find it, as one of the earliest examples, in the *Mysteries of Paris* by Eugene Sue, whose hero, the Grand Duke of Gerolstein, turns himself into the worker Rodolphe in order to uncover the secrets of the city, a figure whom we can see as a model for the urban ethnographer as undercover observer. We find identity transformation, too, in the reporter (another genuinely urban figure) Clark Kent, who as Superman fights evil in the city of "Metropolis," with New York City as the obvious model. The essence of the superhero narrative is the same as that of all metropolitan tales: transformation. "The Super Hero," writes Sanderson in his *Marvel Comic Guide to New York*, "represents the potential within every individual to become extraordinary" (Sanderson 2007, 17). In this case, the legend is not from rags-to-riches, but rather from office-bound weakling to muscle-bound hero.

* *

Contained in these stories, if they are broken down to the everyday level, is the idea of the metropolis as a space of possibility, the idea that it embodies the promise of offering every desirable life-plan a chance of realization. Apu, the hero of Satyajit Ray's film trilogy of the same name, also represents the theme of the metropolis as a space of possibility when he prepares to write a novel about a village boy who goes to Calcutta because he feels "the seeds of greatness" within him. This is a central motif of city literature from the very beginning, not least in the novels of Honoré de Balzac, who finds his universe in Paris, the first city to be described as a metropolis. In one of the most famous scenes of the *Human Comedy* (*Comédie humaine*) Rastignac, the hero of *Old Goriot* and other novels in the cycle, looks down from the Père Lachaise cemetery on Paris, which he has sworn to conquer:

> Thus left alone, Rastignac walked a few steps to the highest part of the cemetery and saw Paris spread out below on both banks of the winding Seine. Lights were beginning to twinkle here and there. His gaze fixed almost avidly on the space that lay between the column of the Place Vendôme and the dome of the Invalides; there lay the splendid world that he had wished to gain. He eyed that humming hive with a look that foretold its despoliation, as if he already felt on his lips the sweetness of its honey out of it in advance and said with superb defiance: "It's war between us now!" [A nous deux maintenant!]. (Balzac 2014)

Rastignac's challenge to Paris demonstrates that the metropolis is a place in which one has to prove oneself. Hermann, Count Keyserling, puts it succinctly: "Whoever proves himself in Paris has proved himself before mankind." He therefore acknowledges *en passant* that Paris is *the* classic metropolis, as it also was for Walter Benjamin. It is a cultural characteristic of the metropolis that it serves as a standard, as is shown not least in a song made famous by Frank Sinatra, *New York, New York*, which plays a modern variation on the motif of the metropolis as a place that tests one's mettle: "If I can make it there, I'm gonna make it anywhere." The attraction of the metropolis lies in its character as a space of possibility. The promise of the metropolis is that its own "greatness" will be transmitted to the individual.

> In the 1920s someone who was a leading actor in Hamburg, in Cologne, or in Munich was very far from being so in the metropolis of the time, Berlin. It was there one had to go to prove oneself, there one failed or became—like Gründgens—a star. (Sens 1987, 20)

Three interlocking processes are constitutive of this space of possibility: the process of differentiation; the process of linkage; and the process of condensation. In 1971, Geoffrey Moorhouse wrote about Calcutta that

> there may not be another city containing such a hotchpotch of people as this one, with so many crucial differences of subculture, of race, of religion, of caste and of language riddling them and holding them apart even when they are thrown most crushingly together. (Moorhouse [1971] 1974, 176)

It may well be that Moorhouse's observation is no longer valid, at least not to the same degree as forty years ago. The quote, nonetheless, provides an impressive example of what constitutes the core concept of the metropolis: variety. This variety can develop to such a degree that the metropolis seems to be a world of its own. As early as 1843, Christian Friedrich Hebbel wrote that Paris was not a city, but rather a world unto itself. Hebbel asserted that no other place on earth could contain as much of the world in a single place. New York City, again, is the example for the modern metropolis. Understanding New York as a world of its own was a topic for a whole series of journalists. When one of the first newspapers sold on the street in New York City is called *The World*, it does not mean in the first instance that this paper reports on the entire world, rather that the world consists, above all, of New York City. We recognize as paradigmatic the 1924 *Around the World in New York* by the Romanian immigrant, Konrad Bercovici, based on preceding newspaper reports. The book guides the reader through Little Italy and Chinatown, Harlem and the Jewish East Side, through Syrian neighborhoods and the French district, the Russian colony and the Hispanic neighborhoods, through Germany, Austria, and Bohemia, convincingly conveying that one does not need to leave New York City in order to travel around the world.

In a study of the immigrant press that also appeared in the 1920s Robert Park, the founder of the Chicago School of Urban Sociology, emphasized that no language group in New York City is so insignificant that it does not maintain a press of its own:

> The Albanians, Armenians, Bulgarians, Chinese, Czechs, Croatians, Danes, Finns, French, Germans, Greeks, Italians, Japanese, Jews, Levantine Jews, Letts, Lithuanians, Magyars, Persians, Poles, Portuguese, Rumanians, Russians, Serbs, Slovaks, Slovenians, Spanish, the Swabians of Germany[!], the Swedes, Swiss, Syrians of New York City all have a press. (Park 1922, 7)

Undoubtedly, the special status of New York City as the point of entry to the New World and the initial site of immigrant settlement, particularly at the turn of the twentieth century, plays a role here, but, in principle, it is the diversity of people of different origins that distinguishes a metropolis. Closely linked to this ethnic diversity, moreover, is the diversity of religious denominations in the metropolis, which one finds in such abundance only there, clearly evident in the places of worship that in part determine the appearance of the city: churches, mosques, synagogues, and temples (cf. Park 1915, 1922).

Religious and denominational diversity also characterizes Kolkata, where in addition to Hindus, there are Muslims, Christians, Jains, Sikhs, Buddhists, Jews, and Parsis, to name only the major religions. It is altogether possible to say that in the metropolis there is room for the strangest ideas and practices. I was quite astonished, for example, to discover just how many faith healers, shamans, hypnotists, and "magi" (individuals possessing magical powers) there are in Berlin. Such individuals reveal one further characteristic of the metropolis, to which Robert Park had already drawn attention in 1915: In the big city even the most unusual aptitudes, skills, and bodies of knowledge lend themselves to professionalization. One consequence of such observations was that the Chicago sociologists became the pioneers not only of urban research but also of the sociology of labor. Nowhere else does the metropolis as a site for possibilities reflect itself more explicitly than in the creativity opened through the invention of new fields of activity, business, and service. In concrete terms, this no doubt manifests itself differently in Kolkata than in Berlin, because the economic conditions, social determination, and cultural forms of articulation are different. In Kolkata, occupational practice may more often be peripatetic in nature, for example, with street hawkers or those offering transport services. Christopher Dell has given us an impressive description and analysis of Kolkata's sidewalk economies (Dell 2009; see also Dell's chapter in the present volume). The principle of the metropolitan differentiating possibilities of employment, however, is basically the same in most cities.

The Swedish social anthropologist Ulf Hannerz discerns access to diversity as a further characteristic of the big city. This access may not always be planned; serendipity may be built into city life to a certain degree. In general, however, metropolitan life creates remarkable opportunities for social relations that are actually achieved as opposed to those that are only ascribed. Here, too, there may be differences between and among different cities, thanks to specific historical, social, and cultural determinants. It is nevertheless true that the threshold to the emergence of new group cultures in the largest cities can more easily be crossed, not least because the requisite number of like-minded individuals is more likely to be present:

> It is in the bigger city, usually, that one finds not just a single pianist but a musicians' occupational culture, not a quiet political dissident but a sect or a movement organized around an ideology, not a lone homosexual but gay culture. (Hannerz 1980, 115)

The city acts as a cultural catalyst: Only through such social linking does it become possible to translate private status as a pianist, dissident, or homosexual into a cultural statement.

The third fundamental process in addition to differentiation and linking is spatial concentration and the related cluster formation. This process refers to the whole variety of spatially segregated and culturally differentiated worlds of work, residence, and experience. To describe this process the Chicago sociologists coined the terms *natural area, social world,* and *moral region.* Socially homogenous residential quarters, ethnic enclaves (e.g., Chinatown), subcultural niches, monostructural service and industrial areas (e.g., the newspaper quarter, printers' row, or the garment district), a museum quarter, entertainment districts, or a government quarter affords the metropolis the qualities of a mosaic of smaller worlds. In 1971, Moorhouse offered an example such clusters in Kolkata:

> You find people living in communal pockets in Calcutta, just as you find its varieties of trade concentrated in what must be uncomfortably competitive huddles. You find, for example, that almost all its native Christians . . . are concentrated along a broad corridor of streets extending eastwards from the Maidan; and you find, if you turn left into Lower Circular Road at the bottom of Park Street, that the next three quarters of a mile are occupied by men selling bits and pieces of motorbikes, internal combustion engines, mudguards, axle grease, bicycle lamps and almost everything else concerned with getting you or maintaining you awheel. (Moorhouse [1971] 1974, 176)

Such neighborhoods and occupational clusters may have changed since the 1970s, but Moorhouse's description still illustrates the variety principle. It is this variety of origins, practices, and value systems, their contradictory cooperation and juxtaposition, and the frictions between them that constitute the raw material of individual life projects, the yeast of social visions, and hence the cultural capital of the metropolis. It is the feeling of being able to choose from among an almost unlimited number of professional orientations, fields of experimentation and opportunity, and, significantly, social circles and networks that forms the subjective dimension of the space for possibility.

∗ ∗ ∗

The culture of the metropolis is, therefore, a culture of possibilities, possibilities that encompass the most ambitious life plans—"the seeds of greatness." The fulfillment of ambition also implies that another aspect of a culture of possibilities, its dark side, is the culture of failure. Nothing is more humiliating than the uncelebrated return of the great son of the province from the metropolis, exposed to the mockery of those who stayed at home. Such humiliation, too, is a theme of Balzac's *Human Comedy*, for example, in the figure of Lucien Chardon (alias Lucien Rubempre) in *Lost Illusions* (Balzac 2014). As a space of possibility the metropolis is an individual, cultural, and social laboratory, a place of experimentation, in which one can succeed or fail through a process of trial and error.

Analogous to the *fait social total* of Marcel Mauss, we can also understand the metropolis as a total cultural fact. The specificity of such a total cultural fact lies in the orientation function that the metropolis performs for the society as a whole. Succinctly stated, a metropolis needs no model: It is the model. In a statement during the 1955 Berlin Festival the poet Gottfried Benn clarified what happens when this model is absent:

> I would like to state one cultural viewpoint, which relates to West Germany. To sum up my thoughts in one concise sentence: West Germany is being ruined because Berlin is no longer there. . . . If one may be quite open: We see in West Germany provincial metropoles with their local leading lights, theater and broadcasting conglomerates with competing cliques, academies seeking a role for themselves, but which does not exist—there is no reference point to which to look, for it would need to be Berlin. There is a lack of anything against which one could measure oneself, from which one receives stimuli, above all, something that produces embarrassment. (Benn 1987, 21)

One looks to a metropolis, to stay with visual imagery, to experience new ideas, innovations, trends, and lifestyles, to discover what's "happening," what's "in," what, in both the positive and the negative sense we're "in for." In other words, *the metropolis is the most important cultural medium of a society.* As such, it functions both centripetally and centrifugally—centripetal, in that it attracts, real or supposed, talent from all cultural spheres and from all points of the compass (and this becomes an act of self-fulfilling prophecy when, like Paris or New York City, its status as a national or global metropolis is uncontested)—centrifugal in that it diffuses the ideas, tastes, and models it generates across the whole of society and announces future social and economic developments. In the critical assessment of Berlin, particularly in the 1920s, this double movement is expressed in the paradoxical formulation that the metropolis at once drains the provinces (i.e., of their talent) and floods the provinces with its products. In 1924, Bercovici wrote:

> New York is the arbiter. What New York accepts is accepted. What New York dislikes is disliked. If New York has put its seal of approval on a book, or a play, or a painting, that book, that play, that painting is accepted. If New York has put its approval on a musician, or an actor, or a preacher, he is accepted by the rest of the continent. . . . And even the people on the other side of the continent, though reluctantly, also come to ask the approval of New York. (Bercovici 1924, 21)

Much the same is true at the national level of the Berlin of the 1920s. In the context of the present volume, that raises a final important question: What are the conditions whereby a metropolis sets cultural standards? Metropoles quite evidently experience shifting tides, their highs and lows. What regulates such tides? Paris, as the classical European metropolis, has an aura that is hard to remove, and, interestingly, it was also German writers such as Walter Benjamin with his "Arcades Project" who helped create that aura (Benjamin 2002). There were two decades of the twentieth century in which Paris possessed an almost magical attraction: the 1920s—captured in exemplary fashion by Ernest Hemingway's *A Moveable Feast* (Hemingway 1964)—and the 1950s, when existentialism was not only a philosophy, but also, and above all, a lifestyle. In both decades Paris became the location of an artistic avant-garde that operated across genres and media: Surrealism in the 1920s and Situationism in the 1950s. With surrealism an idea of the metropolis appears almost as an ideal type, that is, as a place for the testing and representation of new individual life projects and of collective projections, "the dream images in which both deeper needs express themselves and the fashions with which it entertains itself" (Schwarz 1987, 90).

How, we might ask, do these dream images come into being? From the outset we can dismiss such mechanistic models as the TTT formula (Technology, Talent, Tolerance) proposed by Richard Florida, which so many civic leaders have blindly followed. We might ask, instead, whether or not it is a matter of historical conjuncture, in which structural, cultural, and generational components converge in time and space in such a way that independent momentum develops at a certain point. Berlin seems to me to be the best contemporary example. As recently as the 1990s, the assertion that Berlin was a metropolis comparable to New York City sounded merely boastful, typical of the caricature of many native Berliners. Today, in the second decade of the twenty-first century, Berlin has achieved such a degree of international attention that the city has become a magnet of worldwide attraction. How did this happen? Many underestimate the degree to which the New Berlin is influenced by its recent past, and how much it still draws on the Old Berlin prior to the fall of the Wall, a place of pretending, "in which it is possible to do things that cannot be realized elsewhere, as a place of innovation and cultural openness" (Höynck 1987, 99).

The major attractions of the 1990s—Christopher Street Day, the Love Parade, and the Carnival of Cultures—were either taken over from the old West Berlin or created in its spirit. Techno, *the* sound of Berlin and its famous clubs after the fall of the Wall, even took one of its sources from the Ingenious Dilettantes Festival of 1981: "It was here that later ringleaders of [Berlin] techno first took to the stage," as Wolfgang Müller of the art and music project, "Die tödliche Doris" (Deadly Doris), explained in an interview (Müller 2005). It is not least the subcultural heritage of both East and West Berlin, combined with the blank spaces in the urban landscape—spaces of playful experiment—that triggered a cultural process that attracted creative people of all kinds. We still do not know enough—I, for one, surely do not—to say exactly at which point a process becomes self-generating, spreading, like a self-fulfilling prophecy, the message that one just *has* to be there, that one must live in the metropolis. In the case of Berlin, that point, obviously, has already been reached.

Rolf Lindner

References

Balzac, Honoré de. 2014. *Verlorene Illusionen*. Translated by Melanie Walz. Munich: Carl Hanser Verlag.

Benjamin, Walter. 2002. *The Arcades Project*. Translated by Howard Eiland and Kevin McLaughlin. Cambridge, MA: Belknap Press of Harvard University Press.

Benn, Gottfried. 1987. "Das kalte, kritische Berlin (1955)." *Ästhetik und Kommunikation* 17 (61/62): 21.

Bercovici, Konrad. 1924. *Around the World in New York*. New York: Century Co.

Cassirer, Ernst. 1922. *Die Begriffsform im mythischen Denken*. Leipzig: Teubner.

Dell, Christopher. 2009. *Tacit Urbanism: Hawkers and the Production of Space in Every Day Kolkata*. Rotterdam: Post Editions.

Hannerz, Ulf. 1980. *Exploring the City: Inquiries toward an Urban Anthropology*. New York: Columbia University Press.

Hemingway, Ernest. 1964. *A Moveable Feast*. New York: Scribner.

Höynck, Rainer. 1987. "Mythos Berlin—Wahrnehmungsgeschichte einer industriellen Metropole: Ein kulturpolitisches Gespräch." *Ästhetik und Kommunikation* 17 (59): 93–116.

Joerges, Bernward, Barbara Czerniawoska, and Richard Rottenburg. 1995. *Metropolen: Ordnung und Unordnung—Überlegungen zu einem gemeinsamen Forschungsprogramm*. Berlin: Wissenschaftszentrum Berlin.

Kiecol, Daniel. 2001. *Selbstbild und Image zweier europäischer Metropolen: Paris und Berlin zwischen 1900 und 1930*. Frankfurt a. M.: Peter Lang.

Konrád, György. 2004. "Die Herausforderung der Großstadt." In *Wien um 1900: Aufbruch in die Moderne*, edited by Peter Berner, Emil Brix, and Wolfgang Mantl, 259–75. Vienna: Verlag für Geschichte und Politik.

Lüscher, Rudolf, and Michael Makropoulos. 1982. "Revolte für eine andere Stadt." *Ästhetik und Kommunikation* 13 (49): 113–25.

Moorhouse, Geoffrey. (1971) 1974. *Calcutta*. Harmondsworth: Penguin.

Müller, Wolfgang. 2005. "Ingenious Dilletantes?" Interview in Tøni Schifer and Rolf S. Wolkenstein, *Berlinsuper 80: Music & Film Underground Berlin (West) 1978–1984*. Berlin: Monitorpop Entertainment. DVD.

Park, Robert E. 1915. "The City: The Suggestions for the Investigation of Human Behavior in the City Environment." *American Journal of Sociology* 20 (5): 577–612.

———. 1922. *The Immigrant Press and Its Control*. New York: Harper & Brothers.

Sanderson, Peter. 2007. *The Marvel Comics Guide to New York City*. New York: Pocket Books.

Schwarz, Karl. 1987. "Berlin: Kulturmetropole und Industriemetropole neuen Typs." *Ästhetik und Kommunikation* 17 (61/62): 85–100.

Sens, Eberhard. 1987. "Der Traum von der Metropole: Zur neuen Sehnsucht nach Urbanität." *Ästhetik und Kommunikation* 17 (61/62): 17–22.

Süddeutsche Zeitung. 2011. Article on Metropole Ruhr. 27 January.

Zohlen, Gerwin. 1995. "Metropole als Metapher." In *Mythos Metropole*, edited by Gotthard Fuchs, Bernhard Moltmann, and Walter Prigge, 23–34. Frankfurt a. M.: Suhrkamp.

3

"Thank You for Listening Kindly": Musical Agency in Trans-Metropolitan Spaces

Sebastian Klotz

On the CD entitled *This Is Not Fusion* (2007), the UK- and Kolkata-based literary theorist, singer-songwriter, and writer Amit Chaudhuri offers a subtle musical reflection from cross-cultural experiences, embracing influences from George Gershwin, North Indian classical music, rock, and jazz. The geographical connotations feed into a set of original tracks that seem to contradict the title of the CD, though Chaudhuri firmly believes "all music is fusion."[1] It turns out the title is directed against a commercialized notion of fusion, reminding us that real fusion has to do with "time and with ambivalence."[2] The "non-fusion" presented here could be taken as "a striking metaphor for the urban sensibility, which today is increasingly the condition of everybody, even those who stay at home" (Chaudhuri 2007).

How can music articulate these cross-cultural urban sensibilities? Chaudhuri detects similarities between Eric Clapton's "Layla" and the Hindustani *rāg todi*, between the pentatonic blues scale of Gershwin's "Summertime" and *rāgs Malkauns* and *jog*, and between the warning an-

---

[1] Quoted by Ananda Lal in the liner notes of *This Is Not Fusion* (Lal 2007).
[2] Ivan Hewett in the liner notes of *This Is Not Fusion* (Hewett 2007).

nouncement on Berlin's subway (*einsteigen bitte*, please board) and the fourth and fifth scale degrees in Indian music.[3] Chaudhuri's dialogical exploration of these similarities exceeds the merely musical realm as it spurs reflective processes that address matters of cross-cultural identity and aesthetic expression. For those who leave aside these reflections, the music may still be a rich auditory experience. Still, Chaudhuri injects so many cross-allusions, some more explicit than others, that the topic of what cultural fusion is and how one could articulate it will hardly escape the attention of listeners.

Chaudhuri has been afforded the invitations and academic travel grants that brought him to the United Kingdom and to Berlin and that enabled him to produce the CD in Kolkata. Another layer of trans-metropolitan connections has been brought about not only by the *musical* impressions of the Professor of Comparative Literature at the University of East Anglia, but by the geography of *musical instrumentation, borrowing, production,* and *international marketing.* Traditional Indian instruments, such as the *dotara, dhunuri,* and *tabla,* mix with tambourine, bass, acoustic guitar, snare drum, keyboards, and trumpet. Apart from British and German cultural agencies and funding institutions, the recording geography ranges from Kolkata to Norwich in England (recording and mixing) to the mastering studio in Melbourne, Australia. The CD was released by the Times Group of India. Despite the international division of labor that one would expect in much more mainstream projects targeting big sales, the CD gives the impression of a highly personal journey across the hybrid identities of current cosmopolitan citizens.

Next to the imagined similarities of blues and rāga, Chaudhuri performs very explicit geographical locations, both in the lyrics and in the auditory material[4] he develops for these geographies, ranging from imagined to quasi-documentary strategies. While "Moral Education" sets classroom charts to music to signal correct behavior for British school children, the track "Trucker" picks up on the imaginative and colorful writings cov-

---

3   Lal (2007) and Hewett (2007), with Chaudhuri's comments in the liner notes to *This Is Not Fusion* (Chaudhuri 2007).

4   The CD artwork also incorporates local representations; see figure 21 below.

ering Indian trucks. From the familiar curses directed against aggressive drivers to the pacifying "OK—Ta Ta,"[5] the song mimics a ride across inner-city traffic in an Indian metropolis. Through "OK—Ta Ta bye bye/this is how we live and die," the refrain adds an existential dimension. Another site is addressed in two songs situated in Berlin, "Berlin" and "Motz."[6]

Before considering such songs, the exemplary character of *This Is Not Fusion* needs to be discussed. Are the experiences that Chaudhuri articulates *representative* in any way? Which criteria do we have to measure this representativeness? Listening communities and listening situations have undergone vast differentiation since the 1980s, making it almost impossible to penetrate them and to arrive at solid conclusions. *This Is Not Fusion* mirrors this proliferation by offering an eclectic, multi-sited auditory ethnography, inspired by individual experience, but capable of reaching out to an audience that has itself become multi-sited.

Given this situation, trans-cultural musicologies may try to establish complex positions for observation. They may not tap old-school explanations and causalities, but may instead aim to offer contextualizing perspectives. Chaudhuri himself is fully aware of trans-urban and trans-cultural soundscapes, which he actively molds throughout the album. He is an alert and informed observer, engaged with this cultural field. While trans-cultural musicologies ask which experiences this new condition proffers, the tracks on *This Is Not Fusion* articulate these experiences in forms both aesthetically persuasive and sociologically reflexive.

The album makes manifest a new mode of experiencing time/space (English, glossed as chronotope), which has been addressed in current German cultural theory by the notion of cultural *Flexionen* (English, glossed as flection or inflection; Heeg and Denzel 2011). Such reflexivity takes account of the non-linear processes of space and underlines the intermingling of structure and action. In the pluralism of space- and time-based events, "culture" emerges as a discontinuous process of reflexivity that af-

---

5   Tata Motors is India's largest automobile company, itself one part of an international industrial conglomerate.
6   Motz & Co. e.V. is a local charity that issues the street newspaper *Motz* and supports the homeless in Berlin.

fects structure and practice. Proponents of the theory of *kulturelle Flexionen* (cultural flections) situate actions and their structural and transformational effects against the background of confused and shifting time/space relations. Musical material can seamlessly evoke full cultural contexts and expose them to cultural reflexivity. We need to ask, therefore, how and under what conditions music is able actually to capture and enhance cultural flections and how these affect the urban condition.

This Is Not Fusion enacts a specific semantics of a transcultural chronotope. Familiar auditory references ("Summertime") are being brought into unfamiliar contexts to merge with them. The writings on Indian trucks appear next to the announcements on the Berlin subway. Such semantics configure the process of appropriation. The metropolis stimulates and allows actors to act reflexively on their experiences, and to share these experiences with other actors.

Academic analysis should engage this reflexivity in imaginative ways in order to capture their dynamic, social, and cultural repercussions. The multi-sited component of productions such as *This Is Not Fusion* finds an equivalent in scientific procedures that reflect the multi-sitedness of experience, production, and distribution procedures.[7] Consequently, accounts of trans-cultural processes can never be closed or brought under complete academic control. In the present case, a set of trajectories that helps to understand cultural flections draws on notions of musical *conjunctivity* and *fungibility*. The trajectories will cover the role of music and its related social values in city marketing advertisements in Chicago, Berlin, and Kolkata, the profusely pro-urban and imaginative band names in Kolkata, the post-governmental slogan "Be Berlin," the role of global musicians in real-estate marketing, and the contested notion of musical fusion.

The notion of overlapping spaces, which was developed in critical urban theory, perhaps not by chance in connection with an in-depth study of the city and history of Kolkata (Chattopadhyay 2012), is helpful in delin-

---

7 The TransCoop project from which the present book emerged used comparative ethnography to respond to the multi-sitedness of Berlin, Chicago, and Kolkata. The imaginative musical coupling of Kolkata and Berlin on *This Is Not Fusion* exemplifies the hypothesis that specific musical connections exist between these cities.

eating the social, aesthetic, and political aspirations that easily connect to musical materials and contexts. Music connects in ways that surpass existing models of music communication in the sociology of music. The proliferation of potential connections has become boundless in a trans-cultural setting. Music can shape realities and create a realism of its own. It can display dramaturgical power by enacting cultural aspirations that cannot be measured as right or wrong, but according to their aesthetic and social plausibility (Brandl 2006). Under trans-cultural conditions, the perspectives from which to judge such plausibility have in themselves proliferated, thus complicating a theoretical approach to these cultural situations. Musical material can create conjunctions within a split second, evoking a whole cultural tradition, a specific style, artist, or mood.

Yet the full effects of music's conjunctural potential need to be gauged within the context of meaning construction during musical appropriation. Conjunctivities by far exceed mere homologies. Due to the complex semantic texture of auditory material, ambivalent and at times contradictory communicative situations may arise. Unraveling situations that invite cross-cultural projections remains an important task. In addition, current auditory cultures are driven, among others, by strong market forces that seek to translate such conjunctivities into commercial value. This had become manifest in the recording industry's coining of the term "World Music" to increase the consumption of recordings (see Taylor 1997), and it has become even more urgent in the era of social media and algorithmic marketing with individual consumer profiles. Media content is being marketed across various formats and access regimes. Individual profiles serve to generate emotionally and commercially custom-made recommendation lists for consumers. Music's immanent conjunctivity translates into fungibility.[8] In the global age, this fungibility is being orchestrated in a manner so as to be locally and situation-specific and still capable of achieving

---

8   Again, Swati Chattopadhyay has led the way toward using this term in critical urban theory. Fungibility is derived from the "fungible quality of money or labour." It appears in the form of exchangeability and repeatability and helps adopt capitalism to "place-specific claims of community" (Chattopadhyay 2012; see esp. chap. 7, 229, in which she describes "the ephemeral geography of the Durgapuja" of Kolkata as fungible).

global outreach. Any specific exploration of trans-cultural musical agency (i.e., the opportunities for individuals and social groups to develop subject and collective positions in a variety of trans-cultural social situations) needs to take into account the entanglement of music. In the absence of more suitable terms, I address it here as conjunctivity and fungibility.

A case of consolidating locality with an eye toward international competitiveness and city-marketing campaigns makes use of cultural and musical credentials in order to distinguish one city from another. The leveling effects of late capitalism and globalization are thus countered by an explicit insistence on locality and the specificity of place. As international capital flows standardize the procedures, work habits, and criteria of urbanity, marketing campaigns need to find a balance between a potentially exchangeable openness and a uniqueness that recommends the city for investment.

Because no single institution can advance an accepted image of what a city is, the discursive analysis of marketing campaigns can provide initial concepts for how a present imagination of a place is being crafted by at least one influential voice. These easily available marketing videos and documentaries offer themselves as suitable points of departure. As frames they provide a sharper profile when read against the city-specific self-images in which, surprisingly, the arts, culture, and music hold a high stake. Berlin, for example, fashions itself as the pluralistic, individualistic city, as a hub between Eastern and Western Europe, and as a truly international and creative metropolis, combining a complex past (the ruins and fragments following World War II) with rapid progress. The lack of a city vision is modulated through reflexive hedonism, which in turn has become part of the city's marketing campaign. In the long documentary film project, *24h Berlin—Ein Tag im Leben*,[9] the metropolis is presented as a permanently active city that achieves a synchronicity through its abundant citizens and institutions, as well as its cultural background. Seizing the persuasive power of a documentary "reality" film, *24h Berlin* features no

---

9   Eighty camera teams sought to document the city and its residents. The project, which relied on public and private funding, is documented on eighty DVDs, which were released in 2009 by the zero one film company (*24h Berlin* 2009)

single aesthetic ambition comparable to the perception that the urban was revolutionized by cinema in the early period of modernism. Instead, the accumulation of specific moments constitutes what Berlin is during a single day. Berliners from all walks of life, from unknown emergency nurses to Daniel Barenboim, from the city's garbage collectors to mayor Klaus Wowereit, come together in the film and merge into a flow of images and activities, whose only reference point is locality and the twenty-four-hour timeline. Not surprisingly, clubbing hot spots such as Berghain and its resident DJs are featured prominently, yielding fascinating synchronicities with other sectors of the working world (public transport, hospitals, energy plants, police), whose late-night and early-morning shifts are mandatory. *24h Berlin* is not exactly a city image campaign documentary. Key agencies, nonetheless, such as Hauptstadtkulturfonds (capital city cultural funds) and the mayor's office provided funding (see zero one film 2017).

Chicago cultivates itself as the multi-ethnic metropolis, the dynamic city, as the city of neighborhoods, fostering the "harmony and diversity of its neighborhoods" (see City of Chicago 2017). The promotional film, *Welcome to Chicago* (see World Business Chicago 2009) cultivates classic values, features highly aestheticized settings, and portrays Chicago as a city with a firm historical and economic base. With a reassuring attitude, the film's producers stress persuasion through distinction. The rhythm and atmosphere of the city, in which the possible and the impossible intersect, play an important role. The repeating theme of the promotional film is continuity based on economic power, thematically in line with the official city vision:

> As a multicultural city that thrives on the harmony and diversity of its neighborhoods, Chicago today embodies the values of America's heartland-integrity, hard work and community and reflects the ideals in the social fabric of its 77 distinct neighborhoods. (City of Chicago 2017)

In a key statement from a global *business* perspective, the cultural assets appear only fleetingly in the closing sentence:

> Home to an unrivaled economy, workforce, and quality of life, Chicago is a thriving metropolis, yet a tight-knit community for business and residents. The city's dynamic character can be attributed to its people, its location and infrastructure, and its collaborative business and government community.

> Centrally located, Chicago provides easy access to the world. The city has 2,900 daily flights including direct and nonstop service to more than 220 cities worldwide, and serves as a hub for all six Class-One North American railroads, as well as six major U.S. Interstates. . . .
>
> This combination of market access and economic diversity provides the resources a company needs to flourish. Alongside Chicago's pro-business environment, support services, and unique opportunities for growth, the city also offers a vibrant mix of cultural, educational, and social amenities. (World Business Chicago 2017)

In yet another official statement we learn that Chicago's Department of Cultural Affairs and Special Events (DCASE)

> is dedicated to enriching Chicago's artistic vitality and cultural vibrancy. This includes fostering the development of Chicago's non-profit arts sector, independent working artists and for-profit arts businesses; providing a framework to guide the City's future cultural and economic growth, via the 2012 Chicago Cultural Plan; marketing the City's cultural assets to a worldwide audience; and presenting high-quality, free and affordable cultural programs for residents and visitors. (Mission Statement; see DCASE 2017)

In the promotional video "Glimpse Of Kolkata City | Calcutta, West Bengal" (India Video 2009) Kolkata portrays itself as a busy, modern yet empty metropolis, replete with Western commercial iconography. As if elevated highways, trams, and multiple lane arteries plied by yellow cabs, perpetuating a 1950s view of infrastructural development, were not enough, the video's audio track features heavy metal guitar riffs, radiating an active, feel-good atmosphere. Close-ups show anonymous citizens during daily routines, and even the ubiquitous rickshaw, but these shots are framed by the overwhelming presence of cars and panoramic views of colonial architecture on the Esplanade and Park Street.

How do artistic production and cultural appropriation of music reflect such visions? Kolkata's ambivalent position toward global modernization and the fostering of classical Bengali traditions and history are evident in the names given to bands and musical locations alike. A kind of contemporaneity borne by tradition is manifest in the way metal bands refer to the heritage of Rabindranath Tagore and insist on Bengali lyrics only (see Ghose in this volume). This attitude arises from a long experience at the Bengali-Western crossroads, like the one that exposed Chaudhuri to Western guitar playing in his childhood (see the opening of the

present chapter). The imaginative band names, moreover, capture a long-
ing for globalism, visible in its use of English, which deliberately expresses
non-conformism. As metaphors of escape (see Ghose in this volume), the
names stake out an imaginative territory that embraces a reflexive post-
colonialism and the awareness of the precarious shortage of legal music spaces in which a younger generation can express itself. In this way,
Kolkata's urban politics resonate in these names. Some popular musical
venues in downtown Kolkata have names such as Someplace Else (Park
Street), Big Ben, and Princeton Club. Album titles frequently evoke a proud
Bengali heritage, as in the case of *Tagore 4 2moro*. The CD series *The Underground Kolkata* (2008), which itself is a remarkable initiative honoring
and marketing recent cultural processes, features bands that had regularly
performed at Someplace Else: Urban Reflektions, Parallel Universe, Class
Apart, Alienz, and Crystal Grass. Other bands appearing at Someplace Else
included Hip Pocket, Skinny Alley, Orient Express, Krosswindz, Insomnia,
The Supersonics, and Pink Noise.

The label Saregama that markets this music is consciously reflecting
its roots, which date back to the earliest recording facilities during colonial
times. This flashback again underscores the prominent position of Kolkata
on the international music and recordings market:

> With over 300,000 songs, 23,000 artists and 50,000 contracts, Saregama is the
> custodian of over half of all the music ever recorded in India. It is the pre-
> mier destination for all types of South Asian Music and the most authorita-
> tive source of the region's musical heritage. The proud history of Saregama
> stretches back to 1901, formerly known as The Gramophone Company of In-
> dia Ltd. and more popularly as HMV (His Master's Voice), Saregama was es-
> tablished as the first overseas Indian Branch of Electrical & Musical Industries
> Limited (EMI), London. . . .
> Our objective is to create cultural harmony and unite in community
> through collaborative musical events. (Saregama 2017)

The intentional creation of togetherness cultivates a self-image of Kolkata
that relies on harmony, love, and mutual understanding. While listening
to tracks in heavy metal style, one is impressed with the tender and subtle
musical and vocal articulation, striking a warmhearted lyrical tone usually
absent from Western heavy metal. These observations are surely subjective, yet they may lead to methodological considerations that allow us to

understand how cultural self-images translate into musical articulations, and how music affects the dynamics of metropolitan self-images. These processes receive particular exposure in cross-cultural situations, as in *This Is Not Fusion*, when ascribed images ("a singer from India," the "Western" metropolis of Berlin, and the "genuine African American" experience of *Porgy and Bess*) coalesce into something for which fusion, following its superficial use, is not the right term.

To market itself, the city of Berlin has undertaken a particularly bold move in implementing the "Be Berlin" campaign as the official new slogan for the metropolis. The slogan is powerfully ambivalent, evoking the earlier slogan, "Wir sind das Volk!" (We are the people!), which was coined when East Germans took to the streets to tear down the Berlin Wall in 1989. That slogan possesses a Leviathan-like perspective, coupled with a Prussian and Protestant imperative. "Be Berlin," however, appears to be a congenial adoption of recent urban theories asserting that a city is not just the sum of its institutions, but rather is made up of citizens and their actions. Poised between a confession of powerlessness from the politicians and the performative turn, "Be Berlin" is an attempt to socialize an individual hedonism and eccentric creativity that the official discourse on Berlin's potential has been cultivating since the mid-1990s. Still, its potential sociality has no specific direction, and no new government agenda seems to lurk behind the slogan. While marketing figures for the turnover created in the music industry may be helpful in gauging the commercial impact of the industry, an exploration of the texture of Berlin's musical practices requires other tools. In the research for the TransCoop project, the following constellation of interests and institutions has emerged:

1. A strongly subsidized network of musical and cultural institutions, implementing a series of thematic festivals
2. A broad cultural field that is electronic and design-driven (related to 1)
3. Independent musical and social scenes that distance themselves from both 1 and 2
4. A highly qualified creative stratum in precarious social situations that faces cultural and intellectual self-exploitation

The situation has led to a cultural conflict and struggle over funding and the general vision for development in this sector. High-level saturation of an officially funded, low-risk culture is confronted with new cultural attitudes and a new imagination of what the city is all about, with new developments in temporary places and strategies. Both factions mobilize musical and auditory action to make themselves heard.

Actors and institutions in the subsidized sector raise a number of questions: How do actors and institutions reflect, target, or shape urban social processes? How do they negotiate urbanity? How do they define their relation to a specific place? Do they seek a direct impact on the city (mission statement, cultural role)? Do they encourage new forms of expression that cannot be encountered on the open culture market?

Initial observations on the independent sector can be summarized thus: Actors in the field turn the official rhetoric of "Be Berlin" against itself and use the potential of grassroots movements to achieve specific ends, without being explicitly political. They enhance an experimental attitude, a parasitic rehearsal of familiar urban regimes, and they prefer to work in low-hierarchy environments and to cultivate the temporary. While they seek a specific atmosphere, they are not disillusioned about the presence or absence of opportunities. Finally, they do not articulate a grand narrative or programmatic vision, and they do not represent all of Berlin's ethnic groups. The resulting experiences and discourses, nonetheless, have become quite influential. Urban images and concepts, such as the second-hand metropolis and lo-fi culture, have emerged, flirting with a tentative, non-postmodern futurism. The virtues of amateurism are most welcome here and serve to counter the officially funded cultural sector. The metropolis as a *space of possibilities* (see Lindner in this volume) becomes most tangible in these contexts.

Among the musical and affective strategies fostered in these temporary environments, one encounters a laid-back, pensive attitude, a control over meter and rhythm as metaphor for the independent structuring of capitalism's important resource: time. Their musical designs are non-teleological, potentially endless, lending the right sounds to the chill-out culture, which works against or suspends the temporal regimes of the service metropolis (see Rippert in this volume). Participation in sound material is preferable to coining a hit tune. Sequential resemblance, the re-cycling of sounds, the use of "dirty" auditory surfaces, and a preference for non-dramatic music prevail in comparison with mainstream popu-lar music. All in all, one encounters discrete, unobtrusive, and adaptive mood management. The latest musical and social trends from this environ-ment are unplugged rooftop concerts, the new genre of take-away music, and improvised kitchen-music parties that blur the line between private and semi-public spheres, and a superabundance of street music (see, e.g., Nowakowski 2016).

Music, thus, is a key form of expression in this environment. The new electronica scene and urban bohemia provide sound- and music-driven sites for negotiating urban norms. The image of *a second city* as the actual city (Schwanhäußer 2010), linked to Berlin's underground and subculture, plays into this. The paradoxical simultaneity of interconnection and isola-tion particularly comes into focus.[10] Alternatives to neoliberal consumer strategies can thus be anticipated, though nobody can escape negotiating the flexible and adaptive self that present cultural processes require. Music and auditory practices reach into affective households and are the media of *audio-governmentality*, which extends imperatives of profitability and convertibility to music and to sound charted as "information" and trans-lates into commercial benefit through consumer profiles available in the data cloud and social media. These practices affect the realms of affects, feelings, and intuitions (Holert 2009). The tension between a potential *audio-heterotopia*, as Terre Thamelitz refers to the phenomenon, in which manifestations and the ownership of music as personal taste are replaced by participatory strategies concerning music and the city (see ibid.). The actors in the reflected electronica scene and digital bohemia are alert to these conversions and resist audio-governmentality in creative ways. One way to act is to resist the prescribed technical formats and usual strategies of diffusion and distribution. By highlighting the uniqueness of an event, personal participation is ranked higher than follow-up content marketing of CDs and videos. These observations affect the international community

---

10 This was the case at the "Dancing with Myself" conference on "Music, Finance and Community after Digitalisation," held at Hebbel am Ufer, Berlin in 2009.

that clusters about these fields and is not Berlin-specific. In Berlin, these processes achieve a specific visibility, as we see in figure 17. Still in 2017, residents in Berlin neighborhoods affected by gentrification hang banners from their balconies to draw attention to homes threatened with demolition. Street rallies in Berlin, following the model of the "Love Parade," are usually supported by makeshift marching bands and sound systems mounted on vans (cf. Tempelhof 2017; Volka Polka 2009).

Figure 17. Banners for the 2017 anti-gentrification campaign on Rigaer Straße in the Berlin Friedrichshain-Samariter Viertel neighborhood, hung prior to a demonstration on October 20, 2017. Photo: Philip V. Bohlman.

In order to grasp the distance between these informal projects and attitudes that seek no public funding from the low-risk, funded sector, it is useful to gauge the networks that stand behind the landmark cultural institutions and festivals in Berlin. The following survey shows that it becomes increasingly difficult actually to separate the environments. The 2010 Worldtronics festival was introduced in the following way:

WORLDTRONICS 2010. Electronica Surprise. December 1–4, 2010

Club or concert hall? Neo-classical or Ghetto-Tech?—In recent months, the experts have been engaged in increasingly intense and worried discussions of the future of electronic music. It's as if this child of the eighties has emerged from its wild teenage years and is now grown-up and statesmanlike. Those seeking youthful rebelliousness are increasingly hunting among HipHop bastards and Indie-Rock mash-ups.

The four evenings of this festival aim to show that there are other approaches to electronic music, too. The Catalan Rumba, held in contempt for so long, is being redefined in Barcelona while musicians from Berlin learn alternatives to the straight bass drum in Nairobi. In Russia, Soviet Pop, Art Rock and old folk adages fuse and we get the vaguest notion of what's going in Mexico when we learn that the global electronicist Matias Aguayo, commissioned as curator, has selected acts as diverse as a folk band and a one-man-show from the beach at Acapulco. Four musical packages that could not be more different, four helpings of ELECTRONICA SURPRISE. (Worldtronics 2017)

Geographic and stylistic projections interfere and are aimed at producing a "surprise." Artists from abroad are in great demand, injecting new flavors into electronica deemed to find itself in a crisis. International networks, residences supported by various civic institutions, grants, and the prestigious roles played by festival curators are the currency in which the reputation of artists, curators, and producers is measured. Cross-cultural perspectives are taken for granted, though the exoticizing perspective rings through the references to Catalonia and Acapulco. The networks and funding policies create opportunities and enhance the festivalization of public spaces, while a real reason for celebration need no longer be provided.

One of the most influential media festivals, Transmediale, accompanied by Club Transmediale, covered digital responsibility in its 2011 version:

TRANSMEDIALE.11—RESPONSE:ABILITY
Festival for Art and Digital Culture Berlin
Conference, Exhibitions, Workshops, Awards, Film + Video, Performances
February 1–6, 2011

This year's festival transmediale, entitled RESPONSE:ABILITY, features contemporary artworks, spectacular live performances and screenings, as well as renowned theoreticians and activists discussing topics related to the radically changing digital culture and new bio-political, economic and affective dimensions of a society that is increasingly living "live" and "online." The transmediale.11 examines the Internet beyond the era of Web 2.0 with regard to its users' responsibilities and opportunities: how can the Internet be formed and defended as a central trading zone in the light of growing political and legal influences? (Transmediale 2017)

In the second decade of the twenty-first century one recent development has been the outreach programs by renowned institutions of classical music adapting the American model of foundation support. The Berlin Philharmonic and the Berlin Staatsoper unter den Linden, for example, can rely both on public and on private funding. Through these programs they seek to open new dialogues between social groups in the city that rarely interact directly with each other:

Toward the Future

The fundamental aim of Zukunft@BPhil is to make the activities and music of the Berlin Philharmonic accessible to as wide an audience as possible. . . . Above all we want to reach school children of all ages and from all districts throughout Berlin. . . .

The goal here is to create a number of different links by means of music-related projects: between the Philharmonie and various Berlin districts and social groups as well as between the generations. (Berliner Philharmoniker 2017)

Major cultural organizations in Berlin now boast considerable financial support from public and private agencies. The Haus der Kulturen der Welt (House of world cultures), the site of Transmediale and many other cultural events, issued budget figures for 2010, including the following:

- 1.2 million Euros from the German Federal Foreign Office
- 1.9 million Euros from the German Ministry of Culture
- Ca. 1 million Euros from project-specific funding
- 4 million Euros for maintenance and services
- Total budget for the Haus der Kulturen der Welt = 8 million Euros[11]

---

11 Cf. Walter 2010.

The complexity of these networks leads to the questions, Which *social compositions*[12] do musical practices produce and maintain, and under which *spatial and temporal imperatives* can music be situated? Music's potential to evoke and create alliances and projections that transcend the actual auditory material being produced, distributed, and consumed—what Swati Chattopadhyay refers to as "conjunctivity" (2012)—is not a privilege of the present-day Western metropolis. Christopher Dell has gathered music-related material from his study of street hawking in Kolkata (see Dell in this volume). The appendix of Dell's *Tacit Urbanism* includes a newspaper clipping on which the renowned Bengali tabla player, Bickram Ghosh, and his wife, Jaya Seal Ghosh, enjoy an informal cup of tea on the balcony with a large real-estate development project looming in the background (Dell 2009, 145; see figure 18). They advertise Genexx Valley, a lush, metropolitan oasis of high-rise buildings that feature luxury facilities and will be managed like a gated community—an "exclusive neighborhood" in the idiom of the marketing team. To people familiar with the urban appearance of Kolkata, a stretch of blue sky and the apparent calm suggested by the photo, probably feel like a miracle—and a provocation. Similar real-estate projects emphasize their proximity to nature and remoteness from the busy city center, while at the same time highlighting their proximity to other city locations.

In the case of Genexx Valley, the advertisement reads as follows:

> Welcome to Genexx Valley Complex. A world of luxury and comfort. Of lakes and greenery. Away from the hum and bustle of city life. Genexx Valley is all about living life in a new way, with a new attitude. (Genexx Valley 2017)

How do two artists figure in this context? Why does Bickram Ghosh not display his instruments? To what extent is he impersonating this "new attitude?" Is it meant to bring class and reputation to an environment that looks similar and that could be situated in any location or on any continent? The flavor of locality evoked by inserting a celebrity couple is enhanced by the fact that both artists travel globally and function as icons of globalization. The best medium to achieve this is music. It is no won-

---

12 I borrow the term from Chattopadhyay 2012.

Figure 18. Bickram Ghosh and Jaya Seal Ghosh advertizing Genexx Valley, Kolkata (from Dell 2009, 145).

der that Ghosh's recent projects include *Electro Classical,* fusing the "soulfoulness of Classical to create a completely new sound" (cover of Ghosh 2010) and, even more famous, Ghosh's band project Rhythmscape, which he formed in the first decade of the twenty-first century. Responses to the project include the following statement by the internationally known sitarist Anoushka Shankar:

> Rhythmscape has that unique quality of being at once wildly exciting and also deeply moving. Bickram's uncanny tabla skills and love for intricate rhythmic patterns inject a fire and pulse which are impossible to resist. Delicious flashes of Latin or Middle-Eastern flavours blend seamlessly into his concoction, a fusion which stands above many of today's stale attempts at musical integration which are happening in India. Yet through all the frantic travels among rhythms and cultures runs a wistful, haunting pull that is inherently, timelessly Indian. With mellifluous vocals and achingly beautiful instrumental interludes, Rhythmscape transports me to an India which is often hard to find. (cited in Shankar 2014)

In the advertisement, it appears that Bickram Ghosh has "found" his place on the balcony of a real-estate development. Much as Genexx Valley appears to be a fusion of locality and exchangeable metropolitan high-rise housing, Rhythmscape musically crosses traditions and ways of listening that reach from the traditional to the ubiquitous electronica.

The balcony scene and its configuration of music, musician, and actress, property and promise of happiness, merits further elaboration. The Ghosh family builds trust and confidence. They provide a testimonial that singles out a project otherwise situated in the unmarked nowhere, in the anonymous outskirts of the metropolis. The couple invests the valley with cultural meaning and relevance. Ephemeral music and sounds, and the "solidity" of fluid capital, enter a close relationship here. One could hardly imagine a Berlin drummer or Chicago guitarist marketing real estate in this way. The presence of the artists alone is said to translate musical reputation into real estate capital, affording the economic power necessary to own an apartment.[13]

---

13 The backdrop of the balcony in the ad features high-rise residential structures that appear to be artificial, as if taken from a fine-lined grid rather than from a photo. The backdrop perpetuates a decisively modernist tradition in which the drawings embody

Bickram Ghosh's album *Electro Classical* also merits a closer look. Released by Sony Music Entertainment India in 2010 and mastered in Kolkata, it couples "Indian classical influences" and "their new-age electric avatars" (Ghosh 2010, liner notes). The CD situates itself, unknowingly, in the tradition of the picturesque and orientalist, spanning a range of emotions from "The Awakening" to "The Courtesan" to "Wake My Love" and "Sunflower." Engendering a seamless accessibility for listeners, it lends itself to a variety of uses and a high adaptability. It could serve as background music, it could support an exhibition soirée, or it could acoustically illustrate travel or real-estate commercials. Musically, the intersection of funk, jazz, and rock, and the evocations of rāga are packaged in a manner to allow global, versatile marketing. The abstraction of fusion is the same as in the global names of the new secluded real-estate neighborhoods. *Electro Classical* is the ideal acoustic backdrop for the potential residents of Genexx Valley. It cultivates a hybridity à la Bollywood, in which nostalgia is the prevailing mood. A major showcase of virtuosity, it evokes musical professionalism. In such musical and commercial iconography Ghosh and other Indian classical musicians appear as guardians of tradition.

Few tracks are longer than an average pop track, perhaps a concession to the classical background. Through its very crisp sound mastering, this glossy acoustic studio music offers itself to easy consumption. The CD cover highlights the "completely new sound," encapsulating a move beyond the sound dimensions of Indian classical tradition and more recent electronic music. The CD commentary, moreover, does not address the questions of why sound brightness plays such a role and whether there were competing acoustic ideals in Hindustani tradition.

The Indian divisions of major record labels have long been marketing fusion CDs. The surge of electronica gave this genre a new boost, leading to projects similar to Rhythmscape and *Electro Classical*. The *Urban Grooves* series features a Bengali edition, released on EMI, and marketed and distributed by Virgin Records (India). Post-colonial discourse has had little effect here:

---

the architectural vision rather than real structures themselves. Modern architecture, with its strong roots in Chicago, has spread to West Bengal in the twenty-first century.

Bengal—a place where everything is "sweet" and everyone is "musical." . . .
This edition of the *Urban Grooves Project* brings alive the sounds of Bengal
in a refreshing contemporary format keeping the traditional styles intact (*The
Urban Grooves Project* 2010, liner notes).

One is tempted to ask, What makes the grooves "urban"? Is the urban a
matter of sound? The term appears to function like a catchword that lends
music contemporaneity. The electronic textures are reminiscent of other
kinds of pan-Asian electro pop.

The lyrics make no reference to the urban experience. Quite the con-
trary, they emphasize natural and spiritual topics, as if the urban soul is
haunted by visions that lead away from the urban setting. The orchestra-
tion is equally subtle, as it was on *Electro Classical.* Digital instruments
interact with supporting traditional folk percussion, and with the flute
and string instruments (*dotara*). The dominant solo voice strikes a friendly,
humble air, evoking a meditative quality that portrays Bengal as a peaceful
place. The artwork juxtaposes the Hindu goddess Durga, a Bengal Tiger,
and Howrah Bridge in Kolkata (see figure 19). At the top of the cover, a
rickshaw and a ship on Hoogli River serve as urban attributes, complemented by colorful scenes from the Durga Puja, the festival of the goddess, at the bottom. *Urban Grooves* does not extend locality, however, to
the place of recording and mastering, the city of Noida in the Indian state
of Uttar Pradesh, a major global development and outsourcing center.

While *Urban Grooves* and *Electro Classical* can be placed on a post-
colonial geography that reasserts regionalism vis-à-vis global developments and that can paraphrase regionalism only in terms of a picturesque
and closed tradition, other formats show alternatives to the leveling effects of abstract, sound-oriented fusion. One alternative strategy is manifest on the album *This Is Not Fusion.* In Chaudhuri's interventionist,
deliberately personal experience, which operates with extreme localiza-
tion, the fictive, the documentary, and reflected urbanism synthesize as
a listening experience that is not without aesthetic appeal. It does not
simply illustrate post-global concepts; rather, the artist affords a set of
experiences that confront global cultural processes without falling into
the trap of the picturesque and exoticism. This attitude is particularly
evident in the tracks for which Chaudhuri adopts an unusual perspec-

tive, measured in terms of mainstream global fusion. While the two other fusion albums evoke the clichés of a peaceful Bengal or the soulfulness of its music, Chaudhuri uses poetic material that lies outside their scope. The colorful hand-painted images and texts on Indian trucks serve as the basis for the lyrics of the song, "Trucker." The everyday wisdom of India's subaltern, thus, gain a voice and make themselves heard. Chattopadhyay discusses these visual strategies as means for the subaltern and socially underprivileged to articulate themselves.[14] In this context Chattopadhyay states that we lack the tools properly to address what urban social processes are all about. She summarizes her alternative approach as *un-learning the city*, focusing on new optical strategies in penetrating urban infrastructures and the agency of citizens.

Chaudhuri implicitly pinpoints a new framework for urban *auditory* infrastructures by deromanticizing urban interaction (see figure 21). The line "OK—Ta Ta bye bye/this is how we live and die," encapsulates the everyday, lifelong, and dangerous traffic routine to which there is no alternative for many Indians. The track "Berlin" takes off in the manner of a minimalist Kraftwerk techno track, but instead of hard rhythm the percussion picks up on the intonation contour of subway announcers "Einsteigen bitte! Zurückbleiben" (Please board the train! Step back),[15] which makes up the chorus of the track, accompanied by sustained warnings that are similar to the drone in Indian music (CD booklet, *This Is Not Fusion* 2007). Again, it is not obvious that city-marketing material has been chosen here, but rather material between a mechanical signal and the structural features of classical Indian music. The artist claims the agency for these observations and turns them into aesthetic material. This in itself is as true or untrue as the typecast fusion strategies discussed above, but it stimulates fresh responses when one listens carefully (see figure 22).

The track "Berlin" narrates the experiences on a long subway ride across Berlin, incorporating Roma musicians from Romania, German

---

14 Chattopadhyay analyzes vehicular art in her chapter "Auto-Mobility," providing visual evidence for writings on trucks (Chattopadhyay 2012, 162–98).
15 Station-specific announcements of the Berlin subway can be tracked online. They illustrate the aural geography of the city's technical infrastructure and its implementation of service voices (see, e.g., Haltestellenansage 2017).

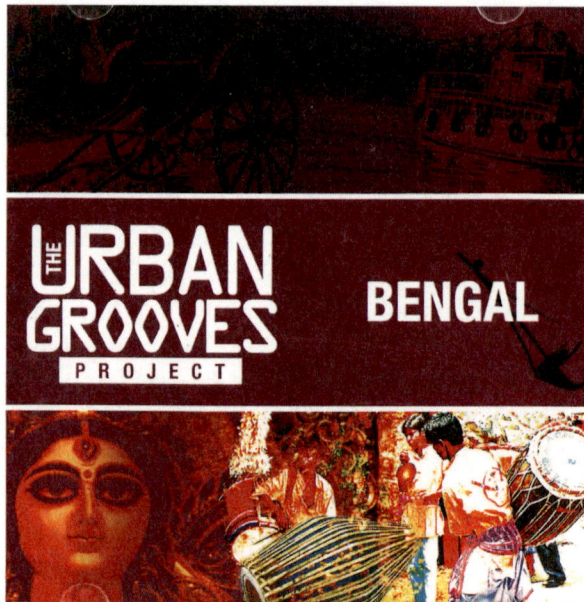

Figure 19. CD cover of *The Urban Grooves Project: Bengal* (2010).

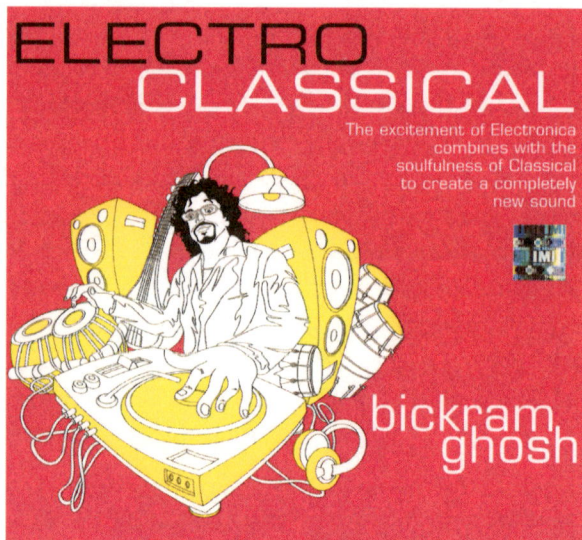

Figure 20. CD cover of *Electro Classical* (2010).

Figure 21. CD cover of *This Is Not Fusion* (2007).

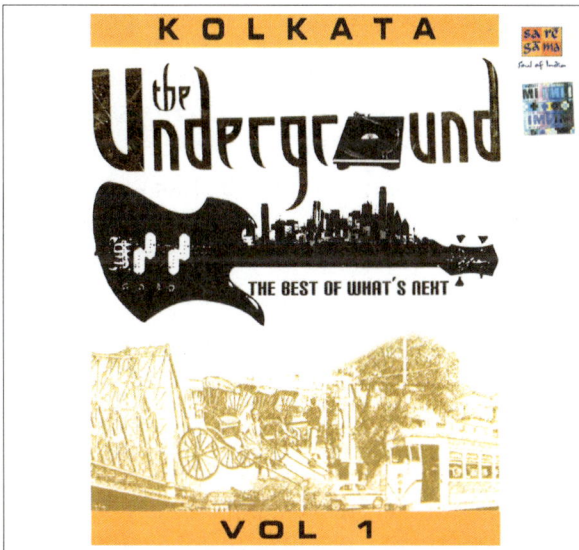

Figure 22. CD cover of *The Underground Kolkata*, vol. 1 (2008).

69

Turkish passengers, a flashback on Potsdamer Platz, the evocation of Bertolt Brecht, and the American army base in the western Berlin district of Dahlem, where Chaudhuri taught as guest professor at the Free University.[16] He adopts various roles and speaking positions in his lyrics, so his itinerary is not touristic, but rather incorporates a great deal of local knowledge. His observations may be typical, but they appear in the new way he paraphrases and contextualizes them. Chaudhuri's moral compass also extends to Berlin's homeless.

On the track "Motz," he lends his voice to a person hawking the street newspaper, *motz*, for charity, with coverage of the homeless.[17] *Motz* vendors receive a share from the street sales. This format allows them to gain a voice in public. Each vendor uses an individual strategy to seize the few minutes between subway and commuter-train stops to make themselves heard. Chaudhuri adopts the role of a fictitious man born in Russia who now relies on German social welfare and who cannot earn his living. He appeals to passengers to donate, playing the role of *motz* vendors as they introduce themselves briefly to persuade potential donors. They sing only rarely, for riders are usually upset by mobile musicians on public transport. The situation is odd, for it is the vendor who fills the interface of anonymity and personalization, although passengers recognize that the vendor is someone in need and whose voice is usually not anonymous. The song "Motz" uses a funky texture, coupled with laid-back, smooth strings, opening a proud, imaginative auditory space for the subaltern.

Chaudhuri lends his voice to the subaltern and to the urban poor. From a trans-metropolitan perspective, this strategy could be termed post-postcolonial. It is not a Western voice that highlights the misery of India's urban poor, but rather an Indian visitor, or rather cosmopolitan, alerting us to the socially underprivileged in the West. Listeners find themselves in the situation of subway passengers, addressed by the vendor, who speaks in first person:

---

16 Dahlem is also home to the 117-year-old Berlin Phonogram Archive, an international center for ethnomusicology research, whose Director, Lars-Christian Koch, is co-editor of the present volume and was a partner in the TransCoop project.

17 The verb, *zu motzen*, in German means to complain or grumble. For the newspaper's mission, see *motz* 2017.

And if you have no small change
I'll settle for a smile.
I know you think that it's strange
I've been singing for a mile.
Thank you for listening kindly
And sparing me a second.
I know you're sitting blindly
And thinking of the weekend.
(Chaudhuri 2007)

The lyrics are reminiscent of the new formats introduced by musical modernism and the new sobriety, as in the case of Hanns Eisler's *Zeitungsausschnitte* op. 11 (Newspaper clippings).[18] These formats were intimately related to the city and its fast-paced social transformation. Through his two Berlin-based tracks, Chaudhuri and his musicians act in the spirit of "Be Berlin" and actually become Berlin.

This Is Not Fusion surveys a geography of its own that competes with geographies of production,[19] distribution, and consumption of the CD. It gives voice to experiences not heard in Berlin's club scene, with its abstract, futuristic, self-referential, and de-personalizing mode. It enriches the auditory texture of cities such as Berlin and Kolkata, as well as of Chicago, all of which contain subway networks. How should the impact of Chaudhuri's CD be measured against the commercial orientation of the two other CDs? Which musical practice has the properly representative weight? And where does the exact task of academic analysis lie?

The observations gathered in this chapter touch upon processes of abstraction and concreteness, in which music is being appropriated, in reflective, trans-cultural urban contexts. Late capitalism reorganizes the matrix of production, distribution, and desire in novel ways. Abstraction and affective concreteness, given the time/space reflexivity in which they take place, appear in new configurations. Why are musical allusions used to make this tension tangible? Why is this tension relevant for capturing

---

18 For a recording of "Mariechen" and "Kriegslied eines Kindes" from Eisler's *Zeitungsausschnitte* by the University of Chicago-based New Budapest Orpheum Society, which participated in the TransCoop project, see New Budapest Orpheum Society 2009, tracks 10 and 11.

19 See above for the recording, mixing, and mastering sites spanning three continents.

the social condition of the urban arena? Why does music emerge as a key medium of urban negotiation? Why does music dramatize the metropolis as a site of potentially endless possibilities?

These questions imply a substantial recalibration of methodologies. Which approach should empirical research take in the case of Chaudhuri's album *This Is Not Fusion*? The album is itself a multi-site experience, thus data from any single city are inadequate.[20] Subjects from other cities may also be trans-culturally informed, but will probably produce very different interpretations. Musical trans-culturality does not possess a prerogative over these challenges. Globalization studies as a whole admit that it is difficult to study globalization empirically (Turner 2010, 5) and that the current toolbox is inadequate to approach the "cultural dimensions of globalization" (Radhakrishnan 2010, 39). The same holds true for our notion of the city and its infrastructure (Chattopadhyay 2012).

In order to articulate a reflexive position of observation and to resist the neoliberal positivism of the metropolis, it is crucial to admit that no objective account can be given. Reflexive observation sharpens the focus of questioning: Do we aim to understand actors, or do we focus on cultural processes of which these actors are a part? Or do we analyze how the urban momentum articulates itself, in transcultural soundscapes? For the time being, music should be approached as a catalyst for trans-cultural and trans-metropolitan processes that enable us to understand how the production of "habitats of meaning" (Hudson 2010, 443), though shifting and temporary, take place.

The challenge portrayed here exceeds disciplinary boundaries. It affects our convictions of what the global city is. If one extends Chattopadhyay's *visually* centered radical reading of urban infrastructure to the *auditory* domain, we might envisage infrastructure for a new *acoustic* field. This alternative view implies that infrastructure is not simply a given, just as much as the social or the aesthetic do not simply exist out there; rather, they need to be actively produced (Chattopadhyay 2012, 248). Processes of infrastructural production can alert us to the permanent between-ness

---

20 One could ask subjects in various cities if "Motz" would persuade them to donate, and to what extent they identify the instruments on the album as local or global.

(*infra*) of the processes and structures that we evoke, use, and modify, and that situate themselves between the politically visible and the hidden, between the expected and the contingent. Chaudhuri, with tracks such as "Motz," risks situating himself in such a between-ness, enacting the social and moral between-ness of a *motz* vendor in real life, not protected by any official discourse or etiquette in dealing with public solicitation. These auditory infrastructures emerge between the hedonistic imperative to "Be Berlin" and the vague, cliché-ridden expectation that Indian musicians will work within a classical-music tradition. They point to ways of articulating a voice, and of performing musical labor, that will resonate in one form or another in the processual structure of the city. Once we widen the perspective and tie the role of music to specific social groups, scenes, and institutions, as well as to the ways they situate themselves within temporal and spatial imperatives, we might gain an even richer perspective on the highly mediated, transcultural metropolis. Music, as one of the most critical cultural practices for the proliferation of perspectives on the city, offers extraordinary potential for interpreting and understanding the metropolitan urbanism of a global era.

References

Berliner Philharmoniker. 2017. "Education." Accessed July 19. https://www.berliner-philharmoniker.de/education.

Brandl, Rudolf Maria. 2006. *Musik als kommunikative Handlung—Musikalische Hermeneutik versus Kognitive Anthropologie: Entwurf einer dramatologischen Musikanthropologie*. Göttingen: Cuvillier.

Chattopadhyay, Swati. 2012. *Unlearning the City: Infrastructure in a New Optical Field*. Minneapolis: University of Minnesota Press.

City of Chicago. 2017. "Official Website of the City of Chicago." Accessed July 19. https://www.cityofchicago.org.

DCASE. 2017. "Department of Cultural Affairs and Special Events of the City of Chicago." Accessed July 19. https://www.cityofchicago.org/city/en/depts/dca.html.

Dell, Christopher. 2009. *Tacit Urbanism: Hawkers and the Production of Space in Every Day Kolkata*. Rotterdam: Post Editions.

Genexx Valley. 2017. "Genexx Valley—Thakurpukur, Kolkata." Accessed July 19. https://www.propertywala.com/genexx-valley-kolkata.

Haltestellenansage. 2017. "Berlin Public Transport Official Station Announcements." Accessed July 19. http://www.haltestellenansage.de/index2_en.htm.

Heeg, Günther, and Markus Denzel. 2011. "Einleitung: Globalizing Areas, kulturelle Flexionen und die Herausforderung der Geisteswissenschaften." In *Globalizing Areas, kulturelle Flexionen und die Herausforderung der Geisteswissenschaften*, edited by Heeg and Denzel, 7–14. Stuttgart: Franz Steiner.

Hewett, Ivan. 2007. "At the British Museum." Liner notes in Chaudhuri 2007 (see Discography below).

Holert, Tom. 2009. "Audio-Gouvernementalität: Subjektivität, Pop und andere Sounds." Accessed July 19. http://archiv.hebbel-am-ufer.de/archiv_de/kuenstler/kuenstler_14358.html.

Hudson, Chris. 2010. "Global Cities." In *The Routledge International Handbook of Globalization Studies*, edited by Bryan S. Turner, 429–46. New York: Routledge.

Lal, Ananda. 2007. "And in Calcutta . . . ." Liner notes in Chaudhuri 2007 (see Discography below).

motz. 2017. "*motz*: Berlinger Straßenmagazin." Accessed July 19. http://www.motz-berlin.de.

Nowakowski, Mark. 2016. *Straßenmusik in Berlin: Zwischen Lebenskunst und Lebenskampf. Eine musikethnologische Feldstudie*. Bielefeld: transcript.

Radhakrishnan, Smitha. 2010. "Limiting Theory: Rethinking Approaches to Cultures of Globalization." In *The Routledge International Handbook of Globalization Studies*, edited by Bryan S. Turner, 23–41. New York: Routledge.

Saregama. 2017. "About Us." Accessed July 19. http://www.saregamaevents.com/about.html.

Schwanhäußer, Anja. 2010. *Kosmonauten des Untergrunds: Ethnografie einer Berliner Szene*. Frankfurt a. M.: Campus.

Shankar, Anoushka. 2014. "Personalities on Bickram and Rhythmscape." Accessed April 4. http://www.bickramghosh.com/about_us_rhythmscape.htm.

Taylor, Timothy D. 1997. *Global Pop: World Music, World Markets*. New York: Routledge.

Tempelhof. 2017. "Tempelhof Blogsport." Accessed July 19. http://tempelhof.blogsport.de.

Transmediale. 2017. "transmediale.11: RESPONSE:ABILITY." Accessed July 19. https://hkw.de/de/programm/projekte/2011/transmediale2011/tm11_projekt_detail.php.

Turner, Bryan S. 2010. "Theories of Globalization: Issues and Origins." In *The Routledge International Handbook of Globalization Studies*, edited by Bryan S. Turner, 3–22. New York: Routledge.

Walter, Birgit. 2010. "Von wegen bedrohte Existenz." *Berliner Zeitung*, November 18. http://www.berliner-zeitung.de/15034346.

World Business Chicago. 2017. "Business Climate." Accessed July 19. http://www.worldbusinesschicago.dreamhosters.com/data/chicago-business-overview.

Worldtronics. 2017. "Worldtronics 2010: Electronica Surprise." Accessed July 19. https://www.hkw.de/de/programm/projekte/2010/worldtronics2010/projekt_detail.php.

zero one film. 2017. "24h Berlin." Accessed July 19. http://www.zeroone.de/zero/index.php?id=461.

Discography

Chaudhuri, Amit. 2007. *This Is Not Fusion.* Times Music India TDFWM 242C, compact disc.

Ghosh, Bickram. 2010. *Electro Classical.* Sony Music India 88697 50734 2, compact disc.

New Budapest Orpheum Society. 2009. *Jewish Cabaret in Exile.* Cedille Records CDR 90000 110, compact disc.

The Underground Kolkata. 2008. *The Underground Kolkata: The Best of What's Next.* Vol. 1. Saregama Soul of India B01A7U58I6, compact disc.

The Urban Grooves Project. 2010. *The Urban Grooves Project: Bengal.* Virgin Records India 50999 095323 2 8, compact disc.

Filmography

24h Berlin. 2009. *24h Berlin: Ein Tag im Leben.* Directed by Volker Heise. Berlin: zero one film, 8 DVDs.

India Video. 2009. "Glimpse Of Kolkata City | Calcutta, West Bengal." YouTube video, posted by "indiavideodotorg," December 8, 2009. https://youtu.be/gamHwNVEO1w.

Volka Polka. 2009. "Mauerpark Demo Berlin 14.11.2009." YouTube video, posted by "Volka Polka," November 19, 2009. https://youtu.be/FdRaZK_QiMQ.

World Business Chicago. 2009. "Welcome to Chicago." YouTube video, posted by "World Business Chicago," October 6, 2009. https://youtu.be/UOCnW4oL2rk.

II
Topographies of the Neighborhood

4

The Rise and Fall of Bar25: An Excursion into Berlin's Techno Scene

Sonja Rippert

Techno has generated a musical pulse vibrating through Berlin since the late 1980s. Names and places like Tresor or Berghain are imbued with historical meaning. Throughout the world Berlin is known as a city evoked by its landscape of clubs. In international youth culture techno is a term that occupies a place in the discourse about Berlin along with the Berlin Wall, *Currywurst*, and the *Luftbrücke* at the height of the Cold War (see, especially, Rapp 2009).

In this chapter I investigate the interrelations between the techno scene, the city of Berlin, and its people. For several years Berlin has observed a major shift from partying in conventional ways—celebrating holidays, rites of passage, and the like—to integrated concepts of event partying. Traditionally, "clubbing" referred to a type of amusement in a specific location, usually constructed of concrete, and at a specific time of day, usually at night. The distinction between dancer and consumer, on one hand, and event staff and DJ, on the other, was always visible, through clothing or bounded areas in which each was active. In the second decade of the twenty-first century, this has all changed. Adjectives such as open, colorful, extensive, expressive, and holistic formulate the new credo for celebration in Berlin. A club's function should not be restricted to one type of amusement as it traditionally has been. Instead, each individual's desires should lead to satisfaction. There is no longer a defined program or a distinction between party-consumer and party-maker. The transformation brought about by clubbing in Berlin today results in the absence of any limitations or restrictions, and it opens the door to basic questions: What does this development imply? Do we observe transformation only within the party scene, or does it hint at further, ongoing shifts across German society and the culture of the city? Is this a phenomenon typical only for Berlin, or do we observe similar developments around the world?

Figure 23. A view from across the River Spree toward Bar 25, couched on the stretch between river, roads, and railroad tracks. © 25films—Bar25 Film—Tage außerhalb der Zeit.

The beginning of the transformation of the club scene goes back to 2005 and the establishment of Bar25. This club first took shape almost as a village of small houses and campers in the midst of a wooded area along the Spree River, surrounded by grass and trees, and separated from the outside world by a fence (see figure 23). The club is separated further from the city by a wall of high-rise residential buildings that date from the 1970s. Until it closed in 2010, Bar25 was the place to be in Berlin's party scene. As the pioneer for such integrated events, Bar25 provides the object of investigation for this chapter on urban transformation in Berlin. I focus, first of all, on the interrelation of the type of party generated by the club with the city in which it originated. Second, I explore the reasons for the predominant use of electronic dance music (EDM) as a soundtrack for this setting. EDM, I argue, serves as the only possible music that fits urban projects like Bar25. During the past decade EDM, particularly that in Berlin, has received growing scholarly attention from a musicological point of view (see, e.g., Garcia 2011 and Butler 2012). It is not my aim, with such research now available, to provide definitive answers to the relation between clubbing in Berlin and the city's urban transformation, but rather to find possible solutions and formulate theses that contain the basis for further analysis.

What was Bar25? The club's name itself does not provide the complete answer. At some moments it was more a bar, at other moments more a club, and sometimes simply a restaurant, cinema, circus, or wellness area. Already with the first parties in 2005, Bar25 became famous for after-hours dancing. Just as every other club was beginning to shut its doors, Bar25 would start to open theirs. "After-hours" came to mean an indefinite period of time. For some at the club it could last for a couple of hours; others would spend several days there. Bar25 was never intended to be a commercial project. Excess earnings were reinvested to expand the club. After a few years it expanded to contain a restaurant, a circus tent, a fireplace, a cinema, a hostel, and a wellness area with sauna. Some people working in Bar25 also lived there. They tried to avoid a club made of concrete that would effectively exclude the outside world. Everything had to be organic and open in some way, for example in the confetti frenzy in figure 24. This concept of openness found fertile soil in Berlin. The city's urban dwellers and many others have longed for an escape of this type. On some weekends, as many as 4,000 guests passed through Bar25's wooden doors.

In 2010, five years after opening, Bar25 celebrated its final party. "Mediaspree," a construction project undertaken by the city for urban renewal in Berlin sounded the death knell. The banks along the Spree had been reserved for investors to install offices and lofts. In 2008, the fight began with slogans like: "Save the neighborhood against capitalism" and "Sink Mediaspree" or "the banks of the Spree are for everyone." Organizing demonstrations and other happenings, many tried to prevent the bar from closing. In the end, it was a futile effort. In September 2010, Bar25 staged its final, closing party—it lasted for 250 hours.

Prior to closing, Bar25 had been a magnet for all sorts of people. An official survey that documents the number of visitors, their age, or the parts of society from which they came does not exist. Instead, I turn to

Figure 24. Confetti frenzy at Bar25. © 25films—Bar25 Film—Tage außerhalb der Zeit.

interviews with regular guests at the club to assist me in my search for answers to questions such as: Why was the concept of Bar25 so popular? Is there a connection with the city of Berlin?

Individuals and Audiences

During the course of my fieldwork I found that the average age of the audiences was between twenty-five and thirty-five. Those who were actively involved were older, some in their late thirties. For the most part, these were freelancers and artists, but many were also students. Taken as a group, Bar25's public did not come from a privileged upper class with leisure time at its disposal allowing it to party more than others. Most patrons, instead, lived in precarious situations, not knowing whether they would have a job next week. Many seemed to be following the slogan, "party as if it is your last one!"

Hagia, Alexandros, and Lena, all of whom I interviewed in January 2011, were each typical of what I would call Bar25 patrons. In their mid-twenties and university students, they discovered the club more or less by accident. After their first visit it was clear that it would not be their last.

They all had several summers in which they made extensive use of this entertainment-paradise. "It was something like a metropolitan circus. . . . For us big-city youth, an evening in Bar25 functioned as anti-structure against a stiflingly rationalized reality" (Lena 2011).

Over the course of Bar25's history, its patrons became more and more international. In general, tourism to Berlin has been increasing very rapidly: In 2010, nine million travelers arrived at Berlin's airports (9.5% more than in 2009; see Amt für Statistik Berlin-Brandenburg 2013). Statistics report that in 2008, 20% of the total financial earnings of all clubs came from party tourism, in other words, from those who traveled to Berlin to party. By the end of the first decade of the twenty-first century, one had begun to speak of Jetsetter and Easyjet Ravers (see Rapp 2009). EasyJet was one of the first budget airlines to take advantage of Berlin's musical tourism. In 2007, they created the following slogan for all potential ravers: "The 'Summer of Love' with EasyJet: Affordable fares to rave about!" (EasyJet 2009).

Alexandros, who originally came to Berlin from Greece, expressed the international attraction of Berlin as a global party city more directly: "I know people from Athens who came to Berlin just to party for one weekend in Bar25. . . . It had quite a reputation. . . . Nobody cared who was playing or how much it cost" (Alexandros 2011).

During the early years, most partiers came from Berlin, suggesting the club's affinity to the city. Berlin is a city of extreme contrasts. On one hand, it is a center of culture and lifestyle, while on the other hand it has an enormous public debt. With 3.5 million inhabitants, Berlin was 66 million euros in debt in 2011, more than any other federal state in Germany. The unemployment rate was around 14.5%, well above the total rate of 7.6% in Germany (Bundeszentrale für politische Bildung 2013). In certain districts of Berlin, unemployment is as high as 16% (e.g., Bezirksamt Neukölln 2013).

Berlin also used to be the capital of unmarried singles. A survey from 2009 revealed that 30% of the population between eighteen and fifty-nine years of age was single. Still, a new survey conducted by Germany's largest market research institute, Gfk Geomarketing, has determined that Regensburg had become the capital of households with a single-family member by 2011, replacing Berlin, which had held that distinction for many years (Gfk Global Markting 2010).

From 2002 to 2014 Berlin was governed by the Social Democratic mayor, Klaus Wowereit, who had the reputation of being a party-mayor. He coined such popular phrases as: "I am gay and that's how it is," and "Berlin is poor but sexy." Wowereit started a media campaign to promote Berlin with only two words: "Be Berlin!" (see the chapter by Sebastian Klotz in the present volume).

Bar25 grew out of this cultural milieu. It picked up on the sunny side of the city, especially the fact that Berlin has abundant water, parks, and many other green areas, and the club fought against the dark side by setting up a parallel village that had its own dynamic. "Bar25 didn't just sell vodka shots and food—they sold a dream of getting together—people from all over the world meet there searching for harmony and love. . . . We are the city, that was the motto!" (Alexandros 2011).

Another very important aspect of Bar25 has been music. What was its role and how important was the music to the people there? The interview responses given by Lena, Hagia, and Alexandros were contradictory and for me, as a musicologist, disappointing. Music was "not so important" (Lena 2011) and "insignificant" (Hagia 2011). They all, however, agreed on a typical "Bar25 sound": It was always electronic dance music, sometimes very minimalist, at other times more melodic, but always the typical "four-on-the-floor" bass drum with the hi-hats in-between.

Bar25 had its own label with a booking agency for the DJs. Soon the club created a radio transmitter that would send the music live via digital streaming to home computers. In this way, one could hear the club before actually entering its space. This transformed music from an exclusive medium for the crowd that passed the club's door into an integrated part of its holistic concept. It was as if the club was constantly expanding itself, using different forms for creative reconstructions of the location, and thereby leaving the normally strictly-defined borders of a club zone—the case with many other clubs—aside. The club's music functioned in the same ways. Music not only filled the immediate room in front of the speakers, but it was also transmitted to an indefinite number of living rooms, which were not even limited to an urban geography within the city's borders.

Techno was constantly played, whether during the night or during the day. As a form of EDM it gained popularity during the 1990s. It utilizes a style of music based on a constant bass drum, with different patterns of rhythm and melody loops that are layered on top of the bass. Due to the steady four-on-the-floor bass drum, techno tracks can be endlessly introduced into loops, thereby creating sets of several hours or even days. This technical aspect seems to enable EDM to be the soundtrack for events like Bar25; but is it really just that?

Oliver Kautny, a musicologist from the University of Wuppertal, holds the view that there is more to techno than its electronic techniques. He makes the case for a very interesting view of time perception. Kautny argues that a techno consumer actually becomes what he calls a "parasite of time" (cf. Kautny 2009, 129). Techno is based on repetition, thus giving the impression of certainty and regularity, a feeling that has seemingly been abandoned by our society. In the twenty-first century, one can observe temporal conditions of unrelenting acceleration. Every day there are events in politics, technology, or personal life that could and do destabilize one's reality. Young people have few financial and career perspectives for the future, and they become trapped between mini-jobs and internships; this even happens after college and university education. Everything has to be done in a rush.

Techno counteracts such acceleration. Though it is fast music, it does not vary much in tempo. On the one hand, the turntable is technically not capable of accelerating or decelerating more than eight beats per minute. On the other hand, the DJ tends to stick to one type of music (e.g., house, electro, or minimal as subgenres), which in turn is bound to one tempo.

> Acceleration will be outwitted with its own product, tempo. Moments of deceleration can be experienced. . . . Techno has the potential to stop the permanent speeding-up, for example, by means of a constant tempo (*Gleichmaß*) on a high speed level. (Ibid., 129 and 135)

Another explanation for EDM's dominance is the fact that techno is not aimed at a specific target. It is a music determined to set a focus on its repetitive character. Every component of its composition is constructed as a loop. Again, this can be viewed as a reaction to everyday reality. The drive toward optimizing processes aimed at improvement, enlargement, and competitiveness is a constant companion. Habit and routine may end in a deadlock sooner or later. Not so with techno music and not so at Bar25. Here the movement toward a goal was absent. There was no end in sight as morning arrived—no end to the musical set, no end to the socializing music, and no end to dance activities. People were never asked to explain their ambitions and motivation. Partying needed no reason or rationale.

Kautny's theory of outwitting the accelerating world corresponds to many individual experiences. Hagia described it this way:

> Techno is democratic, knows no age, is optional. The regular, highlight-poor 4/4 beat makes you dance for hours. . . . At some point, you enter a trance and you can go on and on. Your daily life becomes meaningless and distant, and ideally, you enjoy a wonderful momentary collective in a bubble. . . . Bar25 was just a time sink. (Hagia 2011)

In 2012, the team from Bar25 shot a movie about their experiences over the previous years. The title of the movie confirms what Hagia and others claim: *Bar25—Days Outside Time*. The club functioned as an oasis and escape for people who felt lost in their daily reality and in stress from life in Berlin. This oasis represented a symbol of unity, creativity, and hoped-for self-fulfillment. These associations were evoked by music: The Bar25-sound was perceived as a medium for deceleration in a constantly accelerating world.

The shift toward more integrated concepts of partying is a general tendency in Berlin. More and more groups (e.g., Bachstelzen and Pyonen) get together to build their own little villages downtown. For all of them, techno delivers the optimal soundtrack, not as a dominant element, but rather subconsciously as part of an integrated party. Techno provides the steady pulse keeping the organism alive. The only way to signal the end of the party in Bar25 was to turn off the music. Techno was indispensable to life in this microcosm.

Because techno and EDM are global phenomena, one might ask whether holistic projects like Bar25 can be found in other cities. Shortly after closing in 2010, there was a rumor that a new opening was being planned in Kolkata, India. "We found a beautiful place at the riverside. . . . In Kolkata we can enjoy a freedom that doesn't exist anymore in Berlin," explained one of Bar25's founders (Vorbringer 2011). Indeed, Kolkata and India in general are known to have an up-and-coming techno scene. At this same time, the first Indian book on EDM, *HUB Indian Electronica 2010*, appeared in Kolkata (Puneet 2010). It describes young artists who try to make EDM accessible to a broader range of people. Though the book sheds light on a rich techno scene throughout India, its contributors also discuss the difficulties with which the artists have to deal. It is one thing to produce such music, and it is another to create a platform on which people can meet and engage with each other. There are few sponsors and venues willing to fund such projects.

Today, we know that Bar25 did not reopen in Kolkata. Even within Germany there is no comparable example of such a club. Bar25's singular history substantiates the assumption that developments within the club scene are closely bound to the specific conditions of the locations for any given club. Despite the fact that Bar25 itself was cosmopolitan, it could not be easily transferred to another urban setting. The founders themselves had to acknowledge this. Shortly after closing, another "Bar25" appeared in Berlin, albeit not with the same name, and not constructed from the same wooden timbers. The club, Kater Holzig, had taken the place of Bar25 as a sort of second edition, located just opposite from Bar25's previous location on the opposite side of the Spree. Today, even that location has shut its doors, but meanwhile Bar25 is preparing to move back to its original spot after managing to buy the land on which the original had been built in 2012 (Schmidl 2012).

Returning to my question about the interrelation between the club and the city, we can conclude that Bar25 was a product of Berlin. As such and with the help of its specific sound, it was capable of creating a point of rest and recovery for those who took part in the event. This, however, did not last for a long time. Today, even as this book goes to press in 2017, the previous owners have called into life new editions of Bar25 on the banks of the Spree it earlier inhabited, now two locations known as Kater Blau and Holzmarkt. Berlin's breathless pace continues to fuel the afterlives of a club that had once provided a space to oppose those very dynamics.

Sonja Rippert

References

Alexandros. 2011. Interview with the author.

Amt für Statistik Berlin-Brandenburg. 2013. "Tourismus in Berlin." Accessed November 4, no longer accessible. http://www.berlin.de/sen/wirtschaft/abisz/tourismus.html.

Bezirksamt Neukölln. 2013. "Arbeitsmarktreport für Berlin-Süd (Neukölln)." Accessed October 19, no longer accessible. http://www.berlin.de/ba-neukoelln/derbezirk/arbeitslose.html (for an alternative website, see https://berlin.de/ba-neukoelln).

Bundeszentrale für politische Bildung. 2013. "Arbeitslosigkeit nach Ländern." Last modified June 3, 2013, accessed July 21, 2017. http://www.bpb.de/nachschlagen/zahlen-und-fakten/soziale-situation-in-deutschland/61721.

Butler, Mark J., ed. 2012. *Electronica, Dance and Club Music.* Farnham: Ashgate.

EasyJet. 2009. "EasyJet Announce 'Summer of Love' Sale." Last modified April 24, 2009, accessed August 1, 2017. http://www.holidayextras.co.uk/news/hx-travel/easyjet-summer-sale-11555.html.

Garcia, Luis-Manuel. 2011. "'Can You Feel It, Too?': Intimacy and Affect at Electronic Dance Music Events in Paris, Chicago, and Berlin." PhD diss., University of Chicago.

GfK Global Marketing. 2010. "Anteil der Haushalte mit Kindern in 2009 erstmals geringer als Anteil der Single- und kinderlosen Haushalte." Last modified February 4, 2010, accessed July 21, 2017. http://www.gfk-geomarketing.de/fileadmin/newsletter/pressemitteilung/BVSD_2009.html.

Hagia. 2011. Interview with the author.

Kautny, Oliver. 2009. "Technoide Zeitparasiten: Die Überlistung der beschleunigten Welt." *International Review of Aesthetics and Sociology of Music* 40 (1): 129–54.

Lena. 2011. Interview with the author.

Puneet, Simar, ed. 2010. *HUB: Indian Electronica 2010.* New Dehli: Goethe-Institut/Max Mueller Bhavan.

Rapp, Tobias. 2009. *Lost and Sound: Berlin, Techno und der Easyjetset.* Frankfurt a. M.: Suhrkamp.

Schmidl, Karin. 2012. "Kater Holzig zieht auf Bar-25-Gelände: Zurück zum anderen Ufer." *Berliner Zeitung*, October 17. http://www.berliner-zeitung.de/3809892.

Vorbringer, Anne. 2011. "Kehren die Betreiber Berlin wirklich endgültig den Rücken? Bar 25: 'Wir gehen nach Kalkutta'." *Berliner Zeitung*, March 9. http://www.berliner-zeitung.de/14640884.

5

METAL PALLY: AN INFORMAL INQUIRY INTO THE UNIQUE HEAVY METAL MUSIC SCENE OF KOLKATA

Patrick Sanjiv Lal Ghose

At some point, urban legends gain credence, not just in their telling, but in the ways they seem to take on a life of their own. My interest in Kolkata's metal music scene began not because I like the music. Honestly speaking, and without wanting to be offensive, I am not at all partial to it. I am, however, a music lover, a classic rock 'n' roll fan, hence always keen to know what musicians are up to, and how they are motivated to keep doing what they love doing in the face of the greatest odds. My interest in Kolkata's metal music scene was piqued because of the urban legends I kept hearing.

One legend spoke of a huge gate that had been erected at one of the main roads leading into south Kolkata's Naktala district, which had the words METAL PALLY inscribed on it. Was this a way of inventing a parallel to the real gate the government had built over the road leading into the Jorasanko district of north Kolkata where Rabindranath Tagore's house stands? Was this legend a way of satirically equating heavy metal with the glorious reputation of Tagore?

A second, more colorful, legend states that, if you ask a bicycle rickshaw driver at a particular south Kolkata traffic crossing to take you to Metal Pally (Bangla, Pally—an area or locality; pronounced Poll-lee), he will do so without further question, asking only which band's rehearsal space you would like to visit. That's the stuff of urban legends, at the very least good for some laughs.

All urban legends have some kind of origin, though it is usually difficult to identify how they come about. In this case, however, Gaurab "Gabu"
Chatterjee, the thirty-something drummer for the Bangla band Lakkhich-
hara, a composer, and the son of the late Gautam Chattopadhyay (or Chatterjee, more of whom later), is the progenitor. An outstanding musician in
his own right, he is credited with having coined the name Metal Pally.
He made the comment while judging a music competition and discover-
ing that many of the participating musicians were from Naktala. Like his
father before him, Gaurab himself is a resident of Naktala.

An extract from the website for the local school in Naktala provides a
telling comment on the spirit of the people who first came to occupy this
area and forged ahead in the face of great odds.

> Our country got independence on 15th August, 1947 and was divided into two.
> Independent nation Pakistan was born. At the time of birth, thousands of peo-
> ple were dead and countless families went refugee due to political blindness of
> our so-called leaders. Some went to Government havel and some started liv-
> ing in vacant areas, togetherly. At that time, Naktala colony no. 1 was formed.
> Despite constant struggle for existence, the refugee families did not lose heart.
> They still had dreams in mind. Naktala High School is an offspring of such
> dedicated dream. (Naktala High School 2017)

After the partition of India and Pakistan, Hindu refugees fled what was
then East Pakistan, and many thousands were accommodated in vacant
areas on the outskirts of Kolkata. One such area was Naktala, now bounded
by NSC Bose Road on the south and Raja SC Mallick Road on the east. A
simple, middle-class colony, with a majority Bengali population, Naktala
remained for a long time on the fringes of Kolkata's urban cosmopolitan
center, not only on the geographic margins, but also on the margins of the
city's awareness.

* * *

If anyone should take responsibility for the radical changes that happened
in Bangla contemporary popular music in the last decade, that honor falls
on the late and arguably great, Gautam Chatterjee. Even in the second
decade of the twenty-first century, his original songs are still covered and

rendered in styles that range from insipid pop to in-your-face heavy metal. Gautam, who died in 1999, was a pioneer in the contemporary Bangla music that broke away from the quasi-classical genre of *adhunik* (modern) popular in the 1970s. He incorporated Baul and Fakir songs and idioms, as well as rock, jazz, and blues, to create a novel sound with his band, Moheener Ghoraguli, thus firing the imagination and interest of young people at the time.

In the cinema of the West, films such as Rob Reiner's rock music mockumentary, *This Is Spinal Tap*, Penelope Spheeris's *The Decline of Western Civilisation Part II: The Metal Years*, Sam Dunn's *Metal: A Headbanger's Journey* and *Global Metal*, and the VH1 channel's *Heavy: The Story of Metal* had all been addressing the musical phenomenon, heavy metal. Why? Because it had undergone transformation from a subgenre of rock 'n' roll to taking on a super identity of its own, thus becoming a lifestyle statement, even a way of life for thousands of young people.

India, never lagging behind in its embrace of influences from Western popular culture, had also begun its metal journey sometime in the early 1990s, mainly in Mumbai and Bengaluru, with bands such as Millennium, Bhayanak Maut, and Demonic Resurrection. Like most bands playing Western music, however, the metal musicians came from English middle- and upper-middle-class backgrounds—the bourgeoisie. Their music was imitative but drew large, youthful audiences, establishing a trend for future metalheads. In fact, Sam Dunn's film, *Global Metal*, includes a bit of the Indian metal scene in 2007, by which time it had begun gathering momentum (for a brief and informal history of heavy metal in other parts of India, see Unni 2017).

The scene in Kolkata was not very different. Western musical styles and repertories, such as classical, rock, and pop, claimed musicians who had borrowed influences from their Indian compatriots. These were basically, an elite subset of society—opinionated, extremely talented, and not known for humility. Their appeal remained limited to their own kind, an exclusive club of the like-minded Indians, quite happy to be big fish in a little pond. As recently as a 2012 "India Ink" blog in *The New York Times*, Michael Edison Hayden would still have us believe that "whereas in America heavy metal has distinctly working class connotations, in India the music is accessible only to the privileged few" (Hayden 2012). Obviously, Hayden had never bothered to check out the scene in the city, because Kolkata, though included in India's contemporary culture, remains on the periphery, largely ignored by Western journalists.

Gautam Chatterjee, who initially played the Kolkata bar and club circuit changed the way young music lovers in the city perceived what could be done with his type of music. Or more likely, it was his death that effected the change. When Bangla rock emerged, it caught the generation by surprise. It began as little more than Western rock 'n' roll, with Bangla lyrics superimposed on elements of Bangla folk and ethnic music. They emulated the English music scene and sang paeans of love, pretentious with anger toward life. Many tried to compete with their brethren across the border in Bangladesh, who, at that moment, were playing a very professional and, in my opinion, superior brand of Bangla rock 'n' roll. Gautam became an icon for mass veneration and little more, like Mohandas Karamchand Gandhi's image on Indian rupee banknotes.

Kolkata's heavy metal scene began to take off in 2008 with bands such as Crystal and the Witches and Aatmahatyaa (both now defunct), playing to small audiences of fifty or fewer, comprised mostly of friends and fellow musicians. In 2010, Arka Das, writing in *The Telegraph* daily in an article entitled "A Para of Music and Its Precious Metal" (*para*, Bangla: neighborhood, area, locality; pronounced paar-rha), stated,

> Naktala and metal music is not an equation every man on the street will crack. Right in the heart of this bustling southern city suburb though lies an old-world *para* that takes its metal seriously. So much so that it's named after the music it hails. (Das 2010)

In the early years of the twenty-first century, metal in Kolkata gained unprecedented popularity within a section of the young who did not entirely associate with what was happening in the more popular forms of music in both English and Bangla. They were a disaffected lot, many unemployable in big firms and corporations because they did not command the global lingua franca, English. Due to a petty whim of India's then-leftist government, teaching English had been suspended in all state schools for over a decade, leaving a generation or two with insufficient language skills for jobs that increasingly required proficiency in the language. Unable properly to express themselves in English, yet identifying with the message that metal brought, they sang their songs in the language they knew best. And so, the Kolkata metal scene gained ground.

In 2007, the first metal concert was held in Naktala, where yet another legend was born. One more of the stories quite fascinates me. The young musicians managed to raise funds from their families, relatives, and friends to hold the debut concert in a local community park, to which these benefactors were then invited. The expressions on the faces of the senior benefactors, so the urban legend has it, were sights to behold as the opening power chords and the manic death growl of the lead vocalist tore apart the placid ambience of the peaceful neighborhood. Many of the metal musicians were soundly berated for wasting hard-earned money on the evening, and yet, the scene continues to exist, if not thrive. Given time, parents can be an indulgent lot.

Once again, it is the metal music scene in Kolkata that continues to enchant me. The strong, independent attitude of the musicians and the close bond they have with their audiences have emerged almost as a cult that fractionalizes middle-class Kolkata society. Musicians shun establishment patronage, even mocking it, and they do what they must with their own resources, something no other genre musicians would have the courage to do.

Prasanna, about forty years old, is a software professional by day, but a heavy metal fan in his everyday musical tastes. In 2011, he wrote in his blog, *Musings of a Manic Manipuri Metalhead*:

> Yes, as hard as it may seem Kolkata isn't just about award-winning literature and art-house films and about jazz and classic rock. Heavy metal has slowly but surely made an entry into the local music scene as well, and by the look of things, has every intention of staying. And why not? In these last two years the number of heavy metal listeners and metal converts has increased by leaps and bounds—the number of gigs held by out-station bands [from other parts of the country] has doubled—in fact, most band competitions in Kolkata these days are being swept by promising new local metal acts. A sign of the times. (Prasanna 2011a)

I was one of three judges for the preliminary rounds of a youth music competition that the American Center held in August 2010. The majority of the entries played heavy metal, indeed, with a quality of musicianship that generally surpassed the competitors in other genres. My fellow judges tended to agree, even as they discreetly covered their ears!

Metalheads hold their own concerts once or twice a year, completely without sponsorship from the big financial brands. Sponsors that would normally have jumped at the chance to reach out to a youth market and justified their laughably-low financial support as more-than-adequate for niche events performed for niche audiences are invisible at metal concerts. If one compares what they could have spent on these niche events, however, with what they do spend on endorsements by Bollywood film stars and the film industry, one appreciates why musicians, not just in India but all over the world, prefer independent operations that are tiny but effective, in which one can happily dispense with big-name sponsors.

"Do It Yourself" (DIY) gigs and shows are very attractive for metalheads: DIY provides a way to express confidence, ability, and independence. Since 2009, The Pit has provided a DIY concert venue exclusively for metalheads. Serious metal music fans and musicians have joined together to hold concerts of heavy metal at the Tapan Theatre, a privately-owned auditorium, usually catering to a local Bangla theater audience, in south Kolkata's Kalighat district. Uttam Mancha is a similar establishment in more or less the same area of the city. Metalheads have given these venues the nickname, "Brutal Theatre." For the organizers, some of whom are also in the band Rashbehari Extreme Music Society income comes from gate sales, with one or two small firms temporarily loaning musical and audio equipment for the event free of cost by way of "sponsorship." A tattoo parlor and a t-shirt vendor pay for advertising and display space. The Rashbehari Extreme Music Society breaks even by charging a flat fee to each performing band. The venue is always packed to capacity and often overflows, from 11:30 am to 11:00 pm. There are no real profits, just a whole truckload of enthusiasm to keep the scene alive.

In 2009, Kolkata's *The Telegraph* included a quote from one of the musicians: "The idea was to get heard and make our music available to metal fans in Kolkata. There is no platform for metal bands, and they don't get as much media attention, win as many competitions or get to perform in pubs and clubs like bands playing other genres," said Kabya Ghosh of the now-defunct band, Cicatrixx. "Thus came about The Pit 1, which took place on January 27 at the same venue" (Ghosh 2011).

As Prasanna recalled in his interview with me:

> With all the red-tape and high-handedness prevalent amongst the guys who pull the strings in the Kolkata rock music circuit, musicians are more apt to think of ways to survive this system rather than think of ways to improve the circuit as a whole. Because doing the latter is not just about time and money, it's almost like going up against a brick wall trying to get things done. (Prasanna 2011b)

Having been in the local music-event production business for longer than I care to remember, I empathize with what Kabya and Prasanna have to say. It is the music lovers who keep the scene alive, even if at a subsistence level. There is no corporate, and surely no government, patronage to speak of. What support there is trickles down with meager and mean-spirited grants, with the consequence that musicians either sell out or seek employment at an underpaid job. The frustration level is extreme. The few musicians who find music labels and companies to distribute their music suffer not only from frustration, but also from a serious deprivation of rights and opportunities. The lack of support fails to deter them in any way. The Pit Volume 7 took place in February 2013, and a Volume 8 followed at the end of the year. Eight self-organized concerts in five years is more than any of the classic English-language rockers in Kolkata or Bangla bands can claim during their many years of performing.

Within this space, therefore, the choice to remain independent is preferred, and that is how an organization such as Naktala Metal Pally was born. Das writing in *The Telegraph* in April 2010 stated:

> Over the past three years, Naktala Metal Palli (or NMP, as its founders and followers refer to it) has grown into a bona fide neighbourhood, critics be damned. And what started with a handful of youngsters passionate about their music and musical idols has grown into a full-blown subculture where not just metal but all forms of original music are encouraged. (Das 2010)

Roopam, Johnny, and Tushar were dedicated to the cause. As NMP (Naktala Metal Pally), they released two compilation CDs in 2009 and 2010, featuring bands from India, Bangladesh, Europe, New Zealand, and elsewhere. They facilitated the growing tribe of hopefuls trying to make their mark. Studio facilities, music sequencing, session players, and the production and distribution of EP CDs were just some of the services they had to offer. NMP, one must not forget, organized the first heavy metal concert in Kolkata in 2007. Like many start-ups before them, however, reality hit, and the three went their separate ways in search of more lucrative opportunities.

Chronic Xorn formed in 2007. Today they have climbed the charts, not just in Kolkata, but all over India, as an outfit to be reckoned with. They say that "something has to change for everything to stay as it was," and they believe that in their music a "new trend is setting in" whereby "things are really changing though everything else driven by emotion remains unchanged." They released their debut album, *Death, Destruction, Sermon,* in May 2010. The band produced an EP and is happy to share their music on their website (Chronic Xorn 2013). They can see a road ahead of them filled with numerous obstacles, but they are prepared to take on anything that comes their way. They are also co-organizers of The Pit. Angshuman Majumder, their bass player and spokesperson had this to say when I spoke with him:

> Heavy metal is a really intense and quite a hard form of music that cannot be done without knowing your instrument. So, it's really important to practice and play really hard to make it sound good. Musicianship is a very important factor when it comes to heavy metal music. . . . I'd say heavy metal is not a culture. It's more like a lifestyle to people who live it and love it. This music gives one the power to speak out and say what you want. Heavy metal is more like an in-your-face thing. It's not a fair world and not a fair society, so it's really important to know it all. I think heavy metal is a very realistic form of music that deals with our everyday lives and people around us. (Majumder 2011)

Kabya Ghosh, quoted earlier, is a twenty-seven-year-old writer and advertising professional, and also the lead vocalist of Not Yet Decided, a band at the edge of heavy metal and alternative music. He told me: "Heavy metal gives us something to hold on to and fight back. It's not just music, it's one of the strongest philosophies ever" (Ghosh 2011). Prasanna makes a pertinent point in his blog:

> Of course this genre of music, being what it is, heavy metal across the country (and even internationally) has always needed to carve out its own path for

survival, not being overly dependent upon the mainstream rules and norms.
In these last few years it had been extremely heartening to see the rapid development of bands from the city. (Prasanna 2011a)

How did this music and its following, in fewer than forty months, suddenly take on a momentum of its own to become the favorite live act at
almost all college festivals, pub-rock shows, and rock concerts, not just
in Kolkata, but all across India? Blogger Dibyajyoti (whose blog seems to
have vanished from the internet) observed three years ago:

> The present scene is believed to have a significant effect on the youth all over,
> well known for their revolutionary thinking and rebellious and inquiring dis-
> position going back to the Bengal Renaissance. Bands . . . continue to make
> rock and heavy metal a source of constant entertainment. (Dibyajyoti 2010)

Some three years ago, an anonymous writer in the online journal *Global
South Sephis e-magazine* wrote the following in a piece called "Changing
Face of Kolkata's Western Music Listeners":

> Internet and the overall availability of international music is the reason why
> the younger generation (mostly sixteen to twenty-five) has become more wa-
> tertight when it comes to preferences and listening nowadays. The forerunners
> of this new wave are the metal heads or the head bangers. Heavy metal music
> all over the world is known for its fans and followers. Probably no other music
> in the whole world has such a clannish following. It is no exception in this city.
> (Anonymous 2010)

I might offer an entirely empirical observation to explain the situation in
Kolkata. For more than thirty years, completely a part of India's democratic political system, a Communist government ruled without interruption in West Bengal. Apart from all the reforms and progress they claim
to have made, the detriment to popular culture caused by the Communist
government is studiously avoided or ignored by critics. Popular culture has
been defined by the ruling Left parties' versions of dialectics. Acceptability
took prime position within the carefully constructed insularity of present-
day Bengali culture. This was ordained by *Diktat*, written or not. It was,
therefore, politically correct to perform, say, *rabindrasangeet* (songs based
on repertories created by Rabindranath Tagore) as a crass though faithful
rendition of the original, but to interpret it in another language or form. To

deconstruct was abominable. In fact, even after copyright lapsed in 2002, the alternative versions of Tagore's music that were produced were timid forays that did little or nothing to enrich or enhance modern Bengali culture. A dramatized performance of a Bangla translation of George Orwell's *Animal Farm* in neighboring Hooghly district, for example, which was understood by some party cadres to be a critique of the Left, was banned. The shooting of a film on the Nandigram land-issue was blocked because some feared uncomfortable questions about the Left's role. Over the course of thirty-plus years, an inglorious tradition of banality, mediocrity, and hypocrisy in the arts and the cultural sphere of Bengal has been sustained. Innovation and invention, the potential to think outside the box, and the will to be really different were all denounced and discouraged.

There were enough artists and cultural performers who happily filled the slots that needed occupying. Mediocre renditions and performances of acceptable, established music run parallel and flood the market even today: Rabindrasangeet, *nazrulgeeti*, Hindustani classical, and *palligeet* (folk music). The same goes for the weak subset of English cover bands that are churning out "originals" while stuck in the rut of performing live cover versions of popular English classic-rock songs to pub and club audiences.

To be fair, the current right-of-center government, which gained a historical political victory and unseated a three-decades-old government on the Left in elections during the 2010s because of their call for change, is just as arbitrary and unconcerned about art and cultural issues. We see two sides of the same coin. The center-right government, in fact, has gone a step farther by placing recorded loops of the Bengali Nobel Laureate, Rabindranath Tagore, at traffic signals to soothe frayed commuter nerves.

Amid all this, metal has, unnoticed, gained ground in Kolkata among younger people frustrated with traditional and acceptable forms of culture. Faced with the depressing prospect of unemployment and underemployment, of never really having enough money for burgeoning consumerism, and of not being competitively qualified, many young people in Kolkata also lack the resources their peers in the other cities seem to have.

As Prasanna, a respected elder of the youthful heavy metal crowd has noticed:

Like all people trying to earn their bread and butter, for musicians as a whole (apart from the lucky few) life is nothing but a huge struggle. I mean, they don't have a steady nine-to-five income like the average yuppie and yet their day-to-day expenses are on par (or maybe even more) than theirs. So unless there is a Mother Teresa in their midst, most musicians would probably rather spend more time thinking about themselves and how to survive in this non-existent rock music circuit in our city. . . . Currently the job market is in a horrendous state, and the youth need more employment opportunities, otherwise they'd end up migrating to other cities—or worse, they'll join a heavy metal band! (Prasanna 2011a)

The heavy metal genre is a way to express this frustration and hopeless-ness. The deep-throated, pained growl of the vocals, the distorted guitars, the manic drumming, the crazy head banging and hair swinging, and the mingling and mangling of the mosh pit in front of the concert stage are all ways to release their angst, albeit temporarily. This is all happening in an organized manner away from the gaze of the public eye, away from the hustle and bustle of other musicians randomly looking for sponsors and patrons to provide them with opportunities, who are desperate to re-main suspended in the public awareness zone. The headbangers are qui-etly but surely getting their act together and becoming truly independent of strictures considered typical and par for the course by musicians from other genres.

Making their own political statement, quite evidently full of irony and frustration, along with a dash of wry humor, an anonymous group calling themselves "Bharatiya Metal Head Community" released a black-and-white poster with Bangla text during the last election campaign, ask-ing people to vote for the symbol, the universally recognized heavy metal sign of two fingers on either side of two folded fingers, enclosed by the folded thumb signifying the horns of the devil (see figure 25).

Given this frame of reference, it is not strange that many of these young people have chosen to be full-time musicians solely performing metal. The frustration still remains as the chances for lucrative advance-ment are slim, but at least they are frustrated doing what they love. This is better than considering suicide while holding a nine-to-five job, or becom-ing an outsourced wage slave. One of the young musicians with whom I spoke said that his parents had bought his guitar and equipment for him

Figure 25. Bharatiya Metal Head Community election poster.

because he had no job. They preferred that he play music, even if they did not understand it, to allowing him to sit idly. We witness what I should like to call a paradigm shift in attitudes.

An article by Shomi Gupta on contemporary music in India in the Goethe Institute's former online magazine, *Art & the City*, states it this way:

> Kolkata, for one, has never really been an important peg in this neo-cultural rub of things. Although the city is well known for its patronage of live music, the infrastructure for the same is still lagging behind that of the others. . . . Thus, even though bands are trying to make their own music and find their way up through winning competitions, it's tough to find a platform beyond that. (Gupta n.d.)

While guitarist Amyt Dutta says that contemporary music in India

> does not provide the spirit of independent music with enough food to keep growing, others are actually glad that the lower cost of living in this metro helps them stay afloat during this period of change for independent music. (Dutta 2011)

Despite all the negative commentary and what the doomsayers claim about Kolkata's contemporary music scene, it is not surprising that the heavy metal musicians are the ones who have hope. Tushar Banerjee, a drummer who began life in heavy metal and was a co-founder of Naktala Metal Pally, states:

With Heavy Metal music, the youth have started understanding the technical aspects of music . . . [and] as a result, the expectations of music lovers have risen and bands are improving too. . . . With the start of the metal movement the youth suddenly are not wasting their time sitting at clubs and passing lewd comments at girls. (Banerjee 2011)

A sense of independence has grown among Kolkata's youthful musicians, and a feeling of being responsible for their actions is awakening. Consumerism has changed them, but it has been a superfluous change. Deep down, they know they cannot afford all that they seek to have. Their lyrics reflect this recognition. Mostly apolitical, their music is concerned with loss and evil: the loss of love or life, the evil of people and desire. They connect with their audience at a very basic level. Angshuman of Chronic Xorn describes their lyrics as "based on the darker part of the human mind or about war or the realistic issues that surrounds us. We prefer to keep our lyrics simple yet realistic in nature" (Majumder 2011). They have captured their generation's interest. No other genre musicians can make the same boast. Their performances are theatrical and powerful shows of aggression. Still, they convey a sense of community, of commonality, of a genuine connection to their listeners. They attempt to be a mirror of their generation.

This generation has come of age in a quasi-liberal, conservative environment, in a middle-class and proletarian space that does not approve of many of the issues needing to be confronted. Niceties are encouraged, and the unknown remains unspoken. When they do have money, they buy cheap equipment and pay to perform. Anything else is too expensive to spend hard-earned cash on. The same is true for their listeners. It is a typical myth, probably perpetuated by those who do not like the music and perhaps feel threatened by it, that metalheads in India are steeped in hard drugs and satanic culture, something more prevalent in the West. Once again, Prasanna makes an acid comment:

The problem is, in our society music is still looked upon as something a person does in his/her leisure time. Music and "serious work" is rarely seen on the same page of a book, if you know what I mean. So until this mentality changes I do not think music will ever be a harbinger for any sort of change that might occur in our society. (Prasanna 2011a)

The Naktala myth has outgrown itself. The musicians now come from all parts of the city, all strata of society and are consequently reaching out to young people all over: Chronic Xorn, Yonsample, Evil Conscience, What Escapes Me, Age of Chaos, Not Yet Decided, Distorted Thought Pattern, and more. In fact the city's first female vocalist and female-fronted band, Crematory Art, have broken the male-dominated barriers, not only because of a woman upfront, but also because they are good at what they do. They are probably the third such girl-band in India, along with Delhi's Hypnotic Sunday and Mumbai's Chronic Phobia. The names of the Kolkata bands themselves are indicative of their attitude and a reflection of where they see themselves in the entire universe.

I cite here what I wrote several years ago in the Goethe Institute's *Art & the City* website:

> As a geographical location, Metal Pally (or Metal Zone) doesn't exist. . . . Metal Pally is a country of their own. Not a Utopian vision, or one that's drug-induced, but a specifically carved out space which is at once typical of the city, and alien to it. They see it as a collaborative space, where no dogma and diktat prevail. With no major sponsors here to provide incentive, they have through sheer hard work and determination held music concerts with their own meagre resources. (Ghose n.d.)

They no longer restrict themselves to Bangla lyrics, except when appropriately inspired, but have jumped onto the global bandwagon. Songs in English mean wider national reach and, as they further aspire, international listeners. The internet has turned everyone into virtual next-door neighbors. Metal Pally of Kolkata can now provide access to the world from their sleepy little suburban homestead, and the reverse is also true.

I have found that serious and sincere musicians, and metalheads are everyday, average young women and men, trying to do something meaningful and positive with their lives. Perhaps they are the same as other young people all over the world, and perhaps they are typical of generations past and generations to come. This does not dilute what they are consciously trying to achieve in Kolkata. For this culture of metalheads music is of highest priority. They do what they can to keep themselves afloat on the choppy sea of competition and one-upmanship. In a world where there may be no jobs and no corporate careers, there is still metal!

Metal musicians in Kolkata may not be out to change the world, but they still want to teach it a lesson.

References

Anonymous. 2010. "Changing Face of Kolkatas Western Music Listeners." No longer accessible. http://sephisemagazine.org/contemporary-south/changing-face-of-kolkatas-western-music-listeners.html.

Banerjee, Tushar. 2011. Interview with the author.

Chronic Xorn. 2013. "Chronic Xorn: Indian Heavy Metal." No longer accessible. http://www.chronicxorn.com/p/music.html.

Das, Arka. 2010. "A *para* of Music and Its Precious Metal." *The Telegraph*, April 13. http://www.telegraphindia.com/1100413/jsp/calcutta/story_12247265.jsp.

Dibyajyoti. 2010. Blog post. No longer accessible.

Dutta, Amyt. 2011. Interview with the author.

Ghose, Patrick Sanjiv Lal. n.d. Text in the Goethe Institute's former online magazine, *Art & the City*. No longer accessible. http://www.goethe.de/ins/in/lp/kul/mag/kus/dam/kol/en9135631.htm.

Ghosh, Kabya. 2011. Interview with the author.

Gupta, Shomi. n.d. Text in the Goethe Institute's former online magazine, *Art & the City*. No longer accessible. http://www.goethe.de/ins/in/lp/kul/mag/kus/dam/en5104122.htm.

Hayden, Michael Edison. 2012. "India's Heavy Metal Scene: From Underground to Mainstream." *The New York Times*, April 11. https://india.blogs.nytimes.com/2012/04/11/indias-heavy-metal-scene-from-underground-to-mainstream.

Majumder, Angshuman. 2011. Interview with the author.

Naktala High School. 2017. "The Brief History of Naktala High School." Accessed July 24. http://www.naktalahighschool.org/history.php.

Prasanna. 2011a. "The Pit v.5—Rising Fists." *Musings of a Manic Manipuri Metalhead*. Last modified accessed May 2, 2011, accessed July 24, 2017. http://cprasannas.blogspot.in/2011/05/pit-v5-rising-fists.html.

———. 2011b. Interview with the author.

Unni, Deepti. 2017. "The Metalhead's Guide to the Indie Scene." Accessed July 24. http://popsplat.in/2013/06/13/the-metalheads-guide-to-the-indie-scene.

III
Interventions and the Experience of Urban Space

6

Kolkata Monodosis: Five Takes on Urban Intervention Research

Christopher Dell

Take 1—Kolkata Monodosis

Inspired by the diverse and exciting social life on Kolkata's pavement, which owes much to the cultural practice of the hawkers who occupy it, I decided to do a project on the streets. I took my concept of monodosis, which is research on musical form, and transformed it into what I here call urban-space intervention. My intent was to use monodosis as a kind of performative plug-in for the city, which responds to specific situations, while at the same time provoking interaction with everyday pedestrians and street hawkers. How did I achieve this? Very simple: A solo-improvising vibraphone meets urban-space production. At the point of encounter, cultural practice starts to work in various dimensions. Performative research on form, material, energy, and transformation emerges.

Because we chose ten locations, scouted out in advance by my Kolkata colleague, Patrick Ghose (see his chapter in this volume), we might also interpret the project as a portrait of Kolkata: It works in different spaces, within different levels of society, on different economic layers. Even the instrument I use is Kolkata-specific, for it is the only vibraphone in the city. In the 1950s the vibraphone was brought to Kolkata by Victor Feldman, who later played as a pianist with Miles Davis, and given to Antonio Menezes, a protagonist of the then-thriving Calcutta jazz scene of the 1950s, 1960s, and early 1970s. Menezes later constructed a frame for the instrument, enabling him to carry it around more easily. This mobility would become very handy for the endeavor upon which we were to embark.

While undertaking the project, we realized that it functions on many different levels. Because my way of playing was very different for the culture of Kolkata, we observed an alienation effect, which in turn opened up experience. People could react directly to the musical performance without having to label it. Reactions from those experiencing the vibraphone and its player on the Kolkata streets might vary from nodding their heads with the music's rhythm to making a video of the performance with a cellphone to asking questions about the performance to telling friends what is happening or, finally, to just passing by, ignoring what is happening on the street.

After each performance a dialogue with the audience unfolded. The question that came up most often was, Why do you do this? What is your aim? Even as this question was being posed, the answer was already being given. The intention of Kolkata monodosis was to raise questions about today's practices, the use of urban space. It further asked what is formal or what is informal, what is used or misused, what is public and non-public, and so on. With this project I wanted to expand creativity, allowing space for alternative perspectives on and readings of the urban. I wanted to generate perspectives that extend beyond the mere application of form, but encourage reflection on how and why forms are created.

In this way monodosis becomes a kind of performative meta-practice that situates improvisation in the focus. Improvisation becomes interaction in real time, the constructive use of disorder in a transforming community. As Joseph Beuys expanded the notion of fine arts to arrive at the *soziale Plastik* (the sculpting of the social), the Kolkata monodosis project could stand for an "expanded" way to interpret musical practice (see Harlan 1984). By widening the aspects of music in this project, I arrived at a social technology that I here call "improvisation technology." Improvisation technology is about the organization of space in time; it is about using economy, not as a given, but as an asset. It strives to enable one to perform, to inform, and to provoke reflection on form. I hope that improvisation technology might open new ways of reading and appropriating urban space in the future.

Once our team embarked on the project, everybody got deeply involved in the process of making it happen. Producing the film with Ranu Ghosh, Patrick Ghose, and Rajak A. was thus not merely intended to be a one-to-one capture of street interventions. The cooperation within the film team was a creative interdisciplinary process in itself, which on a meta-production level stands for an artistic endeavor of finding an experimental form of and in itself. In this way, improvisation technology opens yet another level, another dimension of the possibilities for interpretation, readings of the totality of the project. In addition to the physical objects produced by the project—the film and the webpage—the research resulted in my book, *Tacit Urbanism* (Dell 2009).

Take 2—Site Specific

Esplanade, morning, 9:00 am
My first gig on the street. Esplanade is a flowing space, which at 9:00 am is just awakening. I struggle to find the right way to project, to concentrate.

Park Street, morning, 10:00 am
Traffic here is extremely linear. That makes it easier for me to plunge in and find the rhythm.

BBD Bagh, late morning, 11:00 am
An evening in Paris at midday in BBD Bagh. A cheering and dancing crowd. The site has a very ordered, yet flowing quality.

Shyambazar, midday, 12:00 pm
The people gathering behind me give me back-up and energy. And so the open space becomes dense, and I can accompany the sounds of this multilayered crossing.

Babu Ghat, midday, 1:00 pm
Also a very linear site, topographically located between the river and a main traffic axis. Performing here means playing in an in-between space. From the left I receive maximum silence, from the right maximum noise.

109

The people from the ferry, coming from Howrah, have to pass by, they have no time. The people who live here enjoy what they experience, but do not seem to be accustomed to concerts. They are the ones who react the most to my body-work.

Kumatuli, late midday, 2:00 pm
Narrow and very peaceful. The silence takes me by surprise, after having adjusted to the Kolkata sound level. People and goddesses are watching me. The door, in front of which I perform, seems to draw me into a private space.

City Center, afternoon, 3:00 pm
The open space that is most carefully planned is also the most haunting. People stand very far away from me. The hybridity of the space slows down my playing. Playing here is more observing than acting.

Riverside, afternoon, 4:00 pm
A very mellow place, and in that respect one of the most comfortable to play in. Here I am offered tea. The train that passes by opens yet another rhythmic dimension.

Shealdah, late afternoon, 5:00 pm
I am completely lost in the ocean of streams. To fight it is impossible.

Gariahat, evening, 7:00 pm
The last session, and I am already over the top. But this is the place I am the most acquainted with. I have been here many times because the layering and movement of this site are the most remarkable and inspiring to me.

Take 3—Urban Governance

Urban governance during the past fifteen years has concentrated on economic liberalization. Linking India with the global economy has led to a massive influx of capital from outside the country and also a rise in investment from within. The aim was to increase employment within or around urban centers. Although many jobs have been created, to a much larger extent jobs have been cut in the formal sector, leading to an extreme increase of labor in the informal sector during recent years. The strategy of keeping budgetary deficits low, moreover, has led to a low rate of infrastructural investment. Accordingly, we observe a destabilization of the agrarian economy, causing high unemployment also in rural areas, thereby leading again to rapid urban growth.

At the present time, it is obvious that an urban strategy based solely on the organized sector is not viable on account of its limited capacity to create employment and income for the lower classes. The local Kolkata municipality has stated clearly that as soon as they change the strategy toward the hawkers as a development emphasizing informal organization, workers will become overcrowded, encouraging even more of them to spill out onto the pavement. The truth is, nonetheless, that it is happening anyway.

The HSC (the umbrella organization for hawkers) estimates that about seventy-five percent of the local workforce is working in the informal sector, many of them migrants from rural areas who come into the city during the day and return to the countryside in the evening. Some stay in the city during the workweek but go home to the village for a single day. As we well know, hawking is not isolated to the urban center. There is a high proportion of women laborers in the home, who, in small production units, produce goods that are then sold in the city. Usually, such goods are cheaper than the goods that come through retail markets such as Barabazaar. There, goods from Mumbai, Delhi, and other cities are sold. Because many middlemen are involved, these goods are more costly. It follows that hawking functions as an outlet for regional and local small-scale productivity.

The eastern periphery of Kolkata has been witnessing significant transformation, leading to extensive housing investment for the upper and middle classes. New projects continue to be developed along the highway bypass, including five-star hotels, élite residential complexes, private hospitals, and sites for leisure activity. These units are isolated, and their connections to the city cause huge traffic problems. At the same time we see the widening of streets, the reduction of public space, the construction of barricaded parks by private agencies, and the increase of personalized transport infrastructure, accompanied by a decline in public transport. This can be interpreted as a manifestation of a dualistic conception of urban planning instead of a strategy for heterogeneous development across society.

Low-income housing, as well as organizational issues in the city center itself (e.g., traffic and waste management), have been neglected. The exclusionist agenda of urban growth without resettlement or rehabilitation encourages those ousted by growth to migrate to the center and work there on the sidewalks.

Rajiv Gandhi once stated that Kolkata is a dying city. One of the reasons that it is not dying, however, lies in the thriving informal sector and the continuing interaction with the rural hinterland. Circular migration remains a continuing process, providing a low capital-production network in periods of decline in the formal employment. At the same time, we must recognize, Kolkata's hostile policy environment is also due to the fact that hawking causes traffic congestion, accidents, health hazards, and problems for shop owners, who depend on pedestrian traffic.

Taking these factors into consideration, it seems obvious that there is a need to recognize the explicit role of the informal sector in development plans. This holds especially true for the hawkers, since they work in the open public sphere, implicating them in a political economy of change in the planning and management of the city.

Policy Shifts

In Kolkata the liberalization policy, together with the decline of the industrial sector, led to a massive increase in hawking over the past thirty years. It was only with the start of the national policy that hawking came into the picture of local policy. With the current establishment of the APEX Committee we can observe a policy shift from the eviction and relocation of hawkers to the regulation of hawking. That leads to a more systematic, integrated approach taking into account various interests in the city. Three major players are involved: the KMC, the police, and the hawker umbrella organization (HSC).

The role of the architect in this process, as Manish Chacraborty states (Dell 2009, 84), is to be the enabler, the one who in small-scale projects contributes to both formal and informal measures that can moderate the urban process. The central task of city management, thus, is to provide a framework for dynamic transformation, not only for global financial or information-technology concerns, but also for the local low-capital, informal economies. This is not only tied to physical measures, but also to a change of legal structures and politics. The impact of globalization on urban governance is mostly seen as liberation for cities, removing the tight national control that made them dependent on national policy. As we see in the case of Kolkata's street hawkers, however, it has worked in just the opposite way: It was a national policy that made local change possible.

Reflecting on the relation between space and the ways it becomes part of urban geography, Henri Lefebvre has correctly asserted that physical land results from both the means and forces of production (Lefebvre 1991). Physical space in Kolkata is under pressure. Even though there is an increase in prices for residential as well as business space, there is an increase of only four percent of public space and six percent of street space. Looking at the hawker issue and the negotiation of open, public space accompanying it, we can observe how governmental techniques of controlling society become highly physical. This issue also acknowledges the critical importance of everyday struggle connected to making and unmaking the urban. The conflict over urban space reveals that neither the politics undertaken in secret nor the politics generated solely by laws, governmental rulings, and institutions lies solely in the political configurations of the everyday. The materiality of the process reveals that politics is conducted by the combination of these two, by a dialectical movement.

Working on the urban is essentially a matter of understanding form. It is not a reduction of constructed form, but rather an expansion into the form of politics, problematizing the notion of form in the context of politics, because forms are the concrete problems, with which politics engages. For the hawker it is clear that a small formal change in a national policy can have a major impact. The public presence of hawkers also reveals how a group that formerly had no voice tries to make itself heard in the political arena, by introducing form, thus trying to bridge the gap between the informal and the formal.

Hannah Arendt ([1951] 1959) has stated that, in order to enjoy rights, we require "the right to have rights." This is a highly formal question. In the case of the hawkers, the fight for recognition, in other words, for receiving legal recognition, means yearning to converse anew, beyond pre-established procedure of form. When Jürgen Habermas (1990) observed that there is nothing to invent, that we can only conserve what we have already gained, he was surely concerned about already achieved normative benefits, such as social security. When this is only true for a certain group within society, however, how do you go about bringing it about? And how do you anticipate structural changes, for example, in the economic sector?

We conclude, then, that the complex interplay of political, social, and cultural factors cannot be reduced to a single narrative of city planning. Hawkers are still in a state of "permanent exception," but they, together with the Apex committee, are working on a way to find a form for the informal, to strip away uncertainty somewhat and become legally definable in terms of license, retirement plans, and space. The complex economic and social movement in the city, the territorial expansion of hawkers, on one hand, and the widening of streets and the construction of traffic flyovers, on the other hand, oblige public officials to consider "right-sizing," if only tacitly. In the process of governing a city, the task of governing its population, resources, and other factors becomes interlinked with tasks of governing a territory. A space that has so many other forms—ethnic, cultural, economic, and geographical—acquires a territorial form. As a process of politics nothing can be more material than this. The hawker policy of Kolkata demonstrates it very clearly.

The power to effect spatial reorganization is invoked in the name of a national policy, but as yet there is little alternative to policy-making as a form of regulation, even though regulation requires both self-regulation and legal form. The necessity of including form for the hawkers grows out of their quest for legitimacy and the desire to invoke public authority. In this context they have to connect with a familiar order, which is provided by the government and the police, and they must then transform it into a new policy. Although such tactics may prove costly to the hawker unions, denying them the strategic thrust or "war of movement" at the same time takes nothing from their agency. The regulatory meetings of the Apex committee, educational actions by the union, as well as awareness campaigns through the KMC, demonstrate that a specifically new governance pattern seems to have evolved.

Manuel Castells (1996) and others have argued that the urban is becoming a free-floating network. While this notion may hold true to a large extent, it is also important to acknowledge that the urban is regulated by normative settings. The hawker debate in Kolkata reveals how these normative settings cannot be taken for granted, but rather are a matter of permanent negotiation. This is essentially a matter of form and the critique of form. One problem lies in the fact that, over time, forms tend to be applied rather than reflected upon. Accordingly, the application of forms becomes a hegemonic practice: Established form and order are naturalized and legitimated through their existence without reflecting upon the conflict that went along with the constitution of form. One implication thereof is that the truth of form lies in its liminal nature. That is why critiquing form is not an empty formalism: It is a way to understand how politics works and creates order.

Scholars working in cultural studies have exhaustively studied modes of representation. Such research must now be combined with studying action. The cultural explanation of politics provides only partial understanding of the politics of the city, while liberal theories professing good governance are at the same time too synthetic to be acceptable and too limited to interpret the global market as a natural law. In such a context there arises the need for a dialectical approach to emphasize the physicality of politics and the political dimension of physicality. Built environments and everyday interaction are then seen as the active production of the urban world in which we participate, whether we want to or not. Thus, studying tacit urbanism and making explicit the tacit political and cultural levels of the urban become important parts not only of understanding the urban as totality, but also of understanding how we act as citizens and how we participate in the constitution of urban structure. There is no such thing as neutral space in the city.

Take 4—Hawking Typology

It is surprising to recognize how dense street life in Kolkata really is. What is it about the urban form of Kolkata that allows such imaginative production? We found that, to a large extent, this phenomenon is due to the diverse spatial composition and functional combinations of the hawker sidewalk economy, which is embedded in the informal sector economy of Kolkata.

In this specific situation pure architectural design actually does not hold that much interest for us. It is turning urban space into a resource that makes the Kolkata sidewalks so distinctive. For architects it is far more interesting to take advantage of such practice than to turn away from it. The turn of interest toward the spatial role of sidewalks may start with a change of perspective, putting hawker practice on the map and into the picture. It also includes interpreting hawking not only as an economic device, but also as a cultural practice that contributes to the interaction of everyday life. Hawking becomes an asset that provides good door-to-door directions, and accordingly, it keeps residents from taking the car to a distant shopping mall and causing more congestion in the city. Hawking is not chaos, but rather an expression of the concrete, urban situation of everyday Kolkata.

In our survey we selected the portraits of hawker stands. They are divided into typologies that do not specifically derive from their functions, uses (e.g., food vending or hairdressing), and active or passive presence on the street (e.g., standby). Although such types are not taken into account in urban planning, they explain to a large extent what Kolkata is. The types are, for economic reasons, constructed in a very pragmatic, practical manner, with the possible elements of a given space or situation in mind. The highly economical efficiency is guided by the rule of minimum effort and maximum mobility. At the same time, however, they are not simply physical spaces, but rather they are also connected to the cultural level of the space. Hawkers use whatever is at hand. By taking advantage of already existing elements, such as electricity, municipal street signs, the walls of residential buildings, or specific footpaths, they reuse and reinterpret space and its by-products. The material is present, but also has to be discovered in an innovative manner so that it has utility. Hawking as spatial practice, thus, establishes a secondary layer, a secondary role in constructing environment. An urban ecology of use unfolds, with the pedestrian paths and the buildings performing several roles within multiple urban situations.

By treating the interrelations of the physical elements of the urban ecology as the major issue, we try to see the problem as openly as we can. We try to look at the issue objectively, by obtaining information from all sides: the hawker, the hawkers' union, the police, the architect and the municipal corporation, and the NGO. In this way we show that the physical composition of space is very much connected to the political organization of the city. Urban space is neither chaotic nor confused nor predetermined, but rather it is a process constantly in the making.

Modernism has given us the concept of determined planning, while postmodernism has given us the concept of chaotic fragmentation. Might there not be a new way of describing the spaces of the city that lie outside the well-traveled thoroughfares, instead along the side streets or under the flyovers, that do not form orderly routes connecting the modern to the postmodern? Might there not be something in-between, say, a concept of organizing space in production itself, as a kind of improvisation technology? That would recognize that lived-in space is constituted through the relations and interactions among connected environmental conditions, and by actions rather than by isolated forms like buildings. By looking at the notion of tacit urbanism that unfolds as urban interaction, might we not try to learn from hawking about how to make the potential of a situation visible and project that into a future of enabling the urban to perform better?

The hawker's practice can become embodied comprehension of our understanding of urban reality. Our interventions in Kolkata attempt to capture an important part of the living condition of the city, a part that, for a long time, was neither on the map nor in the consciousness of the public, though it was prominent in everyday space and life. As our study of Kolkata's public spaces proceeded, we found that, since the national policy had been enacted in 2004, a policy shift has also been noticeable in Kolkata. This gives us hope for the future of the living city.

Christopher Dell

Take 5—Improvisation Technology:
Trans-Coherence in the Urban Condition

What makes a city a spatial formation? Steve Pile (1999) identifies three aspects that distinguish urban spaces:

1. Their density as concentrations of people, things, institutions, and architectural forms
2. The heterogeneity of life they juxtapose in close proximity
3. The ways they situate various networks of communication and flow across and beyond the city

In my project I focused on the third point, while taking into account the ways the three factors work simultaneously and complement each other. Consequently, I understand the city as spatially open, as a cross-section of different kinds of mobility, from flows of people to commodities and information. My approach recognizes the fact that urban life is the irreducible product of mixed spatialities and transnational connections. This study, therefore, is not only about systems, which imply that there is an immanent logic underlying urban life, but also about analyzing the numerous systemizing practices of networks and individuals alike, which give a provisional ordering to urban life. My project thus becomes an investigation of the theoretical technology that conceives of the city as space produced through intersubjectivity. This implies that the trajectory of cities is to be understood as a set of potentials that contain unpredictable elements resulting from the co-evolution of problems and solutions. Each urban moment can spark performative improvisations that are unforeseen and unforeseeable.

Improvisation technology, however, does not speak of naïve vitality, but rather, it is a politics of hope. In this way, the contemporary city becomes a space of transition: I believe that the possibility of transformation lies in the actuality of change that can arise from the unexpected reaction to the spontaneous productions of urban life. Therein lies the possibility of transformation, leading, in general, to the invention of new spaces for the political. Improvisation is the practice that enables us to navigate the new urban spaces that are characterized by new dimensions of abrupt change, uncertainty, and insecurity (see also Dell 2011; Dell and Matton 2009).

Originally, the term improvisation was used to describe a stage of repairing situations, to correct in a sloppy way something that had gone wrong. Although improvisation was inherently associated with flexibility and mobility, its application was meant to be temporary. When cities become transit places, the situation turns around: Complex urban space takes on the qualities of permanent improvisation. The lifestyle of transition becomes one of the key features of the everyday life of people living in an improvisatory state, and improvisation technology becomes the technology of the self (Michel Foucault) that enables individuals intersubjectively to produce and use space through intersubjectivity (Martin, Gutman, and Hutton 1988; see also Lefebvre 1991). Improvisation in the everyday life of the contemporary city, though in some ways a product, is very different from the neoliberal regime of flexibility. As Regina Bittner writes in *Kolonien des Eigensinns* (1998), the experiences of East German workers in the workplace became sites of sociality and the formation of informal relationships, which became functional in the new economic order. This process, thus, is not only a submission to a dominant, hegemonic order, but as Michel Pecheux (1982) points out, also implies elements of authentic, emancipatory, and subversive practices that undermine established ideologies.

Improvisation technology does not describe the city as a transitional space, but rather it is concerned with *how* such transitional space is produced and how people navigate constructively in this space. Thus, it not only offers a meta-perspective on contemporary urban practice in transition, but it is also a transitory, micro-structured ensemble of practices. As Henri Lefebvre stated in *The Urban Revolution*,

> To get a clearer idea of the scope of the current problematic . . . we can make use of the philosophical thought—with the understanding that we are, making a transition from classical philosophy to metaphilosophy. (Lefebvre 2003, 144)

Urban planner Ananya Roy writes that

> against the standard dichotomy of two sectors, formal and informal, . . . informality is not a separate sector but rather a series of transactions that connect different economies and spaces to one another. (Roy 2005, 148)

In this process it is important not to romanticize informal practice, but to try to understand its premises and structures to learn from it. In this context we can speak of two poles of informalism: "one of active versatility and one of passive pliability" (Semlinger 1990). We can observe how hawkers maneuver between these lines—between exploiting market niches and quickly responding to orders and submitting to outside pressure from customers, accepting cutbacks, forging wage concessions, health hazards, and employment insecurity.

The conflicts that arise from the issues hawkers face in Kolkata reveal that the work dimension of urban complexity cannot be reduced to a unilinear labor hierarchy. It also demonstrates how space as practice becomes a highly political matter. Or as Jan Breman (2013) states the matter: The tendency to face-off against a particular field of employment has to be seen as an attempt to monopolize certain occupational roles or activities for social equals in a situation of extreme scarcity.

Putting hawking on the map means taking into account its distinctive qualities rather than ignoring them. The optimistic scenario would involve integrating improvisation into a policy and formalizing it to a certain extent into a legalized technology. This process seems already to be underway. The results we seek could turn out as structures in a new pattern of independence among small and medium enterprises, creating a new kind of workforce, differing both from permanently employed workers in large companies and from socially insecure, exploited informal workers. Such approaches and solutions apply not only to the city of Kolkata, but they are also of importance for the development of urban centers globally, all of which, to some extent, must face this question.

References

Arendt, Hannah. (1951) 1959. *The Origins of Totalitarianism.* New York: Schocken Books.

Breman, Jan. 2013. *At Work in the Informal Economy of India: A Perspective from the Bottom Up.* Delhi: Oxford University Press.

Bittner, Regina. 1998. *Kolonien des Eigensinns: Ethnographie einer Industrieregion.* Frankfurt a. M.: Campus.

Castells, Manuel. 1996. *The Information Age: Economy, Society and Culture.* Vol. 1, *The Rise of the Network Society.* Oxford: Blackwell.

Dell, Christopher. 2009. *Tacit Urbanism: Hawkers and Production of Space in Every Day Kolkata.* Rotterdam: Post-Editions.

———. 2011. *Replaycity: Improvisation als urbane Praxis.* Berlin: Jovis.

Dell, Christopher, and Ton Matton. 2010. *Improvisations on Urbanity: Trendy Pragmatism in a Climate of Change.* Rotterdam: Post Editions.

Habermas, Jürgen. 1990. *Moral Consciousness and Communicative Action.* Translated by Christian Lenhardt and Shierry Weber Nicholsen. Cambridge, MA: MIT Press.

Harlan, Volker. 1984. *Soziale Plastik: Materialien zu Joseph Beuys.* Achberg: Achberger Verlag.

Lefebvre, Henri. 1991. *The Production of Space.* Translated by Donald Nicholson-Smith. Oxford: Blackwell.

———. 2003. *The Urban Revolution.* Translated by Robert Bononno. Minneapolis: University of Minnesota Press.

Martin, Luther H., Huck Gutman, and Patrick H. Hutton, eds. 1988. *Technologies of the Self: A Seminar with Michel Foucault.* Amherst: University of Massachusetts Press.

Pecheux, Michel. 1982. *Language, Semantics and Ideology.* New York: St. Martin's Press.

Pile, Steve. 1999. "What Is a City?" In *City Worlds*, edited by Doreen Massey, John Allen, and Steve Pile, 3–53. London: Routledge.

Roy, Ananya. 2005. "Urban Informality: Toward an Epistemology of Planning." *Journal of the American Planning Association* 71 (2): 147–58.

Semlinger, K. 1990. "Small Firms and Outsourcing as Flexibility Reservoirs of Large Companies." Paper presented at a workshop on the Socio-Economics of Inter-Firm Cooperation, Social Science Centre, Berlin.

7

Parallel Cities in Your Ears: Transformations of Urban Experience in Sound Walks

Patrick Primavesi

The experience of urban space is multi-sensorial. While contemporary cities and their particular environments are constantly changing, the modes of our perception are transformed as well, due to the increasing influence portable media technologies have on how we experience urban environments. Sound and noise are part of these environments, inhabited by large numbers of people who need to share the space and to communicate, by mutual exchange or by messages that address groups or the community. Traditional sounds, such as bells, can have different meanings, indicating the hour of the day or the hours of religious service, an alarm signal, or a call for rebellion, but they always relate to a sphere of the common, the symbolic order of the community. Media technology in a neoliberal society offers many kinds of *personalized* sounds, also as a means of escaping the common reality or at least to balance it with different perceptions. The experience of the public environment, therefore, may be contrasted or even marginalized by individual sound systems. Such devices, however, all use a similar set of functions, and in producing a new kind of common sphere—networks, clouds, etc.—they rely on forms of limited access with mechanisms of selection, hidden control, and surveillance.

In the last decades, artistic practices have developed that play with these split and mediated realities, using the same technologies by which we communicate or consume music and sounds as outdoor entertainment: a Walkman or player with tapes or discs; MP3 and other data files; mobile telephone, or radio and web-based services. The analysis of urban spaces, places, and related practices is still focused on visibility and materiality (see, e.g., Frers and Meier 2006), but the *audiosphere* gains importance in times of digital contact. Presence and interaction in public space are dominated more and more by the nodes and networks of "informational access," which creates a *layered space* beyond the visual and physical reality (Willis 2006). As this chapter points out, the artistic use of portable audio devices can reflect our changing perception of urban environments, atmospheres, and everyday life. Guided tours and sound walks, by intensifying an experience of parallel places, times, cultures, and contexts, tend to question the binary logic of oppositions that constitute our understanding of the urban, such as inside/outside, private/public, own/foreign, present/absent, reality/fiction.

Parallel Worlds in Audio Guided Tours

When Sony released the Walkman in 1980, its tremendous success also generated suspicion. It was quickly assumed that this kind of technology would reinforce not only the isolation and the lack of political interest of their predominantly young consumers, but also establish structural assimilation and control of the masses. The Japanese music and media scholar, Shuhei Hosokawa, analyzed the so-called "Walkman-Effect" more closely and described it as an urban strategy by which the mobile individual encapsulates and stages her- or himself in the presence of others. Whereas the *flâneur* of the nineteenth century publicly performed his own habitus on the city boulevards (see Benjamin 2002a; Buck-Morss 1991), the new "audio-flâneur" performs relations to someone or something absent from the real environment. Already in the 1980s, the contact to a hidden sphere via a mobile sound device produced the paradox of an open and public secret (Hosokawa 1984). Much more important than the isolation of an individual audiosphere was its public performance of privileged access to a parallel world (ibid.). Thus the Walkman and MP3 player were already means of simulation, anticipating an effect today perfected by the new generation of smartphones: an openly visible and yet secret theater of communication. The attraction of this theater related to an immaterial sphere is both a subtle revelation of private taste and habits, and an instance of what Walter Benjamin calls the *aura*, the apparent proximity of something distant or absent (Benjamin 2002c).

Looking back at the history of performing arts, we might think it obvious that theater has always played with the re-presentation of absent beings, particularly through an evocation of the dead as historical or mythical figures. Theater audiences, therefore, are used to the experience of a certain parallelism that creates the illusion of a different world on stage, even a kind of time-travel into the past, parallel to our own presence as real spectators. One might argue that reading a novel, looking at a painting, listening to a piece of music—that aesthetic experience in general—have always had the potential to create a parallel, inner world, separated from everyday life. There is, however, a new quality of experience connected to technical media. Radio plays or movies that trigger our imagination in a more or less conventional way can stand as examples for the impact media technology has on our habits of perception. Audio walks and audio-guide tours can be regarded as another example of this influence, as a new format of an artistic practice that is also able to intensify our awareness of how we perceive the world while increasingly relying on media technology.

Since the early works of Janet Cardiff and other mixed-media artists, sound art has developed into a whole new genre of interventionist individual or collective performance that challenges the notion of the public sphere and the more or less explicit rules of behavior in urban space. Sound art, perceived via headphones or earphones, produces a *theater of the imagination*. At the same time while on the street—unlike listening at home, at a concert, or in a cinema—we also perceive the outside space, the real environment, together with its accidental sounds. Last but not least, we perform ourselves, consciously or not, as if we are listening to something secret, invisible, and inaudible to others in our immediate environment, the potential spectators of this scene.

This media concept opens up a broad horizon of possibilities, strategies, and tactics in this chapter, starting with a production by the Swiss artist, Stefan Kaegi, one of the founding members of Rimini Protokoll. In 2001, with one of his first works, Kaegi created an audio guided tour called *System Kirchner*, collaborating with Bernd Ernst on the project, "Hygiene

Heute" (hygiene today). It comprised a one-hour walk through the urban environment of a theater, the sort of area one would normally just cross without noticing any detail of the buildings and their particular atmosphere.[1] Participants started their walks individually, equipped with a Walkman, listening to a story about a scientist who had recently disappeared, kidnapped by an anonymous organization. While following the instructions and listening to the story, one experienced the environment through different eyes. On the one hand, *System Kirchner* was a paranoid crime story with elements of a conspiracy theory, a search for traces and remainders with a certain thrill, propelling the participant into something strange and unforeseeable. On the other hand, *System Kirchner* was an exercise in "psychogeography," a term coined by the situationist, Guy Debord, in the 1950s and meant to describe a way of investigating the emotional effects of particular urban environments and reinforcing them by artistic means (Debord 1955).

System Kirchner used a fragmented science-fiction story to explain seemingly banal elements of everyday reality. A participant's perception of this reality was thus intensified and at the same time called into question. The audio track directed the participant's path and attention toward the unspectacular, for example, ugly backyards, parking lots, or office buildings, revealing their "real" purpose as a factory for weird experiments, as secret prisons, or as missile launch bases. The sound in our ears created effects of *alienation*—the method of epic theater theorized by Bertolt Brecht—to make us look differently at things otherwise considered normal (Brecht 1994). The narrative explanations given by the audio track were not completely fictitious, but rather they were mixed with economic, historical, and political facts. Often there was a rhythmic beat underlying the voice, urging participants to walk faster, or even to run, in order to catch up with another person. Movement through the environment was coupled with a participant's imagination, triggered by audio tracks, sounds

---

1   The performance by Hygiene Heute took place in three different versions: *Verweis Kirchner*, at the festival *Zeitenwende* Giessen, July 2000; *System Kirchner*, at Mousonturm Frankfurt a. M., 2000–2001; and *Kanal Kirchner*, at *Spielart Festival*, Munich, November 2001.

and voices, music and noises. It was still possible to hear the noise of the outside world, which produced effects of coincidence, integrating them as possible events in a particular setting. As this example shows, the format of the sound walk offers a wide range of possibilities for artistic concepts that reflect the transformation of urban experience and the experience of the urban. A precondition of these works is a careful *sounding out* of atmospheres, a research of places and their sounds, in order to create parallel worlds that correspond to lived experience, and to question it.

Rimini Protokoll's *Call Cutta* in Kolkata

The commercial use of parallel worlds linked by audio technology expanded exponentially in the new millennium with the boom of *call centers* in areas or countries with low wages, especially in India. In 2004 the Swiss-German performance group, Rimini Protokoll (Stefan Kaegi together with Helgard Haug and Daniel Wetzel), were invited to Kolkata by the Goethe Institute/Max Mueller Bhavan to prepare a performance production related to this city. Rimini Protokoll is internationally successful and well known for its documentary or reality theater, which involves non-professional actors to perform their own experience and knowledge from working and everyday life. They chose the call center industry, which has a considerable base in Kolkata, as a starting point and entitled their project *Call Cutta*, also playing with the old city name Calcutta. Daniel Wetzel remembered:

> We were looking for a place where India connects with the West, and we ended up with a call center because it's a place where Indians imitate Westerners by adopting their names and speaking their languages. (Wetzel, cited in Hansen-Tangen 2006)

As always in the work of Rimini Protokoll (in 2016 over sixty productions in various formats and styles), the choice of the site—in this case both a production space and a topic—was influenced by the search for institutions, themes, and practices that have their own kind of theatricality. This is the material for the performances, and not just a search for pure reality or authenticity. It is not the mere reality of a call center that provides

127

the focus or message of the production, but rather an exploration of the practices and the individual beings used to *perform* the work. In this case, the group was interested in the fact that a call center functions itself as a theater. By comparison, Rimini Protokoll pointed to the example of New York pizzerias that would use call centers in India for the orders and credit card payments of customers in Manhattan. These customers are averse to being confronted with the reality of globalized business, but prefer instead to being betrayed by accent-free service voices. "So, for the sake of both the outsourcing company and their customers, the Indian performer first of all has to make sure that his theater of service hides the reality of globalisation" (Wetzel, cited in Van Lindt 2008).

After many visits, and extensive research and preparation work, an audio guided walk was developed that would lead through an old part of the city center of Kolkata, directed via mobile phone from a call center in Kolkata's Salt Lake district. This was the first phase of the whole project. In its notes to the project Rimini Protokoll referred, without exaggeration, to "the world's first mobile phone theater," as they have called this production probably without exaggeration:

> The Kolkata chapter of the project was connecting two parts of the city of Kolkata: the high-tech area new "Shining India" with the old and traditional district of Hatibagan that once was an area of Indian wealth during colonial times, and also an area where the Indian freedom fighters could operate very successfully because the big mansions and palaces of the rich are separated by very small lanes, ideal for the guerrilla uprisings against British soldiers. The audience came one by one to booked time-slots in the well-known Star Theatre. Here, the visitor got equipped with a mobile phone. The received call connected him/her to Rimini Protokoll's call center unit, located in Kolkata's northern new IT-sector, Salt Lake. In ten-minute intervals the play started for each visitor individually: A bright young cheerful voice speaking accent neutralized English called you and started talking, became your guide, your actor, your blind date and helped you step by step, through the streets of Kolkata. (Rimini Protokoll 2005a)

When they had found a call center that allowed them to use the workspace for the project, Rimini Protokoll, together with a team of twelve call center agents, started by developing a script, based on self-made maps and images of Hatibagan. The narrow lanes of the quarter close to the old University

Figure 26. Call center in Salt Lake/Kolkata, hired for the production of *Call Cutta* (2005). Photo: Rimini Protokoll.

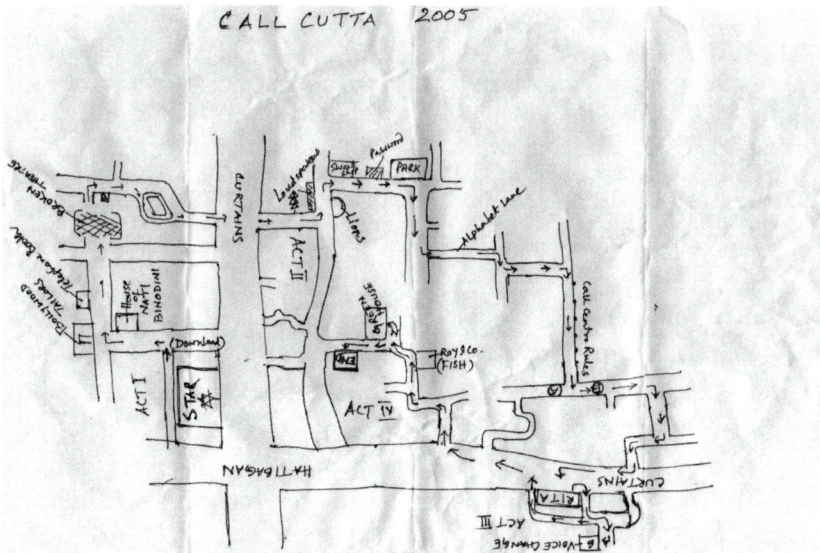

Figure 27. Map of Hatibagan/Kolkata, with the path and stations of Rimini Protokoll's audiowalk (2005). Drawing: Madhushree Mukherjee.

of Calcutta offered many stories and historical contexts. In this lively environment one would meet old craftsmen in their workshops next to the street, as well as children playing on dusty squares or entire families living on the sidewalk, but street names are rare, and orientation is quite difficult, at least for foreigners. The dramaturgy of the production developed from the idea that the participants would receive instructions that helped them make their way through the streets and also find various clues that would connect to the overall story. The story was not completely scripted, but the related narrative remarks, instructions, or questions were put into the format of a powerpoint presentation on the desk screen of the call center agents. The beginning of the script, linked to photos of the starting point, was a brief introduction establishing contact to the listener in the theater foyer and already addressing the issue of experiencing street life as spectacle:

> Hello. (*wait for response*) Am I speaking to _____?
> My name is _____.
> Please make yourself comfortable and look out of the window. Relax. Take a deep breath.
> Can you hear me well? Tell me if you need it louder or lower? *Adjust headset if not.*
> I used to sit where you sit now, every afternoon in the old Star Theater, watching the people moving across the pavement. You might think, they are your actors—and you are their audience. In that case, don't you think cars are like little curtains—showing or hiding people.
> But I'm no longer living in Hatibagan.
> Now I am exterritorial. Not here—not there—just somewhere in between.
> I will show you where I lived. (Rimini Protokoll 2005b)

Some basic rules are given: to follow the indicated directions; not to mistake left for right; in case one gets lost, to stop and orient oneself anew by describing the environment to the caller; and, last but not least, to confirm the arrival at a target point by saying "Download!"

This code word already makes reference to the film *The Matrix* (1999), one of the most successful and influential attempts to represent, in the language of a Hollywood science fiction blockbuster, the parallelism of worlds that are totally different from each other and yet interconnected. The allusion, therefore, to the film vision of an artificial world that would repress and gradually replace the "real world" of human life can also be regarded as one of the structural patterns for *Call Cutta*. As in *System Kirchner*, the experience of a guided stroll through unknown or alien parts of a city gets intensified by elements of a conspiracy theory about a powerful reality behind the illusory surface of our perception. Instead of the pre-recorded voice from the Walkman, in *Call Cutta* there is a live contact via telephone. Already in the film *The Matrix* the decisive survival tool is the telephone, in particular the connection between a cellphone on the streets of the Matrix world and an operator's phone in the "reality" from where the illusions can be attacked. Among the most thrilling sequences of the film are audio-guided walks, scenes where the hero (the computer hacker Neo, who has become a kind of freedom fighter for real humans) is guided by phone instructions through an unknown and dangerous terrain. In this context it is possible also to regard the connection between the participant on the streets and the call center agent in *Call Cutta* as an almost complete dependence. The guided person perceives and crosses the real environment by using the information and the perspective of the operator from the call center. He will learn something not only about the particular reality of the historic Hatibagan quarter, but also about the reality of media and interfaces that have started to replace this reality long ago.

It is a kind of symbolic statement to let the journey start in an old conventional theater—which in fact was transformed into a cinema some years before—by following the traces of a once-famous actress who performed there and lived nearby. The dramaturgy of the walk definitely *dates* a theater of role-playing, as well as the imagination of the people on the street as actors, hidden from cars like little curtains. Perhaps the street still is a theater, but its spectacle follows other rules now, different from the simple function of a curtain showing and hiding the actors of a stage show. Not to live in Hatibagan anymore also means having established another kind of theatrical and mediated relation to reality *in-between*, as the call center positions him- or herself in the introduction: "Now I am ex-territorial. Not here—not there—just somewhere in between" (Rimini Protokoll 2005b). This in-between is the sphere that *Call Cutta* invites us to explore not just the reality of a call center, but also the streets as they can be seen through a more or less touristic gaze. Even Kolkata inhabitants are

Figure 28. Star Theatre in Hatibagan, newly renovated entrance.
Photo: Patrick Primavesi.

in most cases not very familiar with the old quarter. Crossing Hatibagan means traveling back in time, for its appearance does not differ much from a century ago.

The one-hour *Call Cutta* walk was finally made available to individual participation from February until March 2005. The dramaturgy of the scripted instructions was still playing with dramatic conventions, such as the transformation into another character ("you becoming me") and the overall structure of four or five acts. We learn about the once-famous actress Nati Binodini, pass a street sign with her name and see the house where she lived, in the great days of the Star Theatre at the beginning of twentieth century. Having arrived at some workshops of Bollywood Tailors, in front of a mirror, the participant him- or herself is addressed by the caller as a camera, focusing on his or her own image, which might change as the person passes. In an area where groups of people sit around watching, he is warned: "The spectators are already waiting for you on their benches in front of you, aren't they?" In case of any trouble the advice is simply to say "Don't worry. I am part of a play," thus highlighting the fact that in this area many unforeseen events may happen during such a walk, even more so after the repetitive appearance of many passersby with earphones.

A shabby entrance to a Chinese restaurant turns out to be the former box office of another theater, the old Biswaaropa with nine hundred seats. The participant is asked to enter the now devastated area that was once the stage and to sing a song, as if she or he would be part of the final spectacle before the theater burned down. That happened a few years ago when, according to some "secret" rumors, probably spread for the purpose of investment speculation, there was an attempt to clear the space illegally for a future shopping mall. The imaginary need to escape the fire makes the walk even more adventurous, when one is urged to "look out for a way out of the theater." In the *tension scene*, the path leads through a decrepit building behind the former stage, and with short commands and some percussive musical sounds, there is an escape from the scene. In particular this results from an *action part* that asks the participant to jump through small doorways, albeit cautiously, as if the agents of the Matrix were lurking behind the wall.

Figure 29. Street sign (Nati Binodini Sarani/Raja Bagan Street). Photo: Patrick Primavesi.

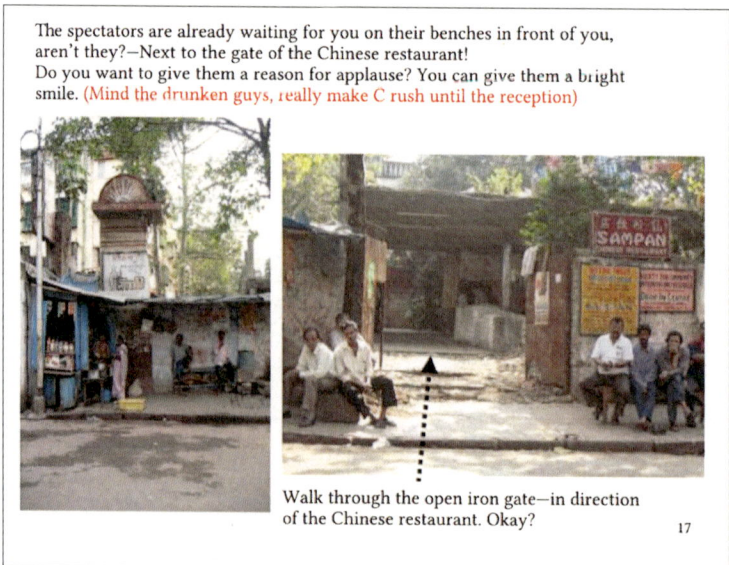

The spectators are already waiting for you on their benches in front of you, aren't they?—Next to the gate of the Chinese restaurant!
Do you want to give them a reason for applause? You can give them a bright smile. (Mind the drunken guys, really make C rush until the reception)

Walk through the open iron gate—in direction of the Chinese restaurant. Okay?

17

Figure 30. Extract from the original script used for *Call Cutta* (2005).
Courtesy Rimini Protokoll.

Because the environment of Hatibagan is quite unique in its mixture of various workshops and scenes of private life on the streets, both old and new, there is no absence of interesting and absorbing sights. Further stations of the walk are telephone booths of all kinds, shops, and contrasting street scenes. Act 2, called *Consolidation*, draws the customer into a conversation about telling lies or falling in love on the phone and instructs her or him how to cope with possible call center relations. Entering "Love Park," a playground for children, one can listen to some popular Indian love songs from the 1960s. The participant then crosses a narrow lane with words in Bengali and English orthography painted on the walls, together with phone numbers of various medical services, at which we could donate our blood for several hundred rupees. The melody in the background of the conversation turns into electronic funk, and the listeners are encouraged to transform their stroll into a sort of dancing with swinging hips. Once they have arrived at the "Regional Institute of Technologists and Analysts," they are invited by a voice to enter the world of "Internet," hidden behind one of the door panes. On a computer monitor a call center agent describes his job and compares it once more to the work of theater actors.

At this point, asked to "step outside into reality," the participant is already in Act 3, and a second caller takes over the conversation, claiming that he just hacked into it. The new voice convinces the listener not to follow the advice of the first caller, who had finally recommended joining the call center company named Garurh, or Garud Ltd., named after the divine eagle figure Garud,[2] in order better to fight against this company, which would constantly look for "new outbound-slaves." Act 4 draws participants into a revolution, in pursuit of Indian freedom fighters hiding in these lanes sixty years ago, and it introduces the new battle "to redefine what Indian call centers could be," independent of business plans imposed by foreign countries. On the balcony of another internet café building listeners are asked again to look around the streets to see if someone was following. The tour then ends with a cup of tea or coffee, offered by the

---

2   The name is also used by a special unit of the Indian Air Force, the *Garud Commando Force*, founded in early 2004, mainly for airfield seizure and air assault operations against terrorist attacks.

Figure 31. Hatibagan/Kolkata: Site of the destroyed theater. Photo: Patrick Primavesi.

friends of the call center activist, in a room where the walls are covered with sketched maps of the quarter. This could be Act 5, with the possibility of another transformation. The "customer," as the script of the call center agents describe a participant in the language of their trade, becomes an actively reflecting performer.

This tendency comes close to the media theory of Bertolt Brecht, who in 1932 claimed that radio should be changed from an apparatus of distribution into one of communication, and who also aimed for a theater that would activate the audience, or even make them dispensable in a theater for performers (Brecht 1994). While the plays of Brecht's epic theater are even today popular in Kolkata and other Indian cities, the more radical part of his practice and theory is not well known, in particular the *teaching plays* (*Lehrstücke*) that anticipated and strongly inspired the Western media theater today. Even without direct links to Brecht contemporary performance often relies on alienation effects, moments of interruption, and the exposure of acting and performing. In fact, the majority of local reviews treated *Call Cutta* as a breakthrough into new forms of theater, which were, moreover, different from the usual street theater. The walk in Kolkata, however, was only the "First Chapter" of this production. The follow-up was set in Berlin, transforming it to a kind of *parallel city*.

Call Cutta in Berlin and *Call Cutta in a Box*

For an overlapping period of some weeks, the call center agents in Salt Lake operated for the customers in Hatibagan district, as well as for those participating in the *Call Cutta* projects. With the evening shift they talked to participants of a similar walk that took place in the middle of Berlin, following the tracks of the former Anhalter train station. Again the starting point was a theater, the café of Hebbel am Ufer Theater, which coproduced *Call Cutta* in Berlin. After some introductory words the caller established the rules for the walk. If a particular goal was reached, the participant should not say "Download," as was the instruction in Kolkata, but rather "Ich kaufe" (I'll buy this),[3] as if she or he were in contact with a trader at a stock market.

The path began by crossing through the lobby of a big Postbank office building and a parking lot, where the first clue to the theme of the walk was posted: a photo of two Indian men in a café, supposedly in 1942 at the very same place where the participant was standing today. In a garbage can nearby she finds another photo, waiting to be picked up. Next to Mahatma Gandhi there is a man from the earlier picture again, now introduced as Netaji, the Leader of an Indian liberation army. He had traveled to Berlin because he wanted to convince Hitler to support the fight against the British occupation. This story is strange enough to serve as a trigger for the imagination and to provide a historical backdrop for the actual relation between the contemporary caller from India and the listener/participant in Berlin.

---

3   Unless otherwise indicated, the quotations in the following paragraphs are drawn from the operator's script of *Call Cutta* in Berlin, an unpublished PDF-file from Rimini Protokoll (Berlin 2005b).

55 Min.

You see the picture? The submarine-crew. Do you see Netaji with glasses in the front row?
My grandpa stayed in Berlin meanwhile, he kept broadcasting Free-India-speeches over the radio to India... In 10 different languages... Together with others, former forced labour workers of Daimler-Chrysler...

Siehst du das Bild? Das war die U-Boot-Mannschaft 1943. Siehst du Netaji mit der Brille in der ersten Reihe?
Mein Opa blieb unterdessen in Berlin. Er sendete Befreiungsreden in 10 verschiedenen indischen Sprachen über Radio nach Indien.
Zusammen mit anderen, ehemaligen Zwangsarbeitern von Daimler-Chrysler...

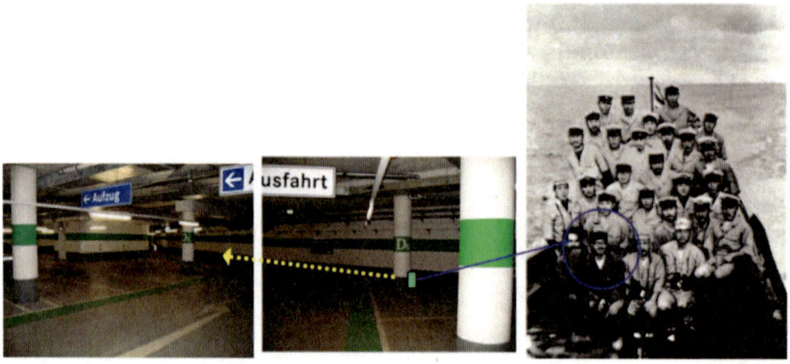

Now walk on. Keep following the arrow.

Geh weiter. Folge den Pfeilen um die Kurve.

100

Figure 32. Extract from the original script used for *Call Cutta Berlin* (2005). Courtesy Rimini Protokoll.

Act 2 begins at the Tempodrom Building. From the top of its crown-shaped roof the remains of the Anhalter train station platforms and tracks are still visible, now covered by trees and bushes. On the ground again, the voice leads us to track 5, where Netaji is said to have arrived in Berlin in 1941. The call center agent mentions that his or her own grandfather was finally convinced by Netaji to join the liberation army, "Freies Indien" (Free India), changing his name from Samir Muckerjee to Martin Heynold. German support for this army followed a simple logic, "The enemy of my enemy is my friend," and the participant is directed along a narrow mud path toward an old bunker.

A shortcut through a broken metal fence reaches Act 3, with its theme of "personal attitude." In the middle of a courtyard between apartment buildings participants are encouraged to take position by loudly articulating the password "Ich bin dabei," by imitating the gesture of a Netaji sculpture, by pointing in the direction of India, and by singing an Indian military march, all the while standing on a playground for children and attracting attention (for such moments of personal "encounters," see also Roselt 2005). Additional hidden photos show Netaji as a soldier in the jungles of Burma and as statesman meeting Hitler, who finally sent him in a submarine to Japan, while the soldiers of his liberation army were fighting against British and American soldiers along in western Europe or back in Berlin against the Russians. Again, participants are asked to imitate the sounds they hear—the cries of Bengal tigers, as well as cats and birds from India.

The noises of auto rickshaws and auto scooters are added to the sonic conversation, now getting more personal with questions such as "Have you ever lied on the phone?" or "Did you ever fall in love on the phone?" Participants are urged not to jump from a bridge that crosses the modern rails: "Wir brauchen dich noch" (we still need you). The password is changed again into "Hatcha," meaning "okay" in Bengali. After singing a melancholy tune, the caller asks if the listener would ever use violence to free his own country, or prefer to fight in the underground struggle in a foreign country? In the "underworld" parking garage contact with the telephone guide gets lost for a while. Once telephone connection is reestablished, the listener learns that Netaji is said to have died in a plane crash shortly after Japan lost the war. Act 5 is once more about personal relations and leads the listener to an electronic media store, suddenly confronting the guide "live" on the screen of a computer, who introduces her- or himself as a member of a new secret foreign legion, ready to liberate the Indian call center agents.

Similar to the walk in Kolkata, the tour in Berlin—from early April until the end of June 2005—not only provides a guide through an urban environment with a quite particular atmosphere and history, but also it addresses the situation of call center agents today. A parallelism is thus established between the call center and the environment, and between today's reality and the historical past. Since the Salt Lake district of Kolkata and the Hatibagan quarter are two completely separate worlds, symbolizing different pasts and related to different cultures, and yet connected through simultaneous experience, the connection to a city on another con-

Figure 33. Site of the former Anhalter Bahnhof, during *Call Cutta Berlin* (2005).
Courtesy Rimini Protokoll.

tinent is almost the same. The call center industry is based on the possibility of guiding and influencing phone users all over the world by a fixed
set of information. The only requirement is that the caller remains in the
position of knowledge and authority granted her or him by the medium itself: the power of a bodiless voice that reaches you from an invisible realm
of control (cf. Benjamin 2002b; Ronell 1989).

In everyday life this phantasm is effective enough not only to convince people to accept bargains, contracts, and obligations, but also to direct their steps. The efficiency of the commercial calling practice in combination with its aforementioned theatricality offered a particular potential
that the first two chapters of the *Call Cutta* project had just begun to explore. If we keep in mind the current process of stratification, by which the
informational access to immaterial and invisible spheres of contact produce a layered and multidimensional space, we may also regard the two
parts of the project as a *test run* for a future urban experience, ironically

reflected by a plot of personal engagement. How personal, however, can this test run really become in a framework of standardized and scripted call center contact?

Reflecting upon the quite successful series of remote-control audio walks in Kolkata and Berlin, Rimini Protokoll shifted its interest to the question of how the particular relation created by the media setting and the parallelism of cities and places between caller and participant could be intensified again:

> These tours were very much shaped by the guiding task, conversation was rather limited because to stop walking and start talking was not really fore-seen. Also, technically the connection was just not so good—it was too fragile and noisy. We asked ourselves what would happen if we reduced the compli-cations along the way and offered the option to really talk. (Wetzel, cited in Van Lindt 2008)

In the context of this project that explicitly played with the (re)location of seemingly placeless and disembodied voices, the idea of a more "real" conversation was a step back to an easier setting of just two individuals connected by the telephone line, now both of them in rather neutral office environments. Opening at the "Kunstenfestivaldesarts" in Brussels in 2008, the new version of this telephone theater under the title *Call Cutta in a Box* offered time slots through which individual participants could enter a simple office where he or she still can view a part of the city, but remain inside a building, without physically experiencing the urban environment.

The new setting was structured by the attempt to create a situation of personal contact as opposed to the professional distance of call center communication that still dominated the earlier versions of *Call Cutta*:

> The whole attention has shifted from the outside to the inside of this simple connection. To dealing with your imagination regarding this person you talk to. Yes, there are windows, one in Brussels and one in India. Here it's the af-ternoon or early evening, there it is dark already; here you can see different things than there. But the subject of the interaction is more you. This is much riskier of course, because matters are in your hands this time; the attractions in this performance are, to a much larger extent, self-created attractions. (Ibid.)

The reduction of the urban environment to the space of an office provides greater proximity between caller and participant. What makes these parallel situations different from a mere business call, however, is again a shift of the focus that lies more with the connection itself, with the apparatus, and with its own theatricality.

Interest in continuing the project and moving it into a "box" was focused, as Wetzel points out, on a particular kind of theatrical behavior related to mobile phones in general: "The mobile phone lets you integrate a person into your imagination much more strongly than if you saw the same person on stage, wherever you are" (Wetzel, cited in Hansen-Tangen 2006). The disembodied voice coming through the cordless Skype contact on the computer in the office introduces her- or himself under a real name and with some personal stories, likes and dislikes, confessions about the biggest mistakes thus far in life, and other biographical details, while expecting the same from the participant. A virtual tour through the call center on the other side mirrors a chat about the office room and its equipment: a desk with a computer workstation, a couch, a table with a kettle, a mug and tea bags, some potted plants, and various pictures on the wall. Again, the conversation is partly scripted, divided into various scenes, and directed by the caller, but there is much more space for a freely developing chat than in the street walks of the earlier *Call Cutta* versions. Because the voice is not yet linked to an image of a body, the listener creates the voice's own images. The "separation of the elements," a means of epic theater and also a quality of early media technology (silent movies, radio broadcasting, and telephone as well), produces a certain tension of contrast and juxtaposition. Making use of the computer and an online contact, *Call Cutta in a Box* places the participant in an intermediary setting for an experiment in communication during times of globalized connectivity.

The conversation draws not only on personal memories and feelings, but also on cultural differences in standard of living, the value of religion and family life, weather conditions, and experiences of the everyday. Some technical tricks are involved, when for instance the kettle is magically turned on by the caller, or his or her image suddenly appears on the screen of the desktop computer as if it had suddenly hacked into the participant's account. The dominant part of the game, therefore, is still on the side of the caller, who asks the participant to walk through the office, sing a song, and perform a little dance, before making him discover a little web camera producing video streams for the call center. The relation, however, is balanced to an extent that makes the participant feel more involved than in any other kind of theater. Whereas for the earlier *Call Cutta* walks the callers were instructed to adopt a character or attitude (e.g., imagining one's own grandfather as a member of the Indian liberation army and preparing a new liberation army for call centers), the agents of the Box version required an everyday personality as a mirror for the participant, performing him- or herself.

With *Call Cutta in a Box* Rimini Protokoll installed a theatrical audiosphere, offering a virtual experience of a call center and at the same time the possibility of a mutual exchange through the creation of theatrical behavior, gestures, and utterances. Although initially turning back to dialogue as a means of traditional theater, this production instead created an intermediate laboratory for theatrical potentials in phone calls and informational contact in general, testing a situation that in those years became more and more common through Skype technology and other communication platforms. Theater was in this case almost completely transferred to the audiosphere, with sounds replacing sight and eye contact, thereby triggering the imagination.

Fascination with this setting, however, was still determined by the fact of distance. By interconnecting urban environments through remote encounter the *parallelism* of the related cities was exposed. As Anjan Dutt, who created a television documentary about the project, described the idea of his film: "It would be interesting to see how much of Calcutta can be Berlin and vice-versa" (Dutt, cited in Saha 2004). On this level of media-based urban performance, the cities themselves become players. In fact, *Call Cutta in a Box* functioned as an audio interface between the call center in Kolkata and festivals all over the world. Starting simultaneously in Zurich, Mannheim, and Berlin (April 2008), then in Brussels, Helsinki, Wrocław, and Dublin (May–July 2008), followed by Groningen, Copenhagen, Seoul, Oldenburg, Paris, Amsterdam, and Moscow (August–November 2008), then New York City, Athens, Johannesburg, Cape Town, and Sharjah (2009), and finally Minneapolis and Heidelberg (2010). Thus the project explored the interrelation of parallel worlds by a call center connection as an experience of globalized realities, turning the individual performance of vocal contact to a distant audiosphere into a theater of cities.

Stefan Kaegi and Lola Arias's *Ciudades Paralelas*

Stefan Kaegi undertook a related project, this time with Lola Arias (Buenos Aires), which was a kind of festival on tour, combining eight performance installations by different artists. The project started in 2010 as a coproduction between the Hebbel am Ufer Theater of Berlin and the Schauspielhaus Zürich, funded by Pro Helvetia and the Goethe Institute. The first performance took place in Berlin, followed by one in Buenos Aires. *Ciudades Paralelas* (Parallel cities) then moved to Warsaw and Zurich, with a shorter version in Copenhagen and Kolkata. All eight works were produced by the same artists in each city, each relating to the particular environments in which the *Ciudades Paralelas* took place. The project, thus, opened new horizons for site-specific works by productions that reflected the interchangeability of institutions such as a library, hotel, train station, courthouse, shopping mall, apartment building, rooftop, and factory. The tours or walks that combined these various stations enabled the participants consciously to perceive the theater of the everyday. Over the long run *Ciudades Paralelas* created a framework for the perception of differences between the cities as well. A courthouse in Buenos Aires has a different history and atmosphere from one in Berlin or Zurich. In each city the tours intensified comparison, more focused than the average mix of individual productions at usual festivals. The installations, walks, or performances challenged the participants—reflecting their behavior as voyeur or as witness, while perceiving daily life in urban environments as an interaction among various parallel worlds.

In most of the performances sound and audio devices played an important role, for instance, in the installation *The Quiet Volume* by Ant Hampton (London) and Tim Etchells (Sheffield). Two registered participants were placed together at a table in a library, provided with instructions by a notebook and earphones. Whispering voices asked them to read a few pages in prepared books, also drawing attention to all the small noises in the library—pages being turned, patrons breathing or walking through the library. This imaginary journey through texts and through different library reading rooms (e.g., in Berlin at the new library center of Humboldt University) opened an intimate approach to urban life, in the library as one of those places that, as in Michel Foucault's idea of hetero-topia, can integrate extremely different times and places. In particular the experience of the smallest sounds in a common quietness is interesting, for it makes the listener reflect on the relation between sensory percep-tion and the creation of space.

The next station of this tour is an Ibis Hotel, in which Lola Arias's in-stallation confronts the listener with the otherwise invisible working life of the hotel's chambermaids. These laborers, mostly from Asia, normally clean a room in only ten minutes, servicing hotel guests they never meet personally. In the rooms prepared for this installation, the participants were alone with the traces of their otherwise unknown hosts: everyday objects, and pictures or films showing the daily life, labor, and dreams of the cleaning staff. In some of the rooms the obligatory televisions display their messages; in other rooms voices are audible, as is their favorite music via earphones.

Again, the sound transports a quality of experience different from the visual appearance of a place. This difference can also be perceived on the second tour, organized in a Mercedes Benz factory by Gerardo Naumann (Buenos Aires). Here visitors are guided from one employee to the next, crossing the management floors as well as the assembly line for motors. In the din of heavy machines listeners strain to hear a personal guide ex-plaining the organization and control of every single movement in the working process, while also including references to the private life of the workers who seem to have completely merged with the factory: Workers and robots labor almost with the same kind of effectiveness.

In the splendid staircase of Berlin's central magistrate court, Chris-tian Garcia (Lausanne) composed and staged a *responsorium* in which a choir of singers dressed in black descends to the audience as in ritual pro-cession. The text of this composition is based on actual court decisions, including judicial formulae and statements. In the name of the people a solemn ceremony is performed, a theater of law and justice. Through the sound of a cappella choral voices the almost sacred atmosphere of the impressive building becomes audible, enhanced by the repeated ringing of little bells that signal the continuation of the procession.

The private life of an apartment house provides the scene for Dominic Huber's *Prime Time* at Mehringplatz in Berlin: five apartments, whose living room lamps and televisions are simultaneously switched on and off, as if in a musical score. After twenty minutes, five mostly German Turkish families step out on their balconies and bow toward the audience, which has participated in their daily life via headphones, following their TV programs and their conversations while preparing dinner. Listening to the privacy of someone else's apartment—not from a secret and voyeuristic position, but openly standing on the street together with others—spectators participated in the very dissolution of borders between private and public, inside and outside, currently taking place on a large scale in postmodern media societies.

Finally, staged by Kaegi on the rooftop of the theater or another highrise, a blind musician told the story of his life and sang a song about the "invisible eyes" of the things around us. This performance subverted the idea of a panoramic overview by an intensified experience of the common audiosphere that is normally ignored. The basic question about ways to experience participation in the city as a whole was addressed by a reduction of the sensory field. Guided by the perceptional habits of a blind actor, participation in the audiosphere seemed much easier than in the widespread visible space of the city. Instead of superiority and control, the rooftop performance offered pedestrians perspective, tactile and shortsighted, but much more intense than any visual panorama. One might think of Michel de Certeau's analysis of the planning and surveying position from the top of a skyscraper as opposed to the perspective from below, thus allowing for a different perception of space and for a poetics of irregular pedestrian ways (de Certeau 1984). Different tours through everyday urban life produced an experience of life in parallel cities and parallel worlds, interconnected temporarily for the duration of the festival. In almost all the works the dimension of sound marked the threshold between the different worlds and spheres, not only playing with the perception of the external reality, but also triggering the imagination of a listener on the go.

LIGNA: *The First International of Shopping Malls*

Ciudades Paralelas also included a work by LIGNA, a group of performance and radio artists based in Berlin, who organize interventions and situations of *dispersal*. Participants are invited to perform movements and gestures that are broadcast as instructions by radio transmitters. Among these broadcasts were scenarios for revolutionary (or at least irregular) behavior at train stations, shopping malls, and arcades. LIGNA's productions are always both interventionist performances and experimental explorations of their environments and the behavior related to these environments. In particular, LIGNA's work suggests experimenting with the social and performative dimension of space (LIGNA 2017). Through a practice of sounding out, broadcasting radio signals, and thereby setting the bodies of the participants in motion, the environment and the participants' gestures become recognizable in new aesthetically and politically charged ways. Tactics of subversive affirmation may transform gestures.

Such tactics also apply to the gesture of *listening*, an everyday practice of technologized consumption and a common practice since the introduction of the Walkman, mobile phone, and iPod. In particular, gestures that have become habitual can be called back into consciousness by repeating and exposing them, like highlighting a quote in a written text. As Walter Benjamin noted in his commentary on Brecht's epic theater, a theatrical performance can make an audience aware of its gestures by an interruption of the normal flow and routine of daily behavior (Benjamin 1998). Many LIGNA works make gestures visible via their playful interruption and transmission. A similar idea of interruption was formulated by Debord, describing the construction of *situations* in the public sphere as something that interrupts the economy of the ongoing spectacle of consumption in capitalist societies (Debord 1955). As opposed to the use of sounds and voices in a society of almost invisible control, as Gilles Deleuze describes it (Deleuze 1992), LIGNA's radio ballets expose the process of receiving instructions playfully. Voice and sound are used not in terms of superiority and control, but rather as a subversive repetition of all the means whereby the public sphere has become a sphere of surveillance and standardization.

For *Ciudades Paralelas,* LIGNA organized a collective audio walk through a large shopping mall. Once again, the participants were equipped in advance with small radio receivers and headphones so that they could listen to instructions on how to become an "agent" of the *First International of the Shopping Malls.* They were advised to behave discreetly, to become someone else by adopting that person's movements, to feel the rhythm of the arcades and also to change this rhythm, to empathize with commodities of consumption, to form small groups with others, and to become subversive in the spirit of Walter Benjamin's *flâneur.* The basic idea of this conspiracy of flâneurs was to avoid drawing attention so that the conspiracy could unfold unnoticed by the security guards. It was nevertheless possible, just as with the *Radio Ballets,* to change the atmosphere of the mall, and to circumvent its norms of behavior. Sometimes there were also groups of participants who accelerated their pace or walked in slow motion, simply to alter the average speed of movement through a given area, not unlike demonstrations that peacefully block traffic while pedestrians cross the street in slow motion. At the same time the audio track informs the listener that, since the 1950s and based on scientific research, the average walking speed has been treated as an important economic factor, to be manipulated for the attraction of customers. Another interesting moment in this conspiracy performance was its conclusion, when everything dissolved unspectacularly, all participants reentering the normal flow of passersby. Before the security service could decide whether or what actions to take, the entire performance was over, dispersing with a final instruction paraphrasing Benjamin from his *Arcades Project* (2002a): "Walk through the house of dreams as if nothing had happened."

Similar to some of Rimini Protokoll's work, LIGNA's productions do not just document or depict a given reality, but rather they use a certain amount of fiction and feigning to question our conventional understanding of reality. Thus the dispersed action in the shopping mall can be regarded as an interruption in an otherwise continuously performed spectacle of capitalist consumerism. One might argue that there is a tendency for this kind of work to become more and more artful and artificial, and aesthetically elaborate, such that the subversive momentum quickly loses its political impact. We should also admit, nonetheless, that similar strategies of interventionist performance, flash mobs, and other forms of culture jamming have already become part of advertising and propaganda campaigns. This does not mean that the constant effort to question and challenge societies of control by creative means and tactics has become dispensable. It may only be that the rigor and pathos of twentieth-century political activism has turned out to be too static and inflexible to cope with quickly changing media and advertising strategies. Theater, in particular, cannot avoid reflecting on different modes of representation, spectatorship, and interactivity in times when the public sphere has almost dissolved into media effects. Productions and activities like those of LIGNA, Stefan Kaegi, and Rimini Protokoll, therefore, are important in the ways they experiment with interrelations between perception and movement, imagination and reality.

The public sphere itself becomes an object of experimental behavior, but not so much as a forum for negotiation and discourse, as publicity has often been defined. It is, rather, a playful acting out and reprocessing of normative orders that control our daily behavior without being noticed at all. As opposed to earlier forms of artistic and theatrical spectacles on the street and in the public sphere, current intervention practices do not seek to garner as much attention as possible, but rather they work because of the quality of attention itself. They reflect the ways in which perception and movement in the public sphere are influenced by sounds, music, and voices. They produce situations of gathering and dispersal that encourage the participants temporarily to transform the norms of everyday behavior within the urban environment. The audiosphere, to which almost everyone in contemporary urban culture is connected for personal entertainment and communication, is used for sometimes individual, sometimes collective imagination of different realities and options for different behavior, thus transgressing and transforming the commercial surface and the multi-layered space of the city. Whether as listeners, performers, or flâneurs in the streets of Berlin, Kolkata, or Chicago, they create a collective performance together as participants in a common everyday life in the global cities of the twenty-first century.

Patrick Primavesi

References

Benjamin, Walter. 1998. "What is Epic Theater?" In Benjamin, *Understanding Brecht*, translated by Anna Bostock. 2nd ed., 15–22. London: Verso.

———. 2002a. *The Arcades Project*. Translated by Howard Eiland and Kevin McLaughlin. Cambridge, MA: Cambridge, MA: Belknap Press of Harvard University Press.

———. 2002b. "Berlin Childhood around 1900." In Benjamin, *Selected Writings*. Vol. 3, *(1935–1938)*, edited and translated by Howard Eiland and Michael W. Jennings, 344–413. Cambridge, MA: Belknap Press of Harvard University Press.

———. 2002c. "The Work of Art in the Age of Its Technological Reproducibility: Second Version." In Benjamin, *Selected Writings*. Vol. 3, *(1935–1938)*, edited and translated by Howard Eiland and Michael W. Jennings, 101–33. Cambridge, MA: Belknap Press of Harvard University Press.

Brecht, Bertolt. 1994. *On Theater—Selected Essays: The Development of an Aesthetic*, edited and translated by John Willett. New York: Hill and Wang.

Buck-Morss, Susan. 1991. *The Dialectics of Seeing: Walter Benjamin and the Arcades Project*. Cambridge, MA: MIT Press.

Debord, Guy. 1955. "Introduction to a Critique of Urban Geography." *Les Lèvres Nues* 6 (September 1955). Translated by Ken Knabb. Accessed July 25, 2017. http://www.cddc.vt.edu/sionline/presitu/geography.html.

de Certeau, Michel. 1984. *The Practice of Everyday Life*. Translated by Stephen Rendall. Berkeley: University of California Press.

Deleuze, Gilles. 1992. "Postscript of the Societies of Control." *October* 59 (1992): 3–7.

Frers, Lars, and Lars Meier, eds. 2006. *Encountering Urban Places: Visual and Material Performances in the City*. Aldershot: Ashgate.

Hansen-Tangen, Torunn. 2006. "Mobile Phones Take to the Stage." Last modified October 3, 2006, accessed July 25, 2017. http://www.rimini-protokoll.de/website/en/text/mobile-phones-take-to-the-stage.

Hosokawa, Shuhei. 1984. "The Walkman Effect." *Popular Music* 4: 165–80.

LIGNA. 2017. "About Ligna." Accessed July 25. http://ligna.blogspot.co.at.

Rimini Protokoll. 2005a. *Call Cutta—Mobile Phone Theatre: About Call Cutta*. Berlin: Hebbel am Ufer, DVD.

———. 2005b. Script for the call center dialogue of *Call Cutta* in Kolkata, PDF file from Rimini Protokoll 2005a.

Ronell, Avital. 1989. *The Telephone Book: Technology, Schizophrenia, Electric Speech*. Lincoln: University of Nebraska Press.

Roselt, Jens. 2005. "Call Cutta in Kreuzberg: Report." Last modified April 3, 2005, accessed July 25, 2017. http://rimini-protokoll.de/website/en/text/call-cutta-in-kreuzberg-1.

Saha, Subhro. 2004. "Call Kutta for Twin City Theatre Tour." *The Telegraph (India)*, October 28. https://www.telegraphindia.com/1041028/asp/calcutta/story_3929710.asp.

Van Lindt, Barbara. 2008. "Call It Call Cutta in a Box: Interview in the Programme Book." Last modified May 1, 2008, accessed July 25, 2017. http://www.rimini-protokoll.de/website/en/text/call-it-call-cutta-in-a-box.

Willis, Katharine S. 2006. "Sensing Place—Mobile and Wireless Technologies in Urban Space." In *Encountering Urban Places—Visual and Material Performances in the City*, edited by Lars Frers and Lars Meier, 155–69. Aldershot: Ashgate.

IV
Trajectories beyond
the Global City

8

Dynamic Diasporas: "The Song of Zion" in South Asia

Philip V. Bohlman

Zion 1980—Whose Diaspora?

Before I left the United States for Jerusalem in July 1980, to begin what would become almost two and a half years of field research for my doctoral dissertation, I had reckoned with the probability that I should have little opportunity to hear Indian music, which I had studied intensively throughout my PhD work at the University of Illinois at Urbana-Champaign. In the 1980s, Jerusalem was a city that hosted an unimaginable influx of musicians and music from every place in the world, and already in 1980, it was my goal to let the many dimensions of the city music of Zion—Mt. Zion is a real place in Jerusalem, located along the southern walls of the Old City—determine the course of my research.

To my great surprise, it was only a week before I happened upon an announcement for a "Concert of Hindustani Classical Music" in the listings of concerts and entertainment options in *The Jerusalem Post*. Other than the time and place—motzeh shabbat, after the close of the Jewish Sabbath, and in a theater near the Great Synagogue of Jerusalem, close to the heart of modern, twentieth-century Jerusalem—there were no other details about who would present such a concert of Hindustani classical music. I presumed these would be visiting artists, and I expected the concert to have some sponsorship from the Indian embassy, which, in 1980 as today, supported a wide range of cultural activities and exchanges in Israel. Official, embassy support, however, was nowhere to be seen. The musicians who performed were not visiting artists, but rather Israelis, and they offered this concert, at least in part, as professionals, to earn a fee.

I was surprised once again when I attended the concert of Hindustani classical music. The musicians who entered the stage—three men who would play *sitar, tabla,* and *tanpura*—wore traditional clothing from two worlds, India and Israel. They wore *kurtas* and *kippot*, the Jewish head cover denoting religious observance, orthodox when worn in a secular setting such as on a concert stage. Jewish religious observance also reminded the audience that the Sabbath had just ended, and this concert would issue in a new week. Each musician bore the same family name, Nagan, a Hebrew toponym approximating "player," musician. Musician toponyms were widespread in diaspora communities; Musikant, Geiger, Fiedler, and even Klezmer, the name of one of the primary characters, a pianist and music teacher, in George Eliot's novel, *Daniel Derronda*, are among the best known, and they provide historical evidence for the ways in which musical professionalism provided a type of negotiation between Jewish and non-Jewish spheres. They designate both the ways in which music closed and opened cultural spaces during the course of centuries of diaspora (see, e.g., HaCohen 2011 for the ways in which Jewish music making was reconfigured as noise to emphasize distance and engender prejudice coded through musical discourse). The etymology of the occupational name, Nagan, extends in numerous directions to describe music making in the diaspora. In Eastern Europe, for example, it is the etymological cousin of *niggun* and *nign*, meaning "melody" in Hebrew and Yiddish, but without words, in the hassidic vocal music of orthodox communities and the instrumental klezmer music of the village wedding.

The family Nagan in Israel consisted of hereditary musicians, in genealogical structure not unlike a *gharana*, from the state of Maharashtra. Professionally, musicians in the Nagan family had played light-classical and theater music, and in the cities, particularly Mumbai and Pune, they were among the finest theater musicians, often sharing that distinction with another religious minority, Parsis (Isenberg 1988; Weil 2007; Jones 2009). The family Nagan played well that July evening in 1980, especially if one recognized that their specific goal was to create an *Israeli* Hindustani classical music. The Nagans were not on tour, and they were not engaged in preserving an immigrant tradition. Instead, they understood Hindustani music also as Jewish, which is to say, no less than Hindu, Muslim, Sikh, or Parsi. As I came to know the Nagans over the next few years, I learned about the ways they understood the Jewish liturgy of the Maharashtrian Jews to be ancient, some parts two thousand years old, the venerable tradition of the Bene Israel, the oldest Jewish community of India (for studies of the history of the Bene Israel, see, e.g., Israel 1984; Katz 2000; Numark 2001; Numark 2012).

Music and ritual practice were intertwined in ways that bound the Bene Israel to the past, and the evidence of such practice had increasingly passed from oral to written tradition after Indian and Israeli independence in 1947 and 1948 (see, e.g., Ashtamkar and Talkar 1882; Fischel 1968; Roland 2000; Schultz 2016). After millennia of diaspora, it was only natural that Hindustani music should take root in Zion. The return of the Bene Israel from India is at least as old as the initial period of modern settlement in the Yishuv prior to Israeli statehood in 1938. During his fieldwork between 1935 and 1938, Robert Lachmann had included metal-disc recordings of the Bene Israel among those he placed in the Archive of Oriental Music at the Hebrew University (see Davis 2013, 510). Musically, India took its place in the multiculturalism of Israel at its founding, also symbolizing the continuity of ancient diaspora.

I turn to diaspora in the present volume on music and urban transformations for several distinct, but related reasons. First of all, diaspora as a historical and social condition is a concept applied to both Jewish and South Asian history. "Living in diaspora," that is, outside a homeland, but bound to that homeland by the prospect of return, is a subject formation claimed by both Jews and South Asians. Second, as a concept, diaspora often carries with it largely negative connotations. It is imagined to begin at some kind of drastic historical moment—the destruction of the temples in Jerusalem—or with the economic inequality, poverty, and overpopulation in colonial and post-statehood India. The reasons one lives in diaspora are, therefore, not always of one's own choosing. Third, diaspora can also produce a certain teleology that is largely positive, above all a teleology of return to the homeland. The prospect of return generates symbols and cultural practices, among them musical practices that sustain connection to the homeland in the everyday, for example, the orientation of prayer in the synagogue toward Jerusalem.

In the present chapter I should like to suggest reasons for turning theoretically to diaspora in a considerably different way, above all because of the role of urbanization in charting the course of diaspora. Examining diaspora as a historical condition of exchange and mobility between and among cities leads me to argue that the teleological move between expulsion and return is inadequate to a proper understanding of diaspora and why it persists. Critical to the theory I begin to open in this chapter is my recasting of diaspora as a means of urban transformation. Diaspora, I wish to state quite unequivocally, responds to specific historical moments as a form of urbanization itself. The city and its subjectivities historically form at the convergence of diasporas, not at their conclusions, thus as ongoing and dynamic social transformation. And music, say, Hindustani classical music giving voice to the "song of Zion," is crucially present at this convergence.

Utopia/Dystopia

Before turning to, or returning to India, the empirical center of this chapter, I should like to propose several theoretical models that offer ways of understanding diaspora as urbanization. I begin with what will necessarily be an initial consideration of city music in utopia and dystopia, and I then turn more specifically toward the notion of the "New Jerusalem" in Jewish history and historiography. Connecting utopia to the New Jerusalem is the relation of each to the place of music, to the city and to city music, and by extension to musical cosmopolitanism, in which music configures space through its mobility. The location of music in cities—the emergence of "city music"—becomes increasingly central in the making of modern global culture. The court and the church, the encounter between empires and religions, the orality of multiple vernaculars and the emergence of literate music cultures—all these give way to the city.

The idea of utopia, which provides me with a discursive, conceptual core, also grows from the moment in which modern music cultures arise through globalization and cosmopolitanism. Even the term, "utopia," invented by Thomas More as the description of an idealized island society (see More [1516] 1965), comes into use in the sixteenth century, coeval with the globalization of empire from the West and the coalescence of urban musical practice in the Renaissance (see, e.g., Feldman 1995). Utopias intervene in the spaces between city culture and music, as they are practiced and idealized. In *Provincializing Europe* Dipesh Chakrabarty illustrates that modern India, no less than modern Europe, becomes an idea in response to utopian thought, though that response may rarely be idealized in practice (Chakrabarty 2000). In the historical *longue durée* of the modern city the search for utopia has motivated action, and few forms of action have exerted greater pressure on global movement than utopia, not least among them the migration movements that create cities anew.

In this chapter, nonetheless, I begin by considering the utopianism of the global metropole in quite traditional ways. My primary theoretical models are Saint Augustine ([413 CE] 1950), Thomas More ([1516] 1965), and Rabindranath Tagore ([1916] 2005), whose aims, in different ways, were broadly theological. It is by treating the work on utopianism as traditional that I expand my interpretive framework to include dystopia. Throughout much of my research on utopia I willingly treat More quite literally (e.g., Bohlman 2013, 237–51). Theologically, More was pushing at the boundaries of a world centered around Christianity until the sixteenth century, for he coined the word, utopia ($o\acute{v}\tau\acute{o}\pi o\varsigma$), to mean "no place." In contrast, the island he called utopia resulted from a flight of literary fancy (More [1516] 1965). Multiplying the meanings of utopia, however, is its similarity to the word, eutopia ($\epsilon\acute{v}\tau\acute{o}\pi o\varsigma$), which means "good place," the most common understanding of the term. Utopia that is "real," therefore, exists only at another time and place. The cosmopolitanism of the utopian city is unachievable. It is in these states that the imagined unity of utopia—all cities on More's island of Utopia are the same—give way to the difference that dominates dystopia and heterotopia.

While tracing the links among global metropoles, I prefer to follow a path toward an understanding of dystopia quite different from common attempts to pair it with utopia. The issue that is for me crucial is not that the dystopian city cannot function or falls into destruction, but rather that its pasts are reimagined as spaces where life and survival insist on their own viability. I connect my theoretical considerations more directly with the history of the Jewish diaspora, which is central to my comparisons of urban transformations in this chapter. The Jewish ghetto of Venice, to take an obvious example of a city quite literally formed from the urbanization of diaspora and also established in 1516, produced much of the same will to survive that characterizes the dystopian cosmopolitanism that followed the expulsion of Jews from Spain in 1492 and from Portugal in 1497. Venice's Jewish history—the history of the ghetto—unfolds as a response to the city's capacity to make survival possible. There is perhaps no more global symbol of urban dystopia in modern Jewish history than the local, in other words, the ghetto (in Venetian dialect, *ghèto*, literally, "iron foundry") the Venetian district in which the iron foundries preceded the arrival of Jews in the wake of the Reconquista. In the history of the modern Jewish diaspora the ghetto provides the modern counterpart to Jerusalem, spreading metaphorically from Venice with the Age of Discovery and the globalization of the Jewish diaspora and the settlement of cities bearing witness to the "New Jerusalem" throughout the world.

The New Jerusalem

As concepts of Jewish polity emerged after the destruction of the Second Temple in Jerusalem in the year 70 of the Common Era, it also became possible to recognize processes of urbanization. Two larger concepts of place and community dominate the ways in which Jewish polity is conceived: *'eda and kehilla*. There are many ways to characterize the relation between 'eda and kehilla, but for the purposes of the present volume, I wish to suggest that 'eda reflects the notion of a Jewish community in the temporality of diaspora, kehilla the formation of a Jewish community in the spatiality of the city.

It is because of the tensions between 'eda and kehilla that the history of the Jewish diaspora becomes one of urbanization, albeit of a rather distinctive kind. Prior to the destruction of the Second Temple in 70 CE, Jewish polity was extensively centralized. The Temple in Jerusalem functioned religiously and politically as a symbol of the city in late Antiquity (Goldhill 2008). Jews spread across the Levant of Antiquity needed to come to Jerusalem to affirm ritual, genealogy, and their symbolic connection to the city as the nation's center. Mobility was crucial to the central role of Jerusalem as a sacred and secular city. This role of the city is still evident in the rituals and biblical texts about pilgrimage, the *aliyah* (lit., going up) to the city, the movement from the peripheries to the center.

Musically, too, Jerusalem was central, with the orchestra and chorus of the Temple, however real, locating music in the urban center (see, e.g., Psalm 150). Historically, the "city music" of the Temple plays an enormous role in Jewish history and ritual. The orientation of the diaspora synagogue to *mizrakh* (lit., east), written across the area above the synagogue *bima*, or altar, is not just the East, its literal meaning: It directs the diaspora worshiper to a specific city.

In the Jewish diaspora, the urban symbolism of Jerusalem was displaced, ultimately and temporarily replaced by the synagogue, which supported a completely different type of worship, ritual, and prayer. The diaspora synagogue replaced the temple in Jerusalem, but only temporarily, assuming what functions it could until the return from diaspora. Urbanization and "city music" remained in the past, but were projected on to the future. The nineteenth-century synagogues of urbanizing Jewish communities—the Neue Synagoge in Berlin (see figure 34) and KAM (Kehilath Anshe Ma'ariv) Isaiah Israel in Chicago, for example—were designed with orientalist styles, not least the minarets and arabesque of a mosque, in order to triangulate local history with the Jerusalem of the past and the future. The architectural history of Chicago's synagogues bears witness to different denominations, but the impact of the Reform tradition of the earliest German Jewish immigrants is evident in the designs of some of the city's most distinguished and distinctive architects, for example, the 1886 Zion Temple, designed by Dankmar Adler and Louis Sullivan (Packer 2016). The synagogue was the space of reconstituting Jewish history and polity. In the synagogue, it was critical that music provided a means of "remembering Zion" (Psalm 137).

In the diaspora, the synagogue also became the place of "remembering" Zion. The synagogue at the periphery could, however, develop a new sense of Zion, of the city, around it. The ritual and musical reenactment of Zion collapsed the distance between periphery and center, providing a way of constituting the city, that is, turning the Sabbath into a virtual urbanization. In Kolkata synagogues, this is why such attention has been given to achieving a *minyan*, the ten male worshipers necessary for constituting the community (Butnick 2013).

As *kehillot* (plural of kehilla) were established and took root in the diaspora, Jewish polity and practice began to undergo further transformation to embrace local traditions, making them Jewish. We witness this clearly in liturgical and musical practice in the concept of *nusach*, melodic form and structure that specifies local, urban Jewishness. In Germany, for example, a north German and a south German nusach took shape by the end of the Middle Ages, finding more and more local forms in early modern Germany, such as in the Mainzer, Kölner, or Wormser *Hazzanut*, to take three of the earliest forms. As German Jewry itself underwent urbanization during the Jewish Enlightenment, or Haskala, nusach became increasingly city-centered, for example, with the Reform movement in Berlin and Hamburg in the late nineteenth century. Jewish music became the tradition of place in diaspora, at once distinctive with melodic idiolect, but bound to history through shared rituals and oral tradition. Gathering the oral traditions of diaspora communities, the Jewish musicologists of the early twentieth century mapped a changing sameness in Jewish music, the urbanizing telos of which was Jerusalem (see, e.g., Abraham Zvi Idelsohn's "Comparative Table of Accent Motifs in the Intoning the Pentateuch," figure 35).

The musical culture of urban nusach was but one sign of the spread of the Jewish city as the "New Jerusalem." Berlin and Kolkata are among the clearest examples of urban Jewish communities that were reimagined as New Jerusalems. Berlin has always seen itself as a new, modern city, and it is hardly surprising that its main synagogue is the Neue Synagoge (New Synagogue), which literally clothes itself in the symbols of the Old Jerusalem (figure 34).

In the nineteenth century, the Jewish community of Kolkata, too, exhibited the urbanity of a New Jerusalem, transforming the Middle Easternness of the already urban kehilla of Jews from Baghdad, who were so critical to the colonial control of the British in Kolkata. On one hand, colonial synagogue architecture borrowed from the British, designing syna-

Figure 34. The Neue Synagoge, or Oranienburgerstraße Synagoge, Berlin.
Painting: Emile de Cauwer (1866).

Figure 35. Comparative Table of Accent Motifs in the Intoning the Pentateuch
(Idelsohn 1923, 44).

gogues that looked like Anglican churches and railway stations, complete with a clock in the steeple, as in the Lal Deval (Red Wall) Synagogue of Pune (figure 39). On the other hand, the influences of a different east were incorporated into the place of worship in colonial Calcutta, as in the Beth El Synagogue in the Lal Bazar district (figure 36). The eastern-style worship space borrows extensively from the Bagdhadi tradition from which the Jewish community originally came. The inner alignment of the synagogue and the kehilla remained toward Jerusalem, but in Calcutta this meant toward the north and west, rather than the east (figure 37).

Zion be-Hodu/Zion in India

Despite the great age of the Jewish communities in South Asia and the considerable impact that resulted from the periodic expansion of the diaspora, the Jewish history of India is less well known than other diaspora communities. Abraham Zvi Idelsohn, for example, did not include South Asian Jews among the communities whose musical practices he recorded and compared (see figure 35). Culturally, nonetheless, Jews were productive and influential, working within Jewish artistic traditions, but even more significantly, integrating these into a larger and more complex cultural matrix, of which music was a part. We have a considerable historical record for the literary impact from South Asian Jewish communities; the Valmadonna Trust collection of "Hebrew, Judeo-Arabic, and Marathi Jewish Printing in India," for example, contains over 730 items (Valmadonna Trust 1999). The record for the musical impact is more difficult to document across history, in part because of oral transmission, also in part because that impact is so often inseparable from other South Asian musical traditions, particularly those responding to expanding urban transformations.

In order to understand better the urban transformations of the Jewish diaspora in South Asia, I should sketch the tension between 'eda and kehilla in the three most important communities: the Bene Israel, the Cochin Jews, and the Baghdadi Jews. Urbanization provides a critical impetus to the history of all three communities, assuming not only different forms, but also increasingly Indian forms during the longue durée of Indian Jewry (for reflections on Jews in urban Bangalore, see Nemichandra 2008).

Figure 36. Beth El Synagogue, Kolkata, external view. Photo: Philip V. Bohlman.

Figure 37. Magen David Synagogue, Kolkata, internal view. Photo: Philip V. Bohlman.

Bene Israel

The history of the Bene Israel begins in the village, particularly in the areas that constitute Maharashtra. The Bene Israel are pre-rabbinic, and they have no history of synagogues prior to the earliest accounts of synagogues in late Antiquity. There is archeological evidence of ritual objects beginning roughly in the seventh century CE. Evidence of Bene Israel trade and craft also survives, for example, the persistence of the specialty of pressing sesame seeds to produce oil. Community life was organized, and there was a ritual specialist, the *kazi*, who was far more like a Brahmanic specialist than a rabbi. The origins of the Bene Israel are difficult to pin down, but it is probable that they had arrived in India before the diaspora that followed the destruction of the Second Temple. The Bene Israel increasingly migrated to the cities with the arrival of the British and the coreligionist Baghdadi Jews, and their main centers are Mumbai and Pune. The strength of their community is clearly evident in their integration into the music theater traditions of Maharashtra, in which they played a considerable role. They draw largely from the structures and styles of modern rāga-based Hindustani music for both sacred and secular musical traditions (see Israel 1984; Schultz 2016).

Cochin Jews

The Cochin Jews settled south from Goa along the Malabar Coast of southwestern India, where the first written and archeological evidence is from ca. 1000 CE. Cochin Jewish communities bear witness to their presence in the culture of diaspora during the first millennium of the Common Era. The synagogue is the center of community life. In a different way, their settlement patterns reflect those of the Syrian Christians, who also claim migration to the subcontinent with the spread of Christianity. In the study of the Jewish diaspora, the Cochin Jews are the locus classicus, the model of a community that returns and leaves only relics in India itself. Their synagogue in Goa is famous more as a modern museum than as a living center for worship. The musical practices of Cochin women have been the subject of important studies by several scholars, especially Barbara K. Johnson (2005).

Baghdadi Jews

The Baghdadi Jews (*yehudim bavalim*) constitute a Middle Eastern community that emerged from a particular history in the Tigris-Euphrates basin, stretching from Aleppo in the north to Basra in the south. The Baghdadi Jews were extremely learned (Babylonian Talmud). They arrived in the mid-eighteenth century with the East India Company (largely from Basra), first to Bombay, but later establishing a strong base in Calcutta as merchants allied with the British. Culturally, the Baghdadi Jews remained Middle Eastern, which is to say, intensively urbanized, with a written tradition arising from the Babylonian Talmud and a vibrant oral tradition in Arabic and Judeo-Arabic. Musically, the Baghdadi community is enormously rich, spreading across Asia, and no less evident in the local traditions of Kolkata. The sacred musical traditions of the Baghdadi Jews are based on the Arabic maqām modal system.

Literate Tradition as Urban Transformation among the Bene Israel

To illustrate the impact of urbanization on the Jewish diaspora in South Asia, I turn briefly to two case studies. In the first, I consider two instances of the transformation from oral to literate tradition. In the second, I turn to empire and the global in Kolkata. In both cases, Jewish musical practices provided agency to the confluence of Indian and Jewish music.

The examples in my first case study come from Pune in Maharashtra, drawing on my own fieldwork, but also extensively on the current research of Anna Schultz (see Schultz 2013; Schultz 2016; Schultz, in press). In 2008, on the very eve of the High Holidays, representatives of Pune's Jewish community, announced that a new *siddur* (lit., order, in the sense of liturgy), or daily prayerbook, was about to be published, "the first ever" in the Marathi language. The announcement of this new edition of a Jewish siddur, whose texts are almost entirely sung, spread through the Pune and Maharashtra press. With Rosh ha-Shana, the Jewish New Year, only days away, the first-ever Marathi siddur was touted as an event of considerable symbolic significance. According to the Pune community, it would connect the centuries-old Jewish practices of Pune to the city of the twenty-first century. With parallel prayer texts in English, the Marathi siddur would also connect the local to the global, and it would enhance the prayerbook's practicality. It located Pune's diasporic position in the time and space of South Asian Jewish history, that is, at the center of a diaspora. Translated into the Marathi of the siddur, the Jewish everyday of Pune was reborn in song, at once Maharashtrian and thoroughly urban. The rich tradition of Jewish writing in Marathi (see Valmadonna Trust 1999) might potentially use written texts, drawn from Israeli ritual practice, to generate a new oral tradition.

As modern as the Marathi siddur is, it is also the latest chapter of a longer history that many might consider unlikely, namely of the exchange of form and melody between Jewish song—in fact, nusach, which I discuss above—and Hindu *kirtan*. Anna Schultz has examined the interaction between nusach and kirtan as a process of cultural translation, moving in several directions at the same time, above all between Jewish and

Hindu vocal practices (Schultz 2015; see also Schultz and Bohlman 2010). In many cases, having relearned Hebrew from British missionaries in the nineteenth century, Bene Israel scholars in Maharashtra had access to a large corpus of scriptures and metrical psalms that they translated into Marathi (Numark 2012; Schultz 2016). The problem remained that many of the Bene Israel, until that point in history rural, could not read Marathi in the literate form of the Jewish texts. To solve this problem, Jewish scholars adopted kirtan, first used to transform the oral to the written by the Marathi Hindu poet Namdev in the thirteenth century, to reach a greater public through oral performance (Schultz 2008; Roland 1998, 120). Anna Schultz has shown how kirtan provided a means to ally Bene Israel identities with a Marathi Hindu past that was becoming a resource in the creation of national identity, though they were careful to articulate what was different about Bene Israel kirtan. For the purposes of education and systematization, in other words, because of urban transformation, the venue for introducing Bene Israel kirtan was a modern and urban institution (Schultz and Bohlman 2010).

Empire and Diaspora

From its colonial beginnings, the Jewish community of Kolkata was more urban than diasporic. Baghdadi Jews were a critical—which is to say, inseparable—part of the British empire, and they were integrated into it because of their urbanity. In a history of colonial Calcutta it is important not to forget just how critical the Jewish diaspora in its capacity to establish the kehilla as a New Jerusalem was to the spread and maintenance of empire. Wherever the British Empire occupied regions of Asia, Jewish communities appeared in the major colonial entrepôts to support the ritual and musical practices of Baghdadi Jews (for a recording and extensive annotation of these traditions, see Kartomi et al. 2007). The history of the Baghdadi community in Kolkata was always hybrid and multicultural, precisely as these would accommodate an urban culture.

One of the most strikingly Jewish characteristics of the Jewish city of Kolkata is its continued witness to past and present, to the multiple diasporas that continuously converge and diverge. The urbanity of the Baghdadi

Jews in Kolkata, therefore, cannot adequately be measured in numbers, or by invoking nostalgia for an imagined past. The three synagogues in the Lal Bazar area of the city support the community to various degrees, for example, by providing a community kitchen for kosher meals during Passover. Accounts of diminished attendance—the first minyan in twenty-five years during the High Holidays of 2013—fail to take account of the ways in which music provides Baghdadi Jewish identity in the twenty-first century, in Kolkata, but also in a highly urbanized Baghdadi Jewish diaspora. Seldom mentioned in discussions of the Baghdadi Jewish community in Kolkata is one of its most vibrant institutions, the Jewish school, which lies across a small lane from the Beth El Synagogue (figure 38). Enrollment is full at the Jewish school, if indeed the overwhelming majority of students are Muslim girls and young women. I might write at length in this chapter about how remarkable and paradoxical this situation could seem, but in fact I prefer to point out that, in the context of the chapter's claims about diaspora as urban transformation, a Jewish school in West Bengal filled with Muslim girls is also quite unremarkable. It is a twenty-first-century manifestation, for example, of the Jewish schools and hospitals built during the nineteenth century in Mumbai and Pune by the Baghdadi Jewish Sassoon family, which also were not primarily intended for Jews. Nor for Hindus nor for Muslims, but rather for the ill of India. The Jewish-Muslim girls' school reveals the possibilities of a modern Jewish presence in a modern West Bengal, in which religion, too, is modern and urban.

Zion on the Spree—A Diasporic Excursus

The chapters in this book, which accumulate around a collaborative research project dedicated to studying music and urban transformation in the three cities of Berlin, Chicago, and Kolkata, provide many ways of establishing comparison for multi-site and multi-history music scholarship. Although I have concentrated largely on the Indian urban examples of Kolkata and Pune, I think it also important to recognize the ways these connect to Berlin through the Jewish diaspora, in which mobility and exchange far outweigh the importance of sheer numbers. What Berlin and Kolkata share—or rather, what converges in their diasporic histories—is

Figure 38. The Kolkata Jewish School. Photo: Philip V. Bohlman.

the possibility of realizing a New Jerusalem. The realization of a New Jerusalem is, in fact, inseparable from the very Enlightenment modernity that transformed Berlin into a city in the course of the eighteenth century. This realization could not be clearer than in one of the most sweeping of Moses Mendelssohn's works, *Jerusalem* (Mendelssohn 1783). It was under the light of Haskala (Jewish Enlightenment) influence that emanated from *Jerusalem*, moreover, that the epithet of Berlin as "Zion an der Spree," competing with "Athen an der Spree," reconfigured Berlin Jewish life in the nineteenth century as urban and modern, as a city in which religion and state could coexist as separate institutions.

It is by no means an exaggeration to claim that the city culture and surely the city music of Berlin in 2013 is increasingly shaped by converging diasporas. The number of Israelis living in Berlin is now estimated as great as 40,000 to 50,000. No profession is identified more repeatedly with the Israeli population of Berlin than music, be this in the city's major classical-music ensembles or in the cabaret scene, which draws nostalgically on the Jewish popular music from the Weimar period. The Jewish population of Berlin is, of course, much greater (depending on the nature of identification, estimates of the Jewish population of Germany run as high as 250,000; see Bohlman 2014, 265–66). The music of Berlin, Jewish and otherwise, has always borne witness to the diasporic urbanization that accompanies Jewish history globally.

In particular, there are urban musics that draw together the narrative strands of parable in Jewish history. I should like to turn to just one of these parables for a brief moment, Dani Levy's 2004 film, *Alles auf Zucker* (the English title is *Go for Zucker*), in which the new, post-Wende Berlin, becomes the backdrop for the New Jerusalem. *Alles auf Zucker* addresses with humor the dilemmas of post-Holocaust, post-unification, postmodern diasporas converging in Berlin. From the moment it appeared in 2004, the film was hailed for its Jewishness, or rather more to the point, the significance of the return of Jewishness to Germany. The film director, Dani Levy (born 1957 in Basel, but since 1980 a Berliner), was Jewish. According to the accolades accompanying the 2005 Deutscher Filmpreis and the 2005 Ernst Lubitsch Preis, both awarded to *Alles auf Zucker*, the film made it possible for Germans to laugh about Jewishness again.

The story of Samuel and Jacob Zuckermann (aka Jaecki Zucker) and their children resolving their differences and joining as a single "kosher family" comes straight out of Yiddish theater and the cabaret stages of the Berlin Scheunenviertel, in which, together with other areas in central Berlin, the film was largely shot. Alles auf Zucker also allegorically re-works one of the central narratives of the Torah, the story of Moses and Aaron, and the journey of the Jewish people to reach Zion. That Samuel comes from one Germany, Jaecki from the other, that is, West and East, is central to the represence of the fractured Jewishness that lies at the center of the film. A new Germany and a new Jewishness, perhaps, but the mish-mash—at moments the mash-up—of music for Jewish stage and film tells a more complex narrative of post-Two-Germany Jewishness in a New Jerusalem. The music in the film paves the way for the return to a city at once ancient and modern: Zion on the Spree (see also Bohlman 2014).

Pune 2008—The "Song of Zion" Returns from Zion

It is with return to Zion that I bring this chapter to its conclusion, indeed, by returning to the diasporic confluence of India and Zion, Maharashtra and Israel. Through this path of return, the chapter comes full circle. It does so, however, incompletely, with end and beginning retaining their counterpoint of consonance and dissonance. The return through diaspora engenders new beginnings, hence rerouting the telos of ending.

During autumn 2008, I was teaching in Pune for the University of Chicago Study Abroad Program at Ferguson College, at the time of the Jewish High Holidays—Rosh ha-Shana, Yom Kippur, Sukkot, and Simḥat Torah—the most sacred period of the Jewish religious year. It is during the High Holidays that Jewish communities gather most publicly, in other words, when the community is constituted by worship in the synagogue. If there were an ideal moment to understand a Maharashtrian Jewish community, this would be it. As the professor and mentor for the Chicago students, leading them in a class on "Religion and the Arts in India," I took it also as my responsibility to attend to their religious needs, and though I am myself not Jewish, to take the many Jewish students to the Lal Deval Synagogue, particularly on Yom Kippur, the Jewish Day of Atonement. As my Chicago students and I entered the synagogue in the early morning, we quickly realized it was full, and that, beyond traditional distinctions between male and female areas, the sanctuary was divided into seating areas by practices of worship and sociability that were for us unclear. Because we spoke Hebrew to the worshipers greeting us at the entry, we were given Hebrew prayerbooks and ushered toward chairs and benches along the side with worshipers dressed in more Western attire. Sari- and kurta-clad worshipers occupied a different geography.

The diverse religious domains of the Lal Deval were reproduced in the prayer, chanting, and song of the Day of Atonement, musically more different than the same. At one level, there were clearly men whose prayers on the *bima*, the altar in the middle of the sanctuary, relied structurally on the modal practices of classical Hindustani rāga. In contrast, there was a third group of worshipers who chanted using the modes of Iraqi maqām. No less striking, there were families more confidently employing the canonic principles of the "Jerusalem-Sephardi" principles of maqām that order the liturgical year in Israel. The three modal systems, drawing from multiple cultures and histories, created an urban music in which the Jewish and the Indian (and the Iraqi and the Israeli) effortlessly coexisted.

The classical-music systems of three different cities were converging. The modal practices layered throughout the service unselfconsciously reproduced the history of the Jewish community, the Bene Israel, for whom Hindustani rāga was deeply embedded in everyday practice, sacred and secular. The two systems of maqām denoted the differences between the communities of nineteenth-century Baghdadi Jews, who had built the Lal Deval temple for prayer, and the twenty-first-century Israelis, who are building the IT temples of Pune for technology. In 1980, the "Song of Zion" resounded again in the synagogues of Pune, bearing witness to diasporas of the past and forming new diasporas in the present. A sacred counterpoint formed from the traditions of Jerusalem, Baghdad, and Kolkata transformed Pune during the 2008 High Holidays into a city at once Jewish and Indian and into a metropolis musically sounding itself as a "New Jerusalem."

Figure 39. Lal Deval, or Ohel David, Synagogue, Pune. Photo: Philip V. Bohlman.

References

Ashtamkar, Benjamin Samson, and Hannokh Shlomo Talkar. 1882. *Abraham Charitra: The Life of Abraham in Marathi Verses*. Mumbai: Kirtanottejakmandali.

Bohlman, Philip V. 2013. *Revival and Reconciliation: Sacred Music in the Making of European Modernity*. Lanham, MD: Scarecrow.

———. 2014. "Afterword – The Beginning of the End: Moments of Represence in Post-Holocaust Germany." In *Dislocated Memories: Jewish Music in Germany since World War II*, edited by Tina Frühauf and Lily Hirsch, 265–76. New York: Oxford University Press.

Butnick, Stephanie. 2013. "Calcutta Finally Makes a Minyan after 25 Years." *Tablet Magazine*. Last modified October 1, 2013, accessed July 25, 2017. http://www.tabletmag.com/scroll/147123/calcutta-finally-makes-a-minyan-after-25-years.

Chakrabarty, Dipesh. 2000. *Provincializing Europe: Postcolonial Thought and Historical Difference*. Princeton, NJ: Princeton University Press.

Davis, Ruth F. 2013. "Sound Archives and Ideology in Israel and Palestine." In *The Cambridge History of World Music*, edited by Philip V. Bohlman, 498–521. Cambridge: Cambridge University Press.

Feldman, Martha. 1995. *City Culture and the Madrigal at Venice*. Berkeley: University of California Press.

Fischel, Walter. 1968. *Hagadot Bene Yisra'el = The Haggadah of the Bene Israel of India*. New York: Orphan Hospital Ward of Israel.

Goldhill, Simon. 2008. *The Temple of Jerusalem*. Cambridge, MA: Harvard University Press.

HaCohen, Ruth. 2011. *The Music Libel against the Jews*. New Haven, CT: Yale University Press.

Idelsohn, Abraham Zvi. 1923. *Gesänge der orientalischen Sephardim*. Vol. 4, *Hebräisch-orientalischer Melodienschatz*. Leipzig: Benjamin Harz Verlag.

Isenberg, Shirley Berry. 1988. *India's Bene Israel: A Comprehensive Inquiry and Sourcebook*. Berkeley, CA: J. L. Magnes Museum.

Israel, Benjamin. 1984. The Bene Israel of India: Some Studies. Bombay: Orient Longman.

Johnson, Barbara K. 2005. *Yefehfiyah: Shirat ha-nashim shel Yehude ḳeralah*. Jerusalem: Mekhon Ben-Tsevi le-ḥeḳer ḳehilot Yisra'el ba-Mizraḥ.

Jones, Jacqueline. 2009. "Performing the Sacred: Song, Genre, and Aesthetics in Bhakti." PhD diss., University of Chicago.

Kartomi, Margaret, et al. 2007. *Out of Babylon: The Music of Baghdadi-Jewish Migrations into Asia and Beyond*. Tucson, AZ: Celestial Harmonies.

Katz, Nathan. 2000. *Who Are the Jews of India?* Berkeley: University of California Press.

Mendelssohn, Moses. 1783. *Jerusalem, oder über religiöse Macht und Judentum*. Berlin: Friedrich Maurer.

More, Thomas. (1516) 1965. *Utopia*. London: Penguin.

Nemichandra. 2008. "In Search of the Star of David." In *Multiple City: Writings on Bangalore*, edited by Aditi De, 178–83. New Delhi: Penguin Books India.

Numark, Mitch. 2001. "Constructing a Jewish Nation in Colonial India: History, Narratives of Dissent, and the Vocabulary of Modernity." *Jewish Social Studies* 7 (2): 89–113.

———. 2012. "Hebrew School in Nineteenth-Century Bombay: Protestant Missionaries, Cochin Jews, and the Hebraization of India's Bene Israel Community." *Modern Asian Studies* 46 (6): 1764–1808.

Packer, Robert A. 2016. "Synagogues of Chicago: Faith, Form, Function and Future." *Jüdisches Museum Berlin: JMB Journal* 14: 24–26.

Roland, Joan G. 1998. *The Jewish Communities of India: Identity in a Colonial Era.* 2nd ed. New Brunswick, NJ: Transaction.

———. 2000. "Religious Observances of the Bene Israel: Persistence and Refashioning of Tradition." *Journal of Indo-Judaic Studies* 3: 22–47.

Schultz, Anna. 2008. "The Collision of Genre and Collusion of Participants: Marathi Rastriya Kirtan and the Communication of Hindu Nationalism." *Ethnomusicology* 52 (1): 31–51.

———. 2013. *Singing a Hindu Nation: Marathi Devotional Performance and Nationalism.* New York: Oxford University Press.

———. 2015. "Performing Translation in Jewish India: Kirtan of the Bene Israel." In *This Thing Called Music: Essays in Honor of Bruno Nettl*, edited by Victoria Lindsay Levine and Philip V. Bohlman, 56–72. Lanham, MD: Rowman and Littlefield.

———. 2016. "The Afterlives of Publishing: Christian Texts for Indian Jewish Song." *Acta Musicologica* 88 (1): 63–86.

———. In press. *Songs of Translation: Bene Israel Migration, Gender, and Textual Orality.* New York: Oxford University Press.

Schultz, Anna, and Philip V. Bohlman. 2010. "Singing the Sacred Together in Pune, India: Jewish Siddur and Hindu Kirtan in the Making of Marathi Modernity." Paper delivered at the Midwest meeting of the Society for Ethnomusicology, DePaul University, April.

St. Augustine. (413 CE) 1950. *Civitas dei: The City of God.* Translated by Marcus Dods. New York: The Modern Library.

Tagore, Ranbindranath. (1916) 2005. *The Home and the World.* Translated by Surendranath Tagore. London: Penguin.

Valmadonna Trust. 1999. *Hebrew, Judeo-Arabic and Marathi Jewish Printing in India.* Leiden: Brill.

Weil, Shalva. 2007. "On Origins, the Arts, and Transformed Identities: Foci of Research into the Bene Israel." In *Indo-Judaic Studies in the Twenty-First Century: A View from the Margin*, edited by Nathan Katz, Ranabir Chakravarti, Braj M. Sinha, and Shalva Weil, 147–57. New York: Macmillan.

9

String Instruments as Urban Icons and Rural Products

Lars-Christian Koch

The city of Kolkata is of relatively modern origins. It is really not possible to speak of Calcutta as a place name or a city until the very end of the seventeenth century.[1] Until the middle of the eighteenth century, the city comprised four different sub-areas: 1) European Kolkata; 2) a residential village with several sacred areas; 3) a traditional Indian market; and 4) a market for the cloth trade stretching along the river. After the battle of Plassey in 1757, the British started rebuilding the city with the goal of making it the capital for their global empire.

From the beginnings of colonial British India until independence in 1947, Kolkata was the cultural center of India, as well as the political center for independence movements. The city has been a melting pot for international and Indian communities, more than cosmopolitan Mumbai (Bombay) and Delhi (Stang 2002, 342–44). The role of Kolkata as a cultural center for India was and still remains true. Kolkata is a city with a strong cultural personality. The mix of varied identities, as well as a strict commitment to traditional ways of life, gives the city its unity. Poetry and music play a crucial role, often imported from nearby villages. From the earliest days of Kolkata, rural Vaishnavite mendicants could frequently be found on the city streets, begging for alms and singing hymns to Krishna and Radha (see figure 40; Solvyns 1799).

---

1 Henceforth I refer to Calcutta by its modern name, Kolkata.

Figure 40. Vaishnavite Mendicant in late eighteenth-century Calcutta (Solvyns 1799, section 1).

Street theater became a major attraction, and the *jatra* theater, especially, was and still is a favorite source of folk entertainment during the winter. Private soirées and dancing girls in the palaces of the *baboos* of north Kolkata were legendary. The lifestyle of the baboo—mostly rich *zamindars* (landowners) with their estates in the countryside—differed from that of residents in the English community. While the baboos lived as if they were British in a tropical climate, they also took the best from the worlds of Bengal and England, smoking the *huka* (water pipe), drinking wine, and enjoying the pleasure of musical entertainment.

This scene became even more pronounced when, for political reasons, Wajid Ali Shah, the tenth and final Nawab of the state of Awadh in Uttar Pradesh, was exiled by the British to Garden Reach, in a suburb of Kolkata in 1857, where he stayed until his death in 1889, receiving a generous pension from the British government. The cultural impact of Wajid Ali Shah on the city was considerable. The Nawab was a poet, playwright, dancer, singer, composer, and great patron of the arts, especially music. Under his patronage all the most important musicians came to Kolkata, though a few did not undertake this early urban migration (Mitra 1990). It was the time when the instrument manufacturing business also started to boom, with the concomitant emergence of new ideas based on different playing styles and techniques applied by the musicians coming from many different areas and different *gharānās* (music schools and genealogical traditions; see Neuman [1980] 1990).

At the same time, as the prosperity of Kolkata's citizens and the neighborhoods and courts increased, the public presence of music and other cultural activities became more important, and the support and patronage of music also increased. Within the urban context musicians tried to please their audiences by changing details within their performance practice. It was necessary for all important musicians and artists to spend at least some time in Kolkata. Many, however, remained where they were even after their patrons came to the city as wealthy landlords, spending most of their time in the city, where they enjoyed life in Bengali baboo style. Accordingly, Kolkata came to develop a very distinctive music culture. Kolkata still supports specific areas in which different communities live and earn their livings. The market area of Barabazar, full of traders and shops is a labyrinth of lanes close to the Howrah Bridge. The shops on either side of Chitpur Road are owned mainly by Muslims. Close to Rabindranath Tagore's home a small settlement of instrument makers continued to ply their trade until the 1980s. The last shop dedicated to the making of string instruments, Kanailal & Bros., closed its doors in 1995 (figure 41).

Figure 41. Kanailal & Bros. (ca. mid-1990s). Rabindra Sarani, formerly Upper Chitpur Road. Kanailal's shop (no name plate) is close to the paint shop. All photographs in the present chapter by Lars-Christian Koch.

This shop was one of the important manufacturing sites for string instruments. Throughout the twentieth century, all important musicians came to the shop to discuss music, musical instruments, and their sound aesthetics. Even more important, this is where their instruments were made. The urban environment, with its remarkable number of musicians from the nineteenth century onwards, became an important transformative space for musical ideas and their conversion into practice. Instrument makers became mediators in this process, translating the ideas of musicians into material objects. This knowledge was transferred within families in the same way musical knowledge was transferred among family members.

To illustrate this transformation I now look at the history of two important families of instrument makers, who worked for at least three generations in the urban environment of Kolkata.[2] The first is the family of instrument makers, Kanailal & Bros. (Koch and Das Gupta 2013). During the period I studied with Murari Mohan Adhikari and Govinda Gopal Adhikari, the history of the Kanailal shop was mentioned several times in different contexts. I soon became aware that the whole family was involved in instrument making over more than three generations. In 1995, I asked Murari Mohan Adhikari to write down the important dates of his family history. It was significant from their standpoint as craftsmen that they always paid respect to associate craftsmen connected to their shop, who are mentioned alongside the family history. Co-workers were and are an important factor in the whole manufacturing process. Murarida began with the genealogy of his male family members connected to the shop of Kanailal & Bros.:

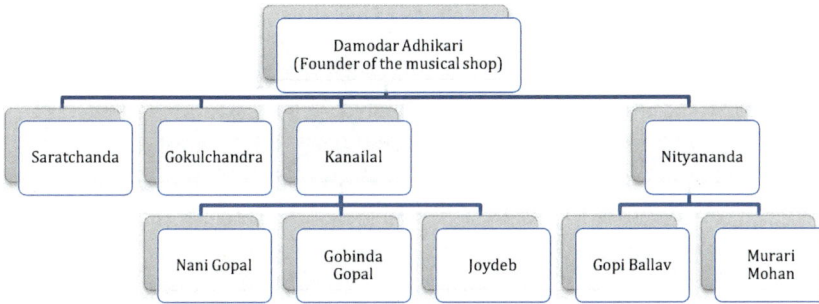

Figure 42. Male family members connected to Kanailal & Bros. (Koch 2011, 29).

Originally working in association with Natabarlal Das, the first important co-worker, Damodar Adhikari, began as a craftsman, founding the shop for

---

2   Other prominent makers of string instruments from the Kolkata urban area, such as Hemen Sen and Hiren Roy, who had their shops in Kolkata's southern suburbs, are not discussed in the present chapter, for they were active in the course of only two generations, beginning their careers first in the middle of the twentieth century.

musical instruments on Upper Chitpur Road.[3] His first son, Saratchandra, was born in 1884, and he entered the shop in 1905 after the death of his father. He himself died soon thereafter, in 1906. His second son, Gokulchandra, was born in 1886, like his brother entering the shop in 1905. He, too, died soon thereafter, in 1907. Damodar's third son was Kanailal, who was born in 1888 and began to work at the shop in 1905, when he was a mere seventeen years old. Kanailal played *esraj* and *sitar*, which he learned in his boyhood from his father. He died in 1945, two years after suffering a stroke due to high blood pressure, from which he had suffered since the age of five. Damodar's fourth son, Nityananda, was born in 1892 and then began work at the shop in 1905 when he was thirteen years old. He worked in the shop until 1960, and he died in 1972 from a heart attack.

The two brothers learned musical craftsmanship from Natabarlal Das for only five years and then concluded their apprenticeship due to his death. Two of Damodar's friends were Paresh Chandra Sen, an accomplished commercial artist and engraver, and Amulya Bhaskar, an accomplished wood carver in furniture manufacturing.[4] The two friends regularly came to the shop in the evening in order to teach woodcarving, drawing, and engraving to their beloved friend's son, Nityananda, who would later develop a distinctive style owing much to the fine arts. Nityananda played the *sitar* and *surbahar*. As a boy he had learned sitar from his father and later from Surendra Nath Banerjee and his two elder brothers, Gopeshwar and Ramprosonna Banerjee. These earlier studies were followed still later by those with Fida Hossain Khan of Jaipur and Mazid Khan, both rudra veena players, or *beenkars*.

---

3 The following list contains some of the preeminent musical instrument makers active during the foundational years for Kanailal & Bros. From Dhaka, and with family members from Dhaka and Kolkata:
   • Nani Ghose
   • Emdad Mian
   • Hinghu Mian
   • Laxminarayan Mistry of Dhaka and other family members in Dhaka and Kolkata
   • Chandrika Prosadji, a highly respected family in Rajasthan and Jaipur
   • Lalji of Benares
4 Furniture carving designs on string instruments became important in the production line of Kanailal & Bros. due to their involvement as co-workers.

Nani Gopal, the first son of Kanailal, was born in 1918 and died in 1947. From 1940 to 1947 he worked in the shop. He was a good sitar player, taught by his uncle Nityananda, and also by Satya Kinkar Banerjee of Vishunupur (1899–1980). Joydeb, the younger son of Kanailal, entered Government Services and therefore never worked in the shop. Gopi Ballav, the first son of Nityananda (1923–1960), was a commercial artist and a good sitar player. Govinda Gopal, the second son of Kanailal (1932–2009), started working in the shop in 1947 and continued until 1995 (see figure 43). He learned his craft—the tuning and making of the sitar, surbahar, esraj, and vīna—from his uncle Nityananda.

Murari Mohan Adhikari, the son of Nityananda Adhikari (1929–2006), started to work in the shop in 1945 (see figure 44). He learned to play the sitar and surbahar, and he acquired his craftsmanship from his father. It was Murari Mohan Adhikari who finally closed the shop in 1995. This family history shows a strong urban network of craftsmen and musicians located in a single music shop in north-central Kolkata.[5]

The Sharmas were another family of instrument makers. They settled in the Howrah district of Kolkata, more or less the other side of the Hoogly River from the Chitpur area in which Kanailal had his shop. A complete and thorough history of the instrument makers in this family must still be written.[6] The family members themselves did not keep any written

5   In the following list I mention a few names of musicians at the time of the period of Kanailal & Bros.:
  • Imdad Khan, Enayet Khan, Wahid Khan, and also his family and students.
  • Feeda Hossain Khan, Mazid Khan, Mohammad Khan—all beenkars.
  • Beenkars from Benares: Laxmi Prosad Misra, Shiva Misra, Pasupati Misra. All were vocalists or vina and sitar players.
  • Ramdas Misra, a vocalist and beenkar; Kanailal & Bros. made a vina for him in 1951.
  • Mustaq Ali Khan and his father, Ashak Ali Khan, were sitar and surbahar players from Benares, though Mustaq Ali Khan learned in Kolkata from an early age.
  • The musicians in the famous Dagar family all admired Kanailal's instruments.
  • Zia Mohiuddin Khan of Mumbai admired their instruments. Murari made a vīna for him, which was, in fact, his first creation.
  • Ravi Shankar's sitar and surbahar were made by Murari Mohan Adhikari.
  • Among the renowned musicians for whom Murari Mohan Adhikari made vīnas were the beenkars, Abid Hossain Khan of Indore and Asad Ali Khan of Delhi.
6   For the information on the family I have to thank Somjit Das Gupta (Das Gupta 2013).

Figure 43. Govinda Gopal Adhikari (1987).

Figure 44. Murari Mohan Adhikari (1992).

records on the history of their family or the development of instrument making. Only oral history and a few details about the instruments allow us to reconstruct the family history.

Shri Mohan Lal Sharma's family tradition of instrument making dates back to the last quarter of the nineteenth century. The family came from what was then the northern province of Bengal. During the last two decades of the nineteenth century, when Ustad Abdullah Khan was at the Court of the Maharaja of Dwarbhanga, the Sharmas were working there as master craftsmen. Later, during the first quarter of the twentieth century, two brothers from the family, Ramlal and Sukhlal Sharma, came to work simultaneously for the zamindars of Rajshashi (the Moitras), the *darbar* (court) of the Nawab of Dhaka and a number of contemporary musicians of Kolkata. Their close associate, Gobardhan Sharma, was also a reputable instrument maker at the time.

Their sons, Gopal and Durga Charan Sharma continued to create instruments with the same tradition of integrity. They further refined the techniques and experimented with the use of several new materials. Gopal Sharma, who was married to Gobardhan Sharma's daughter, died in the late 1950s, while Durga Charan continued his work until his death in the early 1970s.

Mohanlal Sharma, who passed away in 2013, learned his craft from his father, Durga Charan, and uncle, Gopal, and then worked as a master instrument maker until his death. The Sharma family has worked for almost all the great musicians of the past century. Except for the *rababs* and the instruments made by Ustad Abdullah Khan himself, they have made almost all the instruments played in Ustad Amir Khan and Radhika Mohan Moitra's tradition.[7] Members of the Sharma family built some rudra veenas also, but stopped making them due to a myth about the survival of the family of rudra veena makers. Building them in the family ceased

---

7   Instruments made by the Sharmas were played by almost all the great masters of the sarod, among them Abdullah Khan, Md. Amir Khan, Karamatullah Khan, Asadullah Kaukabh (Kukubh Khan), Hafiz Ali Khan, Timirbaran Bhattacharya, Nanigopal Matilal, Ashutosh Kundu, Banikanytha Mukhopadhyay, Enayat Ali, and Radhika Mohan Moitra, as well as some sitar players from Dhaka and Vishnupur.

Figure 45. Mohan Lal Sharma restringing a sitar in a recent photo.

entirely after Gopal Sharma built a rudra veena in 1951–52, just before his demise. Mohanlal made a rudra veena only on very special and limited occasions. Aside from occasionally building sitars and surbahars, the Sharmas generally made sarods, surshringars, surrababs, and some modern instrument inventions, such as the *mohanveena* (1943–48), the *dilbahar* (1956), and the *nabadeepa* (1962–67), as well as different types of esrajs with modern shapes. They made *dhrupadiya rababs* as well, for artists such as Ali Mahammad and Mahammad Ali, and their descendent Shaukat Ali. The Indian banjo was a standard musical instrument sometimes played by sarod players. Almost all banjos of the kind played in Bengal were made by the Sharmas (see figure 46).

Mohanlal Sharma also had associate craftsmen. Dulal Kanji, also a master maker of the sarod, occasionally crafted the skins on the bodies of sarods and surrababs. He was an apprentice under the well-known sarod maker, Hemendra Chandra Sen. Sanat Halder from Majhipara, in the Dad-

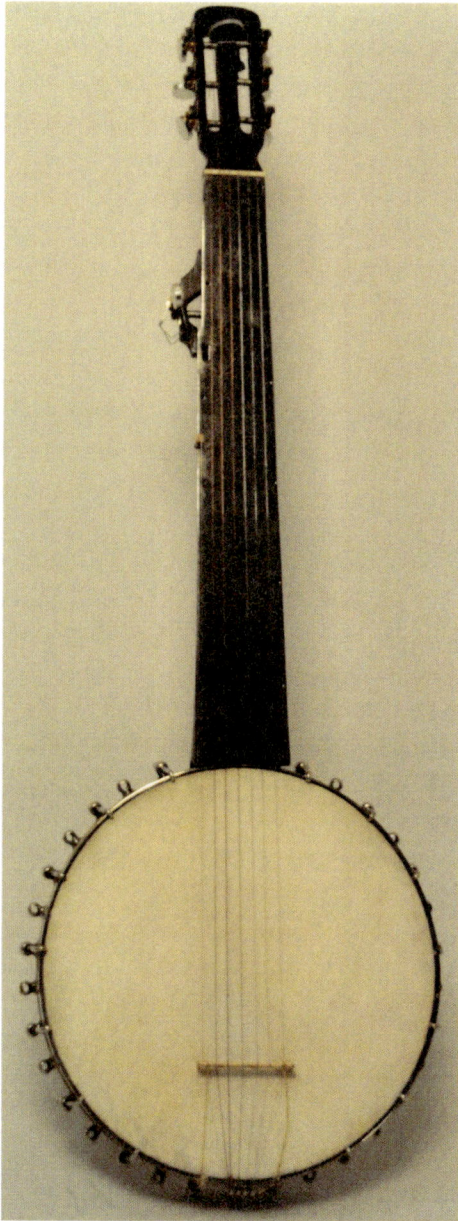

Figure 46. Indian banjo with a metal fretboard.

pur area of the Uluberia subdivision, acquire the intricate art of making instruments from Mohanlal Sharma while working as an associate crafts-man for him.

Today, the two workshops of Kanailal and Mohanlal Sharma are closed, and so too is the shop of Hiren Roy in south Kolkata. Only in the area around Lal Bazar in Kolkata can one still find music shops and those with wares of music instrument makers (see figures 47 and 48).

The Lal Bazar area is still of some significance, for Kolkata is known for its excellent musical instrument production, especially its sitars, sar-ods, surbahars, tanpuras, violins, tablas, and harmoniums, as well as many so-called folk-music instruments, among them: thumbas, bongos, dotara, djembe, drums, violin, flute, khanjira, mandolin, banjo, khamak, matka, handi, guitar, castanets, tambourine, kanshar ghanta, conch, resso, blues harp, pan flute, spring drum, steel drum, melodica, harmonium, piano, moorcing, ektara, recorders, balalaika, dugdugi, dubki, edakkaii, cowbells, chimes, dholak, khol, madol—and more.

Considering the number of musical instruments sold in Kolkata and exported to other countries in addition to domestic distribution inside In-dia, it is obvious that most of them are not produced in the city itself, for there is simply no space for building instruments in the tiny shops of Lal Bazar, not even in the courtyards of the buildings crammed in this dis-trict of the city. How, we might ask, does the city support such a lively production of musical instruments?

When I first began working several years ago with instrument makers documenting their craft, I found it extremely difficult to find out where the basic parts of the instruments were produced. Where did the parts come from that then were taken by the craftsmen in the cities? What were the initial stages of the instrument building that were then fine-tuned in the shops on Lal Bazar, Chitpur Road, or Rash Behari Avenue?

Only when I started a documentation project on sarod-type instru-ments with Somjit Das Gupta did I learn that the initial stages took place in the countryside around Kolkata, which we then began to visit and re-search. Small villages were simply able to make their living from instru-ment manufacturing, at least during those times of the year when their paddies and the fields in which their crops grew afforded them some free

Figure 47. Lal Bazar street scene at night.

Figure 48. Entrance to a music shop in Lal Bazar.

time (figure 49). The output of musical instruments, from the smallest parts to complete instruments, is quite remarkable (see, e.g., figure 50).

The village instrument makers are able to obtain essential tools and machinery, and they have contact with the necessary networks to get the materials. Although the basic knowledge about measurements, selection, and supply of materials still lies with the makers who complete the work in the city, basic production takes place in the villages, generating a substantial network of suppliers, craftspeople with special knowledge, fine tuners, and musicians. The network even extends beyond the city of Kolkata, for the builders from the Uluberia area also supply instrument makers in Varanasi and New Delhi. This is easily visible in Varanasi music shops through the woodcarving in typical Kolkata style, based on the furniture-maker style established in Kanailal's shop in the first half of the twentieth century (figure 51).

The villages in this area are near the old archeological site of Garchumuk, and they are part of an area always known for wood carvers and engravers, as well as the makers of wooden boats and *bajras* (luxury boats). The entire area around Kolkata, moreover, has an economy based on agriculture. Accordingly, due to the needs of agricultural work, it is sometimes necessary to postpone the making of the instruments, thus showing that music instruments do not provide the primary source of income in the area, though in recent years it has become more important as larger orders have been received.

The village in which I conducted my research is called Dadpur, and it lies about seventy kilometers from Kolkata. In Dadpur the farmer, craftsman, and engraver, Sanat Haldar (age 47) lives and works (see figure 52). He learned the preliminary making of sitars and surbahars from his uncle, Anil Haldar, who lived in the same village. From Mohanlal Sharma, Sanat Haldar learned to make instruments such as the dhrupadiya rabab, sursringar, mohanveena, surrabab, sarod, sitar, surbahar, nabadeepa, dilbahar, mayuriveena, esraj, dilruba, sarangi, sarinda, Bengali-type been, and different types of tanpuras and santoor. In other words, he makes all major types of string instruments from West Bengal and North India, and many others from beyond the region. Sanat Haldar informed Somjit Das Gupta about the designs, drawings, and examples of old instruments (Das Gupta

Figure 49. Hut for sitar making, Uluberia district, near the village of Dadpur.

Figure 50. An instrument maker outside a village hut.

Figure 51. Furniture carving and carvings on the body of a sitar.

2013). Das Gupta was also to make further connections to his source, Rad-hika Mohan Maitra, one of Kolkata's most influential sarod players in the twentieth century, substantially contributing to Das Gupta's collection of string instruments tradition.

Sanat Haldar has also worked with Murari Mohan Adhikari on en-gravings for sitars, surbahars, and beens in the Dagar style, acquiring the typical Kanailal engraving style. He has, furthermore, contributed to a project for the Musical Instrument Museum in Phoenix, Arizona, in which he reconstructed old instruments from Das Gupta's collection under Das Gupta's supervision. Additionally, Sanat Haldar took part in the string-instrument training project funded by the Sangeet Natak Akademi, New Delhi, where he was under the guidance of Mohanlal Sharma. His se-nior associate is Dilip Mandol (aged 46), who works with Sanat Halder on engraving, constructing, and varnishing. Sanat Halder has several ju-nior associates and trainees who deserve to be mentioned here, because they are critical to maintaining the network of string-instrument build-ing in the Kolkata area. It is striking to note just how young these as-sociates are, surely indicative of a tradition that has a long history still before it: Pradip Kayal (23), Nabakumar Kayal (21), Abhijit Kayal (21), Mrinmoy Halder (18), Sumit Mandol (17), Krishna Mandol (19), and Sudip Haldar (15), his son.

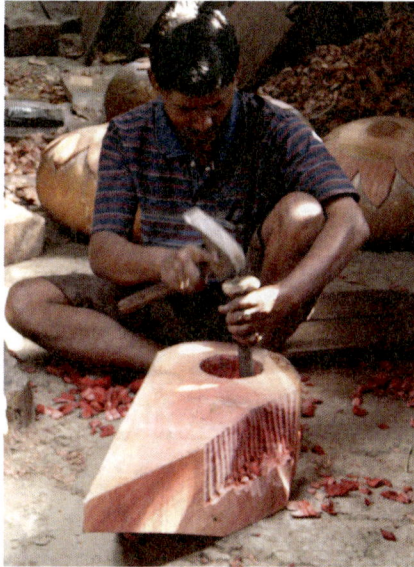

Figure 52. Sanat Haldar working on a sarod.

Figure 53. Apprentices in the Sanat Halder workshop, Dadpur.

Figure 54. The workshop area of Sanat Haldar, Dadpur.

Figure 55. Early stages of sitar construction, workshop of Sanat Haldar, Dadpur.

Instrument Building Networks in Comparison: The Case of the Gibson Guitar

It will surprise many readers to learn that guitars, too, are built at the Sanat Haldar workshop in Dadpur, also using the materials and knowledge in the Ganges Delta region around Kolkata. As local as the instrument-building tradition is in rural Dadpur, it still reflects the cosmopolitanism that characterizes global cities. To expand the local into a global perspective, I make a brief excursion from one of the other cities we explore in this book, to Chicago and the surrounding Midwestern American region, the home of the Gibson guitar.

The Gibson Guitar Corporation was founded in 1902 as "The Gibson Mandolin-Guitar Mfg. Co., Ltd.," in Kalamazoo, Michigan, about seventy kilometers from Chicago. At the beginning, the company focused on manufacturing mandolin-family instruments. In later years, however, the Gibson company initiated the invention of arch-top guitars by using the same construction details employed in violin manufacture, as well as the same woods, especially maple and spruce.

In the 1930s, aside from flattop acoustic guitars, Gibson also constructed the first hollow-bodied electric guitar, used by many jazz guitar players, among them Charlie Christian and Barney Kessel. During World War II, due to the shortage of wood and metal, Gibson was forced to limit the manufacturing of musical instruments, turning instead to the manufacturing of wood and metal parts for the military. In 1944, Gibson was purchased by Chicago Musical Instruments, and a new era started. When Ted McCarty became president of Gibson, the company expended significantly, by creating many new designs, mainly solid-body guitars and high-end production instruments. From single models several thousand units were produced and sold, dramatically changing popular music along the way.

The area around Kalamazoo, Michigan was known for its woodworking industries and its excellent woodworkers from northern Europe. McCarty was aware of the labor history of the area, but also knew that during a period of factory expansion, he would have to employ workers with almost no knowledge of woodworking. Because a strong work ethic

Figure 56. The Les Paul Junior from 1959, which served as the model for more than 4,000 units in 1959 alone (Duchossoir 1981, 179).

connected to woodworking prevailed in the Kalamazoo area, Gibson determined to establish a program of in-house training that would produce a clear division of labor. The marketing of Gibson products continued to be managed in Chicago because the urban structures necessary for successful sale and distribution were in place in the city (Hembree 2007). The network between the rural area and the city, however, expanded, with its flow of well-crafted instruments similar in many ways to that between the villages and the urban areas of West Bengal.

In 1969, Chicago Musical Instruments was sold, and between 1974 and 1984 the production of Gibson guitars was shifted from Kalamazoo to Nashville, Tennessee. The Kalamazoo plant was closed in 1984, but several Gibson employees established the Heritage Guitar Company in the old factory. Still today, they continue to manufacture versions of classic Gibson designs, albeit on a much smaller scale. Due to an expanding world market for musical instruments the direct connection between the regions around Chicago and the city itself may no longer be relevant for the manufacturing and marketing connection. Today, the production of parts or even complete products may be undertaken somewhere in Asia, even for marketing in North America or Europe. The flow of labor, however, still stretches across the networks that developed between the rural and the urban. This is no less the case in West Bengal.

Materialities of the Instrument as Object

To understand the networks and exchange structure of musical materials, knowledge, and labor between urban and rural encounters, it is illuminating to take a look at the materials themselves used for instrument manufacturing. The pumpkin (gourd) used for sitar, surbahar, surshringar, and some other instruments is a product of districts adjacent to the city, such as Hoogly, North 24 Parganas, and other delta areas in West Bengal. Until the 1990s, the best gourds were considered to come from Miraj in Maharashtra state, from which they were imported in large quantities. Today, however, production in Hoogly and 24 Parganas stresses both quality and quantity, thus making it necessary to obtain supplies from all parts of India.

Figure 57. Stocks of gourds in Dadpur.

Previously, the wood used for string instruments was mainly Burmese or Indian teak wood, but it has changed to toon wood due to its lower price, better availability, and lack of restrictions on the trading of this particular wood. This is true also for Indian rosewood and Indian ebony. Teak trees are often tall and massive, growing in dense forests in Madhya Pradesh, but also in northern West Bengal all the way to Sikkim. Harvested elsewhere, the trees are cut to size in sawmills in Kolkata. The process is the same for toon wood, a kind of cedar. The highest quality toon comes from northern West Bengal, Assam, and Uttar Pradesh, again where it is harvested before being sent to Kolkata sawmills.

The tuning pegs for string instruments are made from Indian rosewood and Indian ebony. The bridges are made of sambar, deer horn, and ebony. Today, the horn of a deer is a restricted material, thus it has largely been replaced by ebony or synthetic materials produced and used in urban settings, for example the interior assembly parts made from hard plastic. Indian rosewood, too, is banned and difficult to obtain, thus making it necessary to import new woods from Africa or even from New Guinea. Once again, the import network is controlled by urban sawmills and urban instrument makers. Strings for the instruments use steel, bronze, and copper, also mostly imported to Kolkata. The skins used for the bodies of sarods and surbahars are prepared from goatskin.

The flow of materials necessary for string instruments reveals the extent to which almost all raw materials are produced in the rural areas, before they are processed and evaluated in the city, thereafter traveling back to the rural manufacturing sites, where craftsmen possess the knowledge about design, construction details, and sound ideals recognized in the cities. The pre-manufactured instruments travel back to the city to be fine-tuned according to the needs and sound ideals of actual musicians no less than the special skills of the urban makers.

From this point in the city, the whole circle begins anew, but always with slight changes. The situation for the village instrument maker changes as the system expands. This means that craftsmen like Sanat Haldar are beginning to have more customers from cities outside West Bengal, and they earn more money as they start to sell directly to customers. The instrument makers in the city are aware of this trend, leading them to keep their knowledge about fine-tuning, for example, to themselves. It remains true that one has to go to the instrument maker in the city to obtain instruments of the highest quality. With new routes and changing networks, the creation and distribution of string instruments continue to depend on an environment of craft and labor, located in the city, but extending to the world beyond.

Figure 58. Inside a Kolkata sawmill.

Figure 59. Stocks of toon wood in Dadpur.

Lars-Christian Koch

References

Das Gupta, Somjit. 2013. Personal communication with the author.

Duchossoir, A. R. 1981. *Gibson Electronics*. Milwaukee, WI: Hal Leonard.

Hembree, Gil. 2007. *Gibson Guitars: Ted McCarty's Golden Era, 1948–1966*. Milwaukee, WI: Hal Leonard.

Koch, Lars-Christian. 2011. *Sitar and Surbahar Manufacturing: The Tradition of Kanailal & Brother, Kolkata*. Berlin: Staatliche Museen zu Berlin.

Koch, Lars-Christian, and Somjit Das Gupta. 2013. *Sarodiyo Bin: The Making of Stringed Musical Instruments of the Sarod Family Based on the Collection of the Late Radhika Mohan Maitra*. Berlin: Ethnologisches Museum, Staatliche Museen zu Berlin, DVD.

Mitra, Rajyeshwar. 1990. "Music in Old Calcutta." In *Calcutta: The Living City*. Vol. 1, *The Past*, edited by Sukanta Chaudhuri, 179–85. Calcutta: Oxford University Press.

Neuman, Daniel M. (1980) 1990. *The Life of Music in North India: The Organization of an Artistic Tradition*. Chicago: University of Chicago Press.

Solvyns, Balthazar. 1799. *A Catalogue of 250 Coloured Etchings: Descriptive of the Manners, Customs, Character, Dress, and Religious Ceremonies of the Hindoos*. Calcutta: Mirror Press.

Stang, Friedrich. 2002. *Indien: Geographie, Wirtschaft, Politik*. Darmstadt: WBG.

10

PERFORMING ASSAM IN URBAN SPACES: BIHU ON THE CITY STAGE

Rehanna Kheshgi

In 2009, Khagen Mahanta, known around the world as the "King of Bihu," told me in an interview that "Bihu is the only festival which doesn't have any relation with religion, caste, and creed" (Mahanta 2009). From his home in Guwahati, the Indian state of Assam's capital city, Mahanta narrated to me a story of how the Bihu festival and the music and dance associated with it had emerged from rural roots to become an urban phenomenon, citing himself and other well-known musicians as catalysts for this shift. As one of the eight states of India's northeast region, Assam is unfamiliar to many because of sparse national and international media coverage, which largely focuses on militant insurgent groups, violent bombings, and a continuing immigration crisis. As true of all states in India, a complex array of terms categorizes the people of Assam (see Kheshgi 2016).

According to the 2001 Census, there were roughly 26.5 million people living in Assam, many of whom have appealed to the government on the basis of economic, social, and cultural grounds for recognition as members of unique, marginalized tribal or caste groups. The main goals for seeking recognition are the economic and social benefits conferred by the state upon individuals who can demonstrate membership in a recognized minority tribe or caste. The terms of classification for India's affirmative-action policies, called the reservation system, were drafted after Indian Independence in 1947 by Bhimrao Ramji Ambedkar, whereby "untouchables," previously "outcastes," were incorporated into the caste system as "scheduled castes" (SC) and "scheduled tribes" (ST) (Dirks 2001, 278). Concerns about socioeconomically disadvantaged groups that were not marked by clear, ritually defined categories led to the government-appointed Mandal Commission's recommendation in 1991 that "backward castes" (OBC) be incorporated into the reservation system (ibid., 275). In northeast India, some struggles for tribal recognition have resulted in mass-mobilization and the creation of new states that had previously been part of Assam (Nagaland in 1963, Meghalaya in 1972, Arunachal Pradesh in 1986, and Mizoram in 1987).

As a statewide festival that features music and dance, "Bihu" has been positioned as the symbol of a composite Assamese identity. The opening citation from Khagen Mahanta highlights the powerful ideological vision behind claiming Bihu performance as expressive cultural practice uniting an Assam in which different communities celebrate their own Bihu-s in different ways. Recognized tribal groups such as the Mising, Sonowal Kachari, and Deuri, for example, each have their own way of dancing and singing Bihu. In this chapter I argue that conscious efforts to construct and popularize a standardized form of Bihu, imagined by a growing Assamese middle class, prioritize a normative Assamese identity. It is only through the emergence of this modern identity that government officials, scholars, journalists, and everyday individuals can describe Bihu as the national festival of Assam. This modern Bihu is born in the city, where it becomes possible to de-emphasize or ignore the relations of religious ritual and socio-economic status to performance. The "other" Bihu-s, which are marked by association with a tribal group (i.e., Mising Bihu and Deuri Bihu), are invoked only as a peripheral variety of the modern mainstream Bihu that has earned a place as the most appropriately authentic.

In this chapter I focus on some of the strategies employed by middle-class agents in order to shape Bihu into a performative cultural medium that functions as a resource for defining Assamese identity. Institutional standardization, museum exhibitions, and diasporic performance are some of the elements that contribute in different ways to shaping modern forms of expressive culture. These strategies operate simultaneously, but I locate each in a different ethnographic frame in order to ground the processes in the cultural work that Bihu does for the middle-class agents with whom

I interacted during my research in London during 2008, in Assam extensively from 2009 to the present, and in Chicago. I also draw on my own experiences with Bihu, which were located in urban contexts during my early research, but shifted increasingly to rural areas of northeast India during my PhD dissertation research (Kheshgi 2016). By comparing urban and rural performances of Bihu I was further able to develop a theory whereby the sites of Bihu performance produced modernities in Assam and its diaspora cities (ibid.).

By focusing on these strategies and their realization in global cities and rural Assam, I also hope to complicate the idea of a rural/urban dichotomy by examining performance as a dialogic practice. For the middle-class cultural visionaries I speak about here, bringing the idea of the rural into urban spaces is essential to the project of modernizing Bihu. A modernized Bihu then circulates back into rural areas via various networks, including popular media and Bihu performance circuits.

For my use of the term "middle class," I turn to Leela Fernandes's work, which describes the rise of a new Indian middle class during the colonial period. The political assertiveness of that new middle class was premised on a claim of representation linked with a project of self-identification (Fernandes 2006). Internal differentiation within this new middle class combined with a politics of distinction from elites, the colonial state, and marginalized social groups cultivated a sense of uncertainty. I understand the project of mobilizing a mainstream form of Bihu performance as part of the process of managing this uncertainty. Via the strategies mentioned above, elements of rural folk culture, posited as uniquely Assamese, were gradually shaped into a suitably modern form—"rural modernities"—which the middle class could uphold as representative of a general Assamese public (ibid.).

Before I explore these strategies by locating them ethnographically in different sites, I offer a short description of Bihu. Bohag or Rongali Bihu, is one of three Bihu festivals that mark different points in the annual cycle of the Assamese calendar. Each festival is linked with a different agricultural activity. Bohag Bihu, to which I refer simply as "Bihu," is celebrated during the month of Bohag, beginning in mid-April and ending in mid-May. It is associated with a particular form of music and dance, which will be the focus of my discussion in the present chapter. Bihu is distinct from other Assamese musical genres because its musical instruments, musical structure, and lyrical content. The musical structure gives cues to the dancers who, in contexts of both spontaneous and choreographed dancing, rely especially on the beats of the *dhol* drum to direct their movements. Bihu, therefore, is at once a season, a musical genre, and a dance tradition. In this chapter I focus on the construction of the Assamese Bihu today, to which I refer as "mainstream" and "modernized."

The development of modern, mainstream Bihu is often described according to narratives of past glory, subsequent decline, and later renaissance, corresponding with early patronage by Ahom kings. Mainstream Bihu then underwent marginalization as a result of colonial encounter, only to undergo revival through nationalist cultural visionaries. Since I deal with current performance practices here, I begin by briefly discussing the discourses surrounding these three historical periods as presented in Praphulladatta Goswami's *The Springtime Bihu of Assam* ([1966] 2003), one of the few sources available in English, along with insights from middle-class consultants in Assam, London, and Chicago. These narratives are important because they continue to be invoked in public debates about Bihu via print media, cultural workshops, and everyday conversation.

The legacy of the Ahom kingdom plays an important part in shaping narratives of a valiant, independent, and unbroken past for Assam. Political scientist Sanjib Baruah points out that in 1826, "when the Ahom kingdom passed into British hands, it was the first time in history that the Assamese heartland became politically incorporated into a pan-Indian imperial formation" (Baruah 1999, 21). According to Goswami, the first extant written description of Bihu was recorded by a seventeenth-century historian, Jamili, who claimed that the Ahom king of his time had a field near his palace "specially set out for the purpose" of staging Bihu performance (Goswami [1966] 2003, 21). Goswami sees the king's patronage of Bihu as the first event that "turned the festival into a national occasion," suggesting that the royal promotion of Bihu song and dance led to a thriving tradition throughout the kingdom, whereas performance had previously been confined to discreet and disparate locations (ibid.).

During the eighteenth century, the Ahom king Sivasimha constructed a large, two-story brick palace called Ranghar near today's Sibsagar, in order to be able to enjoy Bihu in a "comfortable manner" (ibid., 22). In the twenty-first century, Ranghar still stands as an important monument to Ahom heritage and is a prominent site for large, open-air Bihu performances. A replica of Ranghar has been constructed in Assam's capital, Guwahati, on the premises of the Srimanta Sankardev Kalakshetra, a cultural center established in 1988 by the state government.

Documenting a change in attitude toward Bihu performance, Goswami points to Haliram Dhekial Phukan's 1829 Assam Buranji, which describes Bihu as a context for "womenfolk of the common people and dissolute men [to] get together and perform dance and music of a very objectionable type" (cited in ibid., 22–23). He also cites William Robinson's 1841 Descriptive Account of Assam, which describes Bihu as a festival in which "large groups of people parade about, attended by numbers of dancing girls, who pause from time to time to exhibit their wanton movements, and charm the audience with their lascivious songs" (cited in ibid., 23). Goswami gives three reasons for the decline: the decrease in royal patronage by the weakened Ahom kingdom in the early 1800s, the rise of Hindu orthodoxy, which deemed Bihu song and dance inappropriate, and the influence of British colonial values on Assamese perceptions of proper public behavior.

The Assamese scholar Paramesh Dutta writes that

> [d]uring turbulent historical times in the last part of the eighteenth and the first part of the nineteenth century, both revolutionaries and rulers used Bihu songs as socio-cultural tools to rally the people. (Dutta 2008, 16)

Dutta asserts that during this period "some elite of the state, under the influence of colonial and western paradigms, disparaged the Bihu festivities as lurid, immoral and having sexual overtones," but due to the patronage of the Ahom kings, "Bihu had already moved away from the fields to the royal amphitheater" (ibid.). In other words, Dutta posits Bihu as a cultural form that had been imbued with enough importance to withstand decades of contempt on behalf of colonial authorities and the Assamese elite who fell under their influence.

In an interview Khagen Mahanta explained to me that, during his youth in the 1950s, Bihu was "treated as a music or a culture of the lower category people" (Mahanta 2009). Traveling to Sibsagar with his father to sing neo-Vaishnavite devotional songs, narrative songs, and progressive ballads, the young Mahanta stayed in the homes of local villagers where he became fascinated with Bihu. He explained that "when I started getting interested to Bihu, that time Bihu was not accepted by our people, our class who were advantageous and who were, a little upper-class people, not only economically, but also class-wise" (ibid.). Mahanta spoke of his early vision for Bihu as a festival with the potential to unite Assam's diverse communities. He claims to be the first artist to perform Bihu at many locations that today have well-established stage festivals in the southern part of Assam. For Mahanta, Bihu was an expression of the song and dance of the "common" people of Assam that all Assamese people could embrace. Through his contacts at Kolkata recording studios, Mahanta recorded albums featuring Bihu songs. Mahanta recalls that these records became so popular that they inspired many families in Assam to purchase gramophone players.

The shift in the status of Bihu over Mahanta's lifetime happened as a result of a process that gained momentum during the mid-twentieth century, whereby Bihu was reinvented as a genre of dance and song that has come to represent Assamese identity through processes of urban transformation to those living in Assam, in the wider nation of India, and in diaspora abroad. To trace these interconnections, I move between and among four cities: Guwahati, Delhi, London, and Chicago. The cities are urban spaces in which modern, mainstream Bihu is created and interpreted by middle-class agents. Guwahati is a city in which middle-class aspirations have shaped this particular form of Bihu. I focus here on processes of standardization that have been implemented through incentive-driven competitions and the training of performers by middle-class culture advocates. Moving to the city of Delhi, I discuss the opening ceremony of the 2010 Commonwealth Games, for which Bihu was called upon to represent Assam as a symbol of Assamese culture within the Indian multicultural formation—detached from its time and place—as an emblem of Assamese unity. In my example from London, I focus on a museum exhibit that interpreted Bihu as an expression of the endangered, remote, rural heritage of India. And finally, my discussion of Chicago highlights modern, mainstream Bihu as an event for bringing together Assamese people, their friends, and their families from the American Midwest. The Chicago Bihu continues to be shaped in dialogue with processes in Assam due to the mobility of middle-class Assamese in the United States and connections maintained through the exchange of popular media, primarily Bihu music albums and video CDs.

Guwahati Bihu

Radha Gobinda Baruah (1900–1977) is often identified as the man behind the first urban staged Bihu in Guwahati in the early 1950s. He is often referred to as the architect of modern Assam, having established the state's first English daily newspaper and having orchestrated the construction of its first sports stadium. Kamal Hazarika, a London-based composer and performer of Assamese songs, told me in an interview that Baruah brought groups from villages to Guwahati, "so instead of the field, they performed on the stage" (Hazarika 2007). Speaking about growing up in Guwahati during the 1950s, Hazarika told me that

> everyone knew about the Bihu, but it was never performed on the stage openly. Radha Gobinda Baruah knew that there were lots of things to learn from here. We must bring it to the stage. At that time, we were not interested [in Bihu]. (Ibid.)

During a visit to Assam in April 2009, I attended a Bihu performance at Lataxil, one of the largest open-air Bihu stages in Guwahati. Following Khagen Mahanta's performance, many groups of young boys and girls performed Bihu songs and dances into the early hours of the morning. Their matching costumes and precise choreography indicated to me meticulous planning and many hours of rehearsal. In contrast, the stage's backdrop featured a picture of a large tree and dense foliage that evoked a rural simplicity, an image often associated with Bihu.

As Assam's capital, Guwahati was the center for the creation of a mainstream Bihu through the urban transformation of music and dance that could represent Assam's rural past in a way deemed appropriately modern for the urban stage. An important vehicle for standardization is the Bihu competition, which emerged at the end of the 1970s as a powerful mode of dialogue between young musicians and dancers, as well as older individuals appointed to judge their performances. Today, Bihu troupes travel from rural areas, small towns, and cities across Assam to compete for large cash prizes. Judges are selected from among a variety of individuals deemed knowledgeable about Bihu, and they assign points to each competitor in solo and group categories. The criteria for success are loosely standardized from judge to judge, and often competitors learn the rules as the competition progresses. The most striking pedagogical moment in my opinion is the question-and-answer session following each performance, where the competitor is asked to reproduce knowledge about Bihu's history and current performance practice. During the competitions I attended in April 2009, the competitors were usually unable to produce the correct answers to many of these questions, and instead the judges used the questions and answers as an opportunity to teach the young performers and the audience about Bihu.

As a state-sponsored institution, the Guwahati-based Kalakshetra plays an important role in shaping Bihu performance practice. The Kalakshetra regularly holds workshops that attract young people from across Assam, grooming them to perform Bihu at the national level. Often, folklorist-performers such as Probin and Rashmi Saikia are invited to lecture on Bihu's history and to present findings from their research in remote locations of Assam where many still believe Bihu to be celebrated in a pure and authentic manner. These rediscovered elements are subsequently incorporated into the choreography taught at workshops for young dancers, thus becoming what I call "rural modernities" (Kheshgi 2016).

Bihu, thus, is constantly changing through attempts to make it more authentic, and at the same time becoming more standardized through attempts to make it more polished and presentable. The rural/urban distinction is dismantled when we recognize that performers from rural and urban areas are exposed to the same Bihu media images and sounds, and that troupes from both rural and urban areas travel across the state to compete. The city, however, mediates both the production of Bihu music and videos, as well as the authoritative stance on authentic performance, in other words, the home of the Kalakshetra, which thereby becomes the meeting place for cultural experts. Guwahati is also a center for shaping young cultural ambassadors. A Kalakshetra representative reported to *The Telegraph* of Kolkata that "[w]e have even tied up with several corporate groups in the country to send Bihu troupes to cultural festivals" ("High Footfall" 2007).

Delhi Bihu

Sending Bihu troupes to cultural festivals is premised on the idea that Bihu can be performed outside of Assam, and, significantly, that it can be performed at a time other than the month of Bohag. The flexibility in the performance schedule illustrates how Bihu contributes to essentializing Assamese identity. Such detachment posits Bihu as modern. In October 2010, Somnath Bora, a well-known *dhuliya* drummer who performs Bihu regularly throughout India and abroad, was commissioned by the Assam State Cultural Affairs Department to organize a troupe of Bihu dhol drummers for the opening ceremony of the Commonwealth Games, held in Delhi. *The Hindu* reported before the event that "Somnath Bora will be creating history since he and his troupe members will become the first from Assam to perform in such a global sporting event" (*The Hindu* 2010). Bora, working within the constraints of his position, chose to present mainstream Bihu, which is identifiable by the drum pattern and the dress of the performers. Mainstream Bihu intertwines a unique imagining of rural agricultural life in Assam with a modern chore-ographed performativity. These two elements allow Assam to participate via Bihu in the spectacle of the opening ceremony of the Commonwealth Games, an event that portrays India as a mosaic of unique cultural units—exemplifying the popular nationalist slogan, "Unity in Diversity" (for a study of music in the 2008 Junior Commonwealth Games in Pune, India, see Bohlman 2009).

London Bihu

In 2002, the curators of a musical instrument exhibition at the Horniman Museum in London identified Bihu as suitable for inclusion in their display. The exhibition "Utsavam—Music from India," which opened to the public in 2008, was created to preserve endangered music practices by presenting musical instruments, audio clips, and video recordings of selected performance traditions collected by a team of researchers specifically for the project. Five different locations in India were chosen based on the curators' understanding that these traditions were in danger of disappearing. A second goal of the exhibition was to direct the awareness of people in India and in the United Kingdom toward Indian music traditions other than Hindustani and Karnatak classical music, and Bollywood popular music. Several different performance traditions were selected from Assam, among them Deuri Bihu, Kachari Bihu, and "Assamese" Bihu (i.e., mainstream). One of the video clips featured a group of teenage girls singing and dancing Assamese Bihu in a field outside Kamalabari village, on Majuli Island, Assam. Incorporating urban aesthetics and mobilized by urban transformation, their choreography was a resounding indicator of the penetration of the standardization project in rural areas such as Kamalabari.

The video clip, an example of the mainstream "Assamese" Bihu, was positioned in the exhibition as one of many Bihu-s. This democratization of Bihu in a London museum, though celebratory, comes with a hidden cost. In accordance with the exhibition's theme and vision, the region was positioned as remote and rural, with traditions and cultural expressions in danger of extinction. In this democratic presentation of Bihu to a London audience, the exhibition reproduced inaccurate rural/urban distinctions about Assam.

Although I am critical of the methods and goals of the project, I benefited greatly from the access it provided to audiovisual material of Deuri and Kachari Bihu performances. I, too, contributed some of my own video footage of UK-based Assamese Bihu events to this exhibition. In conversation with Assamese cultural organizers in London, I became aware of the distinctions between different Bihu-s and the prominence of mainstream Bihu, which I saw performed at various Assamese community events in the United Kingdom. London has a controversial history of displaying Indian culture in museums. Because the portrayal of Bihu in the exhibition contrasts with the perceptions I heard from Assamese residents in England, London features as an important site for the promotion of mainstream Bihu.

Chicago Bihu

On April 18, 2010, I attended the annual Bihu function in the suburban city of Naperville, organized by Assamese professionals residing in the greater Chicago area. As I have noted for the Bihu-s in Guwahati, Delhi, and London, the development of Bihu as an event for expatriate Assamese people to congregate and celebrate their common roots emerged as part of the urban transformation of Bihu to a mainstream festival that bears witness to "rural modernities" (Kheshgi 2016). Assamese families are spread across the Chicago area, and Bihu provides an occasion for people to gather and enjoy Assamese food, music, and dance. The Bihu performances included in the "cultural program," which took place near the end of the evening and featured performances of mainstream Bihu. Jahnobi Bora, who lives in Madison, Wisconsin, travels each year to Chicago to celebrate Bihu with her family and usually performs in the "cultural program." Jahnobi Bora's experience growing up in Assam and winning multiple Bihu competitions prepared her to teach Bihu dance to her daughters and other youth in the American Midwest. In July 2011, she choreographed a Bihu dance for the annual Assam Convention.

The 2011 Assam Convention, which brought together people from across the United States and featured Bihu song and dance as part of the celebrations, was held in Oakbrook, another western suburb of Chicago. Zubeen Garg, Assam's most famous pop idol, was invited as the guest artist that year. Zubeen is the voice behind the majority of Bihu albums and video CDs released in recent years, rivaling Khagen Mahanta, who nevertheless remains an authoritative folk presence in Assam. Assamese expatriate sponsorship of Assamese music and dance in Chicago, as one example of a worldwide phenomenon, plays an important role in continuing to shape Bihu through urban transformations. Annual congregations such as the Assam Convention and Bihu functions are only a few of many ways in which Assamese expatriates maintain relationships with friends and family in Assam.

Whose Bihu?

Throughout the present chapter I bring four cities into focus—Guwahati, Delhi, London, and Chicago—in order to highlight various processes and people involved in creating modern Bihu. Whether on stage, behind the scenes, watching from the sidelines, or viewing a video CD, Bihu music and dance performance is a dialogic process that engages all people present in various contexts. I demonstrate here how the role of middle-class agents in this dialogue has determined the development of mainstream Bihu. In Assam, their voices have emerged more prominently than others due to their privileged position in society. Outside India, middle-class Assamese are the primary organizers of cultural events. The processes described in this chapter—standardization through competitions, detachment from traditional temporal and spatial contexts, a museum exhibition that creates the possibility of democratizing different forms of Bihu but freezes them all in a rural, remote frame, and the diasporic journeys of cultural performance—result from the urban transformation of modern mainstream Bihu through performances of Assamese identity.

The urban transformation is significant because the promotion of one modern mainstream "Assamese" Bihu over "other" Bihu-s does not simply remain on the stage as a reflection of what sells or what is popular among the masses. It is characteristic of the dynamics of social relations in Assam, which may or may not be maintained in the same form among urban communities abroad. Praphulladatta Goswami states in the introduction to his volume of Assamese and Bihu songs that Bihu "has now come to function as a means of social integration, in the sense that most of the inhabitants—Hindu or non-Hindu—observe it entirely or in part" (Goswami 2003, 1). If the project of social integration excludes or marginalizes certain individuals by prioritizing a mainstream construction of Assamese identity, however, the resulting social tensions will manifest themselves not only on stage but also in the everyday lives of people.

The question "Whose Bihu?" invites the reader critically to reflect on the stakes of cultural representation and urban transformations. Here, I have offered but one analysis of cultural representation by focusing on mainstream Bihu shaped by middle-class agents in four cities. Investigating the kinds of work Bihu does for communities who might claim other Bihu-s for the urban settings in which they live sets the stage for a fuller investigation of the ways urban transformation and rural modernities intersect in the cultural interaction of global cities in India and its diasporas.

References

Baruah, Sanjib. 1999. *India against Itself: Assam and the Politics of Nationality.* Philadelphia: University of Pennsylvania Press.

Bohlman, Philip V. 2009. "Music before the Nation, Music after Nationalism." *Musicology Australia* 31 (1): 79–100.

Dirks, Nicholas B. 2001. *Castes of Mind: Colonialism and the Making of Modern India.* Princeton, NJ: Princeton University Press.

Dutta, Paramesh. 2008. "Festivity, Food, and Bihu: A Short Introduction to the National Festival of Assam." *Indian Folklife* 31: 16–17.

Fernandes, Leela. 2006. *India's New Middle Class: Democratic Politics in an Era of Economic Reform.* Minneapolis: University of Minnesota Press.

Goswami, Praphulladatta. (1966) 2003. *Bohag Bihu of Assam and Bihu Songs.* Guwahati: Publication Board Assam.

Hazarika, Kamal. 2007. Interview with the author. June.

The Hindu. 2010. "Assam's Bihu Troupe to Perform at CWG Opening Ceremony." September 6.

Kheshgi, Rehanna. 2016. "Sounding Rural Modernities: Gender, Performance, and the Body in Assam India." PhD diss., University of Chicago.

Mahanta, Khagen. 2009. Interview with the author. April.

PTI. 2007. "High Footfall at Dance Workshop." *The Telegraph (India).* April 2.

11

Making Hindustani Music Work: Avenues of Friction and Empathetic Musicality

Kaley Mason

> Speaking of friction is a reminder of the importance of interaction
> in defining movement, cultural form, and agency. Friction is not
> just about slowing things down. Friction is required to keep global
> power in motion. It shows us (as one advertising jingle put it)
> where the rubber meets the road.
> —Anna Tsing, *Friction*

The year 2007 saw the release of American independent filmmaker Daniel Kraus's *Musician*, arguably the most compelling documentary to explore the labor of music since the turn of the millennium. The second of four films in Kraus's "Work Series" featuring American workers, including *Sheriff* (2005), *Professor* (2009), and *Preacher* (2011), Kraus's *Musician* examines the everyday life of Chicago-based avant-garde improvisational jazz musician, Ken Vandermark.[1] Rejecting conventional use of voice-overs and interviews, Kraus creates an intimate portrait of the musician's labor in a *cinéma vérité* style. The opening scene pictures Vandermark with a tenor saxophone, seated in front of a music stand, alone in a room, presumably at home, working out musical ideas phrase by phrase, playing them first, then notating them with a pencil on staff paper. Visual shots

---

1   At the time of most recent access, each film in the series can be streamed from Kraus's website for a modest fee (Kraus 2017).

alternate between close-ups of closely miked handwork and embouchure-work, and wider frames emphasizing a solitary moment in a musician's craft. Kraus then unfolds a series of scenes using the same observational technique, bringing into relief a range of music-related labor activities, from the entrepreneurial tasks of negotiating payments and securing gigs, to the logistical work of transporting equipment and touring, to the creative labor of recording and performing live.

While Vandermark is the main actor throughout, Kraus also foregrounds social relations that shape his artistry, highlighting the musicians with whom he plays, the sound engineer working on his latest album, the managers and staff at live-music clubs, his life partner and the strain of frequent travel on their relationship, and even the border services officers who give him and his band a hard time. Kraus's emphasis on friction (positive and negative), affect, and mobility (fluid and blocked) grounds the documentary in a perspective of late twentieth-century immaterial labor (Hochschild 1983; Hardt and Negri 2004).

Curiously, Kraus never shows Vandermark playing anything other than avant-garde jazz. There is an awkward tension between the gritty working-class persona and Vandermark's status as a rare musician who can afford to prioritize personal artistic goals due to a lucrative MacArthur Fellowship.[2] Music lessons are equally absent from Kraus's American worker narrative, though few musicians earn a living without supplementary or regular income from teaching. Besides the absence of genre-crossing and pedagogy as interrelated labor activities associated with ordinary musical work, the documentary also invites reflection on how tales of mobility and friction would be different for non-citizens, including undocumented creative workers and holders of temporary employment visas. How would the film's narrative change if a non-citizen musician served as the portal for examining the labor of music in Chicago?

For the scenes that both *did* and *did not* make it into the film, Kraus's *Musician* is a fitting point of departure for this chapter's focus on the

---

2   MacArthur Fellowships are awarded annually by the John D. and Catherine T. MacArthur Foundation to citizens or permanent residents of the United States who are selected for their exceptional creative potential. Vandermark received one in 1999.

Chicago-based musical entrepreneurship of North Indian tabla[3] player, Sandip Burman, and his Texas tour manager, John Gardner. By tracking the development of Burman's artistry through successive stages of movement and struggle, and relating his career to the enterprising alliance these two unlikely co-agents formed, I ask, How did a percussionist from a North Indian working-class background manage to make Hindustani music work for him, for his family in the state of West Bengal, for his full-time manager, Gardner, and for the occasional part-time American workers he hires? Based on direct observation and a series of interviews with Burman, his family in Durgapur (India), and Gardner, I argue in this chapter that Burman and Gardner achieved modest socio-musical gains because of their ability to combine skill sets cooperatively at the crucible of friction, intercultural awareness, and urban mobility affordances. As the ethnographic evidence will show, Burman and Gardner have experienced much of the friction and mobility depicted in *Musician,* and then some. Where their stories diverge, however, is in Burman's strategic decision to concentrate on dispersed music education markets and to cultivate what I call empathetic musicality, the ability to understand and feel aesthetic values beyond one's culturally specific musical frame of reference.

Unlike Vandermark's niche market of transnational avant-garde jazz, Burman realized he could not rely on a conventional Indian music scene at home or abroad. Nor could he rely on the inconsistent support of world-music fusion projects. Rather his approach would need to be more flexible, and, as a result, he went the way of Indian music appreciation. Instead of thinking about American metropolises as market destinations for his labor, he made Chicago his home and hub for travel to short-term teaching gigs at educational institutions in rural communities, towns, and smaller cities in North America, Europe, Asia, and Oceania. Burman would be the first to say that the success of this business model owes much to Gardner's managerial acumen, his communication and organization skills, his knowledge of American mobility systems and cultural

---

3   The tabla consists of a pair of tuned drums played with the hands: the cylindrical wooden *dāhinā* on the right and the larger kettle-like *bāyān* on the left. Both drumheads are made of goat skin (Kippen 1988, xvi).

expectations, his intercultural sensitivity, and his love of music. Without Gardner, there is no touring enterprise, and without Burman, there is no Indian artistic labor to bring to education markets. Together, they developed a highly flexible and mobile Indian music-appreciation service designed to survive the precarious labor conditions under neoliberal capitalism. This chapter is about the work behind bringing Hindustani music to audiences that would otherwise not have opportunities to learn directly from a professional Indian musician. I begin in Chicago with Gardner's account of how he met Burman.

Devon Avenue, Patel's Café, August 12, 2011

There is a new café on the corner of Rockwell Street and Devon Avenue (figure 60; see the chapter of Sonja Rippert in the present volume). The café is buzzing with activity on a summer evening in the heart of Chicago's South Asian commercial hub. Bollywood bhangra-infused hits reach out to passersby in the street. Beneath a chocolate-colored awning and ochre façade, new customers file into an otherwise typical two-story brick building. The brightly lit Patel caste/surname in cursive gold font reflects the success of the Gujarati business community along this ten-block section of Devon Avenue, the second largest concentration of South Asian businesses and immigration services in the United States (Lindberg 1997). Since the Indian Sari Palace became the first Indian-owned business established on Devon in 1973, the South Asian presence grew exponentially in the wake of changes in immigration policy in 1965. With the lifting of restrictions on quotas based on national origins, families were able to immigrate to the United States as a unit, and well-educated workers were given priority, if their skills and knowledge met the demands of the American labor economy (Rangaswamy 1995, 440). In the second decade of the twenty-first century, most of the early immigrant families have moved to more affluent suburbs (Bohlman, Klotz, and Koch 2007), but Devon continues to be an important commercial, cultural, and spiritual center[4] for South Asian communities and newly settled immigrant families. On this occasion, I visit the neighborhood with Burman, a Bengali, and Gardner.

After ordering coffee and savory snacks, Sandipji, John, and I sit around a bistro table in front of a glass display case filled with colorful sweets. This is the last of a series of recorded interviews about the work behind their moderately successful music-appreciation venture. The mood is light, punctuated with

---

4   Besides the Jamia Masjid, a mosque on Devon that serves as an important spiritual center for Pakistani, Bangladeshi, and North Indian Muslims, there is also a Sikh temple, the Gurdwara Sahib of Chicago.

Figure 60. Patel's Café, Corner of Rockwell Street and Devon Avenue, Chicago, August 12, 2011. Photo: Kaley Mason.

laughter and banter. We have known each other for two years, having spent many hours in conversation, over shared meals, coffee, shopping, errands, and appointments. I had visited Burman's family in West Bengal a few months earlier, and since that visit there has been a palpable shift in everyone's mutual comfort level. Casually dressed in a white golf shirt with blue stripes, Sandip seems more relaxed tonight. His slim stature, short straight silver-streaked dark hair, and neatly trimmed mustache stand out next to John's imposing height, burly physique, long auburn-tinged hair (tied back), and wiry beard. Although John has been working with Sandipji for over five years, he only recently began learning from him formally as a student (śiṣya). Gardner may well become one of the first musicians seriously to explore Indian art music on the harmonica, an instrument he came to as a blues enthusiast. His voice is animated when he shares how his knowledge of Indian music has evolved from barely recognizing a sitar or tabla, to distinguishing between different types of ornamentation (gamakas), to appreciating the development of a rāga using rapid improvisatory passages (tāns), to feeling the intensity and release of cadential patterns (tihāī). Originally from Houston, John traveled and worked through many states before coming to Chicago in 2004.

John Gardner: They wanted to build me into what they were doing and I was totally into it, but not totally into it, because it's not music. The only other music I'd ever worked in was directly with an artist. He's a Christian artist, Lanny Wolf. He's won artist-of-the-year many times. He was a pretty established name, but I just, I took company calls and handled duplications if they wanted a DAT recording. That dates it too. But I saw this job. . . . That night I wrote this crazy long email explaining the experience I had working on phones, and that I had worked with this musician. . . . Knowing Sandipji now, there's no way he even looked at it. I'm positive. He scanned through, found the number, and said what is this?

Kaley Mason: So this would have been around 2006?

JG: I think it was late 2006. Someone called and said: "You replied to an ad for music booking." And I was like yes, oh yeah! And he explained a little bit about it. "Where do you live?" I was like . . . Lakeview. "How far is that from Granville (station)." Twenty to thirty minutes on the train I guess. "Well, what are you doing right now?" I said going up to meet you if you let me. . . . I arrived in his house. He had his Mac open. Basically he said, just sit down. No interview, nothing. He said: "I'm booked here and I'm booked here, but I just got a confirmation here, how should I get there?" I was like ah . . . you know I came up with some idea. I think he had two places he needed to fit into the schedule. He's like, okay. . . . "Well do you want to work here?" And I was like, yeah. He didn't ask my name, didn't know anything. I got on the phones right away when I came back in . . . and then over time I phased myself out of my other job, and then ended up doing this full-time, full-time and a half. That's how the whole thing started. An ad on Craigslist. I wrote a long email that he never read.

John continues, recounting his early days on the job working out of Sandip's ninth-floor condominium overlooking Lake Michigan in Chicago's Edgewater neighborhood. He would handle booking, paperwork, tour routing, and website management, among other managerial tasks. While Sandip had already established a network of clients for gigs, the orientation of the business toward planning efficient high-density tours only began when John came on board. Due to visa restrictions, they could only work in the United States for the first couple of years, but that changed when Sandip received an O-1B visa, a temporary worker visa granted to applicants who demonstrate extraordinary ability in the arts. This meant that Burman no longer had to renew his visa annually and could therefore travel outside the United States with less risk of not being allowed back. John gradually formed a network of schools interested in Indian music appreciation stretching over four continents. It would be misleading, however, to overstate the singularity of Sandip's and John's work-related travel. South Asian musicians, like many performers, have historically pursued peripatetic livelihoods by choice and necessity.

North Indian Musicians on the Move

North Indian classical musicians have long viewed mobility as a fundamental condition for improving artistic reputations and meeting basic material needs. Even prior to the decline of feudal patronage in the latter-half of the nineteenth century, enterprising musicians traveled widely across the subcontinent in the service of princely states, often leaving the musical training of successive generations of performers to sedentary elders in hereditary *bradris* (brotherhoods) or community networks (Qureshi 2007, 34). Daniel Neuman summarizes this social fact well:

> If we examine the biographies of musicians in the past, it is clear that in their moves from patron to patron, court to court, from West to East and South to North, Indian musicians have always been characteristically peripatetic. "Home" was not where one typically earned one's livelihood. Home was where one was born, one married, one returned for holidays and other celebrations, and, perhaps most importantly, from a musical point of view, where one experienced one's formative music learning period. But one typically did not carry on one's craft at home. (Neuman 1984, 10)

With the expansion of Indian capitalism and the intensification of British imperialism following the Indian Rebellion of 1857, hereditary performers from varying social backgrounds increasingly moved to colonial urban centers for work. By the early decades of the twentieth century, a growing urban mercantile class offered new patronage in the form of private soirées, public concerts, recording studios, radio stations, and eventually, commercial film. This occupational migration was largely facilitated by the construction of India's railway, which became both the primary vehicle for colonial modernity and the ultimate harbinger of an Indian nation-state. Before the railway, musicians who worked within patron-client feudal arrangements could only travel within a limited geography of regional princely states, but this changed dramatically following the construction of the first lines in the early 1850s. Marian Aguiar has recently shown that what began as a means for extracting raw materials, such as cotton and coal from the hinterland through a single rail line running out of Calcutta, grew into a unifying symbolic and experiential basis for constructing a modern national identity, as "railway tracks became the skeleton that mapped territory and supported the corpus of the future nation, creating a dynamic social geography (although this body would be partitioned in 1947)" (Aguiar 2011, 7).

The combination of railway modernity, capitalist markets, and an emergent culture of physical, virtual, and social mobility was equally transformative for musicians as it was for other occupations enticed or forced to move by shifting labor patterns. In his classic study of the impact of mobility and cities on Hindustani musicians in North India, Neuman drew on census and genealogical data to argue persuasively that the emergence of stylistic schools or trade lineages known as *gharānās* (lit., of the house) in North Indian art music only began to appear in the middle of the nineteenth century, around the same time as the construction of the first railway lines and the increasing urbanization of music specialists (Neuman 1978a). Neuman's study revealed how urban patronage opened pathways of mobility for low status performers (ibid., 206). By the early twentieth century, non-hereditary musicians and Hindu music reformers began combining classroom education with elements of the master-disciple tradition in an urban mission to modernize Indian art music (Bakhle 2005). Trains and cities were catalytic for both the formation of the gharānā system and the institutionalization of courtly entertainment as national music.

What the railway did for the aspirational and physical mobility of music specialists and the modernization of an Indian national art music in cities, aeromobility did for musicians after Indian Independence in 1947. Regional South Asian urban frontiers for new musical patronage rapidly gave way to transnational horizons in the second half of the twentieth century. Although Hindustani music specialists toured Europe and North American cities as early as the last decades of the nineteenth century (Farrell 1997), it was really Ravi Shankar, a non-hereditary sitarist, who established a broader audience, thereby creating new pathways for artistic work and recognition abroad (Slawek 1991). Drawing on a distinguished Bengali Brahmin family history of international experience that began with his father Shyam Shankar's education in London and continued with his elder brother Uday Shankar's intercultural performing arts tours of Europe and North America, Ravi Shankar became India's most celebrated musical ambassador by the early 1960s. His high-profile concerts and collaborations with European art and popular musicians, including Yehudi Menuhin and George Harrison, empowered Shankar and other Indian musicians to help secure an unprecedented prominence for Indian music (ibid., 178).

Notwithstanding Ravi Shankar's musical cosmopolitanism, artistic leadership, and ability "to change his stylistic colors and shadings to meet the demands of his performance context" (ibid., 175), there were also historically specific conditions, as well as musical and pragmatic factors, that prepared the way. These included the melding of superficial interest in South Asian spirituality with countercultural expression in pop-music scenes, sustained state patronage and prestige for classical art forms in India, American familiarity with small ensembles, the affordability of hiring a minimum of two musicians, and the relative portability of limited material to transport (Neuman 1984, 13–14). Another important historical factor was the role that universities and colleges played in legitimizing Indian classical music as worthy of sincere musical interest (Wade 1978). Indeed, the market for Indian music workshops, master classes, and concerts on campuses grew significantly after Ravi Shankar and Ali Akbar Khan opened their music schools in California in 1967.

Despite an increase in employment opportunities for classical Indian musicians beginning in the late 1960s, access to well-paid gigs was uneven, especially for tabla players. Speaking about the situation in Lucknow, James Kippen offers a succinct historical explanation for this disadvantage:

> Tabla players owe their low status to their socio-musical identity as second-class citizens of the music world. Musically, their occupational specialization was the subservient role of accompanying the soloists: singers, dancers and instrumentalists. Socially, tabla players were traditionally recruited from low castes, in particular the *mīrāsī* caste. (Kippen 1988, 87)

Tabla players did not have an easy road to artistry in the Hindu modernizing climate of the twentieth century. This was largely due to the instrument's association with the mīrāsī hereditary lineages mentioned by Kippen, whose traditional occupation included accompanying professional women performers (tawāif), artists glossed as dancing girls and courtesans in nineteenth-century English sources, and later stigmatized as prostitutes following the violent debasement of their unconventional female agency by colonial authorities and Hindu reformers at the turn of the twentieth century (Qureshi 1997). With the democratization and globalization of Indian music, however, a new generation of tabla players—including musicians like Sandip Burman and world-music superstars like Zakir Hussain—challenged the notion that they could never become main performers, that accompanists should always be scaled down in the mix according to classical ideals of performances (Subramanian 2006). Neuman has discussed how accompanists acquire a new sense of self-worth after gaining access to aeromobility and freelance opportunities abroad, a process of socio-musical mobility that finds expression in the informal English epithet of being "foreign returned" (Neuman [1980] 1990, 190; see also Neuman 1978b). Still, tabla players are widely considered inferior in the Hindustani hierarchy of musical roles, a hard reality reflected in the inadequate pay ordinary musicians receive. Drawing from an interview with Burman at his condominium in Chicago on July 21, 2011, the following exchange about his early years freelancing in the United States captures this struggle well:

> *Kaley Mason:* So you made some good connections at events like the Bengali Association. . . .
> *Sandip Burman:* AS YOU PROBABLY UNDERSTAND . . . I can be outgoing . . . for a spark of the moment. At that time I was not afraid. Beggars cannot be choosers. . . . What do I have to lose. So I made that [money] . . . and somehow I made that. . . . And somehow I made that. So then I started this class for twenty bucks, fifty bucks, WHATEVER. . . . I need a place to stay.
> *KM:* So when you go to a new place first, you would go there because you were invited, and then you would stay with a family or somebody for a few days.
> *SB:* And then I'd teach, and then I'd go to your house, and I'd teach.
> *KM:* And move.
> *SB:* And move. It's tough man. Can you think about it? I DON'T KNOW NEXT WEEK WHERE I'M GOING TO STAY. Just THINK about it. And, suppose you're traveling in India. One day you're in Calcutta. The next day you're in Santiniketan . . . but you don't know next week where you're going to stay. . . . How about Panagarh? Panagarh falls apart, then you're done, because Santiniketan people say you gotta get out . . . but your Panagarh fell apart right! And, it's totally not your country.
> *KM:* So did you take trains too? Buses?
> *SB:* I did take some buses . . . but mostly flights. BECAUSE ALL THE MONEY I WOULD MAKE . . . I would spend on flights, and the food was free. You can barely live like this.

Given the asymmetry of socio-musical value facing Hindustani accompanists and the peripatetic precariousness of working in South Asian diasporic networks, it is not surprising that Burman and others like him would seek to reinvent their art with dignity through travel.

A Tabla Artist's Tale of Blocked Mobility and Fluid Crossings

Indian musicians no less than other musicians depend on the fixed and moving materials of occupational mobility. This includes pedestrian ways, railways, ferries, and airports, as well as communication technologies that make moving possible (Urry 2007). While the accelerated pace of global capitalism has widened the horizon of opportunity for some performers, such pathways remain inaccessible to the majority. Embodied musical labor, like most labor, does not have the fluid movement that neoliberal economic reforms enabled for goods and capital in the late twentieth century. The image of pathways is significant here, for as work on pilgrimage and border-crossing has demonstrated, even as pathways cut across boundaries in ways that trouble persistent notions of cultural fixity, they also confront the politics of non-recognition that influence how we grapple with exclusion in our work (Bohlman 1996). Pathways must be understood in relation to blocked access, a point that became clearer for me when I accompanied Sandip and John on one of their encounters with legal mechanisms that regulate the bodily movement of performers.

Belmont Avenue, Dr. Chmiel's Family Practice, January 3, 2011

> I drive west on Belmont Avenue. It is a freezing afternoon in Avondale, one of several historically Polish-American centers in Chicago. Sandip Burman, John Gardner, and I park in front of the Staropolska (Old Poland), a family restaurant that we later hear offers some of the best Polish comfort food in the city. Signs in English and Polish line the block as we walk past a dentist's office, a video store, and a martial arts club before reaching our destination: a medical family practice. A middle-aged woman with blond, shoulder-length hair and a bright smile greets us in Polish-tinged English from behind a counter in a waiting room. I take a seat while Sandip checks in for his appointment and negotiates the method of payment. In the past they accepted checks, but this year she politely insists on taking cash only. After some negotiation, she

makes an exception and Sandip appears relieved, his heavy coat now drawn to reveal a bright yellow and ochre-patterned shirt, a gift from his sister Sima from India. He soon disappears behind closed doors for a medical exam, step four in a long list of annual requirements for obtaining a visitor visa and work permit for Canadian tours. I ask John about these steps while we wait.

Step one: You need an invitation letter from a sponsoring institution. Step two: Once the letter is received you begin planning an itinerary. Step three: You make a request for approval from the Labor Market Opinion branch of Human Resources Canada. As mentioned above, step four is the medical exam, which is a prerequisite for step five: You apply for a work permit. Step six, seven, and eight: You arrange accommodation, organize transit connections and transportation, and try to anticipate changes beyond your control.

John's mobile suddenly sings and he politely excuses himself, explaining that his work is time sensitive and there are problems with a booking in Australia. He takes the conversation outside, and I begin to notice how American patriotism is braided with Polish nationalism in the waiting room: a God Save America flag next to a portrait of Pope John Paul II, an artificial Christmas tree beneath a tapestry of Kraków, and a poster promoting the local Paderewski Symphony Orchestra. According to John, there is only one medical practice in the city authorized by the Canadian Consulate to complete exams for work-permit applications, a monopoly that makes this Polish-American doctor's office a critical gateway for artists with bookings in Canada (figure 61).

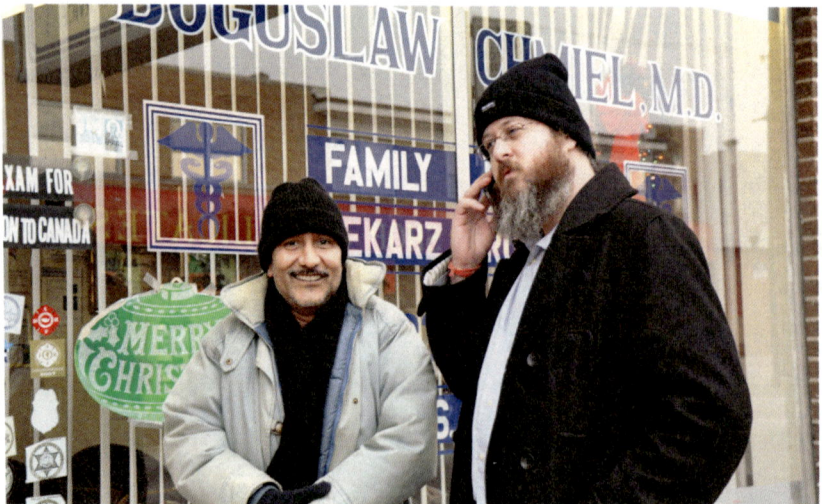

Figure 61. Sandip Burman and John Gardner in front of Dr. Boguslaw Chmiel's family practice on Belmont Avenue, Chicago, January 3, 2011. Photo: Kaley Mason.

The above ethnographic scene underscores why the work of understanding and complying with national laws that regulate, restrict, and reject the movement of musical bodies is an integral part of the labor of music. This, however, is hardly the first gateway for Sandip, a seasoned musician whose career spans many moments of blocked mobility. How did he overcome working-class roots in West Bengal to gain access to international routes to global artistry?

Bengali Avenues, Durgapur, March 2011

The Burman family lives in a middle-class neighborhood on the edge of Durgapur, a relatively small planned city with the second largest industrial complex in the North Indian state of West Bengal. Located around 150 kilometers northwest of Kolkata near large coal deposits, Durgapur was a model for development and Soviet-Indian cooperation in the 1960s because of its large-scale steel, fertilizer, chemical, and machinery industries. Like many families in Post-Independence India, the Burmans migrated to Durgapur for work, and Sandip Burman's father, Siva Prasad, was employed as an overhead-crane operator for the state-owned Mining and Allied Machinery Corporation (MAMC). His mother Manika worked at home. Both parents enjoyed music and encouraged their two children, Sandip and his younger sister Sima, to develop their musicality. While there was predictable friction between father and son when Sandip left his studies to pursue a career in music, parental pride in Sandip's success is today prominently displayed in the form of awards and music-themed portraiture on the first floor of their two-story home. One photograph in particular stands out. Dressed in a full-length beige kurta and standing with hands folded in front with humility, a young Sandip Burman poses beside Pandit Ravi Shankar in what appears to be a green room following a concert.

After a morning breakfast of fried bread (puri) and potato curry, Sandip's parents offer to take me to see some of the significant sites in their son's musical past. We begin at the Durgapur railway station where Sandip would catch the Suri-Howrah line to Kolkata. Next we visit the MAMC working-class quarters where the family lived in a modest two-room row house for twenty-five years (figure 62). This is where Sandip grew up, went to school, and where he purchased his first instruments at a music shop nearby. The contrast between the two-story middle-class home they live in now and the simplicity of the crumbling row house is poignant, and yet, understandably, his parents appear to be overcome with warm nostalgia for the community they left behind. Before we leave, they stop and visit old friends over tea in an identical row house facing theirs on the other side of a clearing. The air is thick with reminiscence. Chicago's Devon Avenue and even the brand-new multi-storied shopping complex near their current middle-class home seem a world away from here.

Figure 62. Sandip Burman's childhood home at the Mining and Allied Machinery Corporation quarters in Durgapur, West Bengal, March 28, 2011. Photo: Kaley Mason.

Burman is the first person in his family to pursue a career in music. Without the professional support of a hereditary lineage or the resources of a middle-class musical family, he struggled to gain recognition and opportunity without the benefit of professional kinship ties. Demonstrating an early affinity for music in childhood, Sandip started learning tabla from his father before he studied formally with Sudhir Ray in Durgapur. After a chance meeting with Pandit Shyamal Bose of the Farukkhabad gharānā, who happened to be attending a wedding in the region, Sandip began learning from him in Kolkata, a decision that he made with the blessings of his first guru. Twice a week he would commute to the metropolitan capital, taking a bus to the Durgapur railway station, then a train to the Howrah terminus, and finally a ferry across the river to the Bow Bazar neighborhood where the late Pandit Shyamal Bose lived and taught. Eventually, he began to get gigs accompanying other performers and this led to a crossroads: a choice between botany and music. He chose the latter and soon began concentrating exclusively on teaching, accompanying, and, most of all, becoming a disciple (śiṣya).

His big break came in the early 1990s when he was selected to play for the Maharishi Music for World Peace project, a global festival founded in the late 1980s by the charismatic leader of the transcendental meditation movement (Reck 1978). Getting selected, however, was just the beginning, as visas were not easy to obtain in the absence of financial resources or contacts in high places. After acquiring a passport, he made his way to an ashram in Delhi where musicians waited for the call to join the festival in Europe or North America. Sandip soon realized that the barrier of economic disadvantage was not easily overcome when he noticed other musicians getting visas and moving on out of turn. With 80 rupees in his bank account and parents with modest resources, he did not have the funds or the connections to expedite the process. Still, he chose to stay rather than open a music school in Durgapur, and so he accepted an offer to teach at the ashram school while waiting for the call. His first time applying for a visa at the United States consulate in Delhi was unsuccessful: He was rejected on grounds that he could not provide enough evidence of his status as an artist. Only after obtaining a letter from Maharishi International University in Iowa did he finally manage to get a visa, followed by a flight to Los Angeles. For the significance of gateway encounters like these, travel and identity documents are powerful forms of network capital, the absence of which has real consequences for the unfortunate majority born into families with fewer means for mobility (Urry 2007; see also Silverman 2012, 150).

Once in California, Sandip struggled to find enough work in a saturated Indian music scene. As his network of contacts grew, however, he began traveling to teach and perform in other states and even accepted a short-term gig accompanying students at the World Music Department of the Rotterdam Conservatory in the Netherlands. For over a decade, Burman taught private lessons, gave master classes and workshops, and accompanied soloists from place to place before finally settling in Chicago. After meeting John, he began expanding his market. To make these tours economically viable, he now plays as many gigs as he can in as small a window as possible. With the financial responsibility of a mortgage, business costs, John's full-time salary, and material commitments to family in India, minimizing expenses is the only way. John looks after planning, organizing, and negotiating the density of bookings for each country, which leaves Sandip free to focus on delivering the musical goods. The musical goods on these international and American tours consist mainly of master classes that teach Indian classical music appreciation in high schools and post-secondary institutions. Although he has also toured widely as an accompanist and performer in public concerts, his formula for bringing Indian music to the classroom has become the primary source of revenue. Finding the right business model, however, is only one part of the job: Coming up with creative ways to meet the expectations of audiences unfamiliar with Indian musical idioms is the real challenge. Recognizing the limits of virtuosic displays for uninitiated listeners, Burman stresses the need to make affective connections with both organizers and audiences in ways that facilitate mutual understanding and interest.

Empathetic Musicality:
Mobilizing Cosmopolitanism from Below

Burman's distinctive brand of international Indian artistry and pedagogy depends on his ability to cultivate intercultural collaborations and friendships. To explain the significance of these affective bonds in his career, he invokes the Bangla term *jogajōg*, meaning the act of getting connected or maintaining connectedness, from the Sanskrit *yoga*, literally union, and *jōg*, addition. It is almost always paired with a verb, as in *jogajōg kora* (to be or make communication with someone) or *jogajōg rakha* (to keep), to keep or maintain relations or state of mutual communication. To keep jogajōg with someone is to stay in touch, an action that simultaneously implies relations, union, and affective connection. A focus on jogajōg in the context of global musical artistry makes relations rather than isolated lives the portals through which we examine musical exceptionality.

Building these relations requires tenacity, serendipity, and, most of all, empathy. Cultivating genuine empathetic musicality demands more than cosmopolitan curiosity and good intentions: It involves working hard to broaden musical horizons in a continuous state of openness to other ways of being musical in the world, and connecting by hearing and feeling sound patterns that shape unfamiliar musical sensibilities. This merger of connecting and sensing into a single capacity for musical empathy resembles the concept of bi-musicality, a classic ethnomusicological method that Stephen Cottrell extends to describe gigging musicians in London who, like "sonic chameleons," invest in becoming polymusical to meet the expectations of diverse urban publics (Cottrell 2007, 96; see also Slawek 1991, 175). My concept of empathetic musicality, however, foregrounds compassionate listening and learning as a pre-condition for making and sustaining jogajōg. Empathetic musicality does not merely imply mastering multiple musical idioms well enough to blend with a given environment like a chameleon, but rather it nourishes a form of intimate musical recognition that makes pathways and mobility possible. The creative sound strategies Burman uses to make and maintain connections are the musical dynamics of jogajōg.[5]

Following a conversation I had with Sandip about the aggressive corporate policies Starbucks uses to push out local competition, he invoked the analogy of an independent coffee shop to explain his approach to musical entrepreneurship. He sees himself as a performer struggling against an overabundance of tabla players and "big chains" of dominant players in music scenes. To differentiate his art from competitors in Indian music, he realized that his best chances for survival have hinged on cultivating unique and diverse qualities, like independent coffee houses, and molding them into his own distinct musical persona so that in his words, "no one can take his job." Innovation, flexibility, and versatility—these are some of the qualities he developed to transcend limited opportunities facing tabla artists in a saturated market. Each quality would eventually find expression in specific musical accomplishments, which would then serve as the basis for making jogajōg with music educators, artistic directors, fellow musicians, and students.

As Burman gained more exposure to the range of expressive traditions practiced in American music scenes, he recognized that if he could acquire melodic skill sets he would increase his chances of getting gigs. Inspired by his encounters with marimba players and a gamelan, he took

---

5   The musical dynamics of jogajōg find visual expression in the color scheme Burman and Gardner use to evaluate interaction with a potential patron.

up the rare art of playing several tablas melodically and harmonically as a separate instrument called *tablātarang*, often translated as waves of tablas from the Bangla. When playing tablātarang, only the higher-pitched wooden *dāhinā* (also called tabla) are used. Although the idea of tablātarang can be traced to the turn of the twentieth century (Wade 2001), it was Pandit Kamalesh Maitra who became the most celebrated master of the instrument in post-Independence India. He revived tablātarang as a condition for joining the Uday Shankar Ballet on its 1951–52 North American tour, a condition likely informed by the positive reviews Vishnu Das Shirali's performance on the instrument received during Shankar's 1932 show in New York (Farrell 1997, 164).

The conventional way of playing tablātarang is to tune between ten and sixteen tablas separately according to the given rāga and arrange them in a semi-circle around the performer with low-pitched drums progressing on the left to higher-pitched drums on the right like a keyboard. In a widely accessible online audiovisual recording of Burman's 2005 performance at the Kennedy Center for the Performing Arts in Washington DC, we see how the series of pitches are arranged in the opposite order, from high on the left to low on the right.[6] Sandip decided to play bass pitches on the right in order to make the instrument more accessible for American audiences familiar with the standard jazz drum kit. Since the late 1990s, Sandip has been giving master classes in percussion departments across the United States, hence his innovative approach to tablātarang must be understood in the context of making and maintaining connections in this scene (figure 63).

The second musical quality that Burman cultivated through his interactions with musicians from different backgrounds was flexibility. According to the *Oxford English Dictionary*, to be flexible implies that one has the capacity to bend, adapt, and yield to external influence. Throughout his career, Burman maintains that he consistently allowed himself to be humbled or as he would put it, "grilled," by other musicians in order to learn from them and ultimately equip himself to make connections.

---

6   At the time of writing, several video excerpts of the 2005 performance at the Kennedy Center were accessible on YouTube (e.g., Burman 2011).

Figure 63. Sandip Burman (left) tuning his *tablātarang* to John Gardner's harmonica before a master class at the University of Chicago, December 2, 2011. Photo: Kaley Mason.

From jamming with South Indian, bluegrass, and Latin American musicians, to hanging out in jazz clubs and studying functional harmony, he invested heavily in diversifying his general musical knowledge base. He attributes his strong ties with percussion departments to his commitment to understanding and appreciating dominant musical frames of reference. Besides securing him more master classes, his pliable musicianship elicited invitations to collaborate with established Grammy Award-winning jazz-fusion artists, including Béla Fleck and the Flecktones. In a scene from their 2002 album, *Live at the Quick*, Burman is in the spotlight for an eclectic arrangement of Aaron Copland's "Hoedown" from the 1942 ballet *Rodeo*. He begins the piece by reciting drum words (*bols*) in a sixteen-beat tāla cycle. He then gives Fleck and bassist Victor Wooten the cue to begin a series of short rhythmic exchanges in the Hindustani tradition of *savāl javāb* (question-and-answer exchange between soloist and accompanist) before bringing the intro to a close with a rhythmic cadential pattern (*tihāi*).

The final musical strategy and quality I wish to bring into relief is versatility. Whereas flexibility implies bending or adjusting one's art on a single instrument, versatility invokes "taking up varied pursuits or tasks with some success or distinction" (OED). It implies the ability to switch to something entirely new, like taking up another instrument. I remember from my own fieldwork how Malayan ritual musicians in South India would refer to an individual who could switch and play multiple musical roles as an "all-rounder," like the cricketer who plays every position. At some point in the 1990s, Burman began learning the sitar to become an all-rounder. While he himself would admit that he is not an exceptional player, he has achieved enough competence to demonstrate the melodic concept of rāga on one of the most popular Indian instruments worldwide. His versatility in shifting from tāla to rāga, tabla to sitar, is particularly advantageous for the master-class market. Instead of hiring two performers, schools gain a more complete and engaging lesson in Hindustani music for the price of one. Few Indian musicians choose this path, which is precisely why he invests in qualities that enable him to craft a unique musical persona to connect with potential patrons, co-creators, and friends. Like Starbucks, Sandipity Sound, the name of Sandip's company, is global, but unlike Starbucks, his company is proudly, even fiercely independent, its narrative shaped by toil and adversity, tempered with moments of serendipity.

The musical entrepreneurship of Burman and Gardner demonstrates that musicians have potential as agents of urban transformation in ways that are not always tied to global cities as sites for performance. Moving against the grain of capitalism's rural-to-urban delivery of wage labor to manufacturing and service industries (Sassen 2001), Burman uses the aero-, auto-, and rail-mobility hub of the American Midwest to go in the opposite direction, back to rural, semi-urban, and suburban margins. By opening up an intercultural space in smaller urban settings where encounters with Indian music are less common, he capitalizes on his pedagogical role as a catalyst for new ways of listening to music and hearing the world. Offering a counterpoint to the theme of music as medium for urban transformation, Sandip's eclectic career invites us to consider the city as a medium for socio-musical change. I recall a conversation I recorded on the way to Café Metropolis on Chicago's North Side, Sandip's favorite

independent source for coffee. Reflecting on the gap separating performers born into pathways of mobility and those who must first acquire the
knowledge and means to overcome immobility, he riffs on movement, privilege, and music:

> *SB:* Listening . . . putting yourself in that situation, that . . . crossing, you know
> . . . what do you call it if it is a four-way street.
> *JG:* Intersection.
> *SB:* That yeah. . . . If you are putting yourself at that intersection, your perspec-
> tive will be four different ways. Correct?
> *KM:* You have choices. . . . And perspectives.
> *SB:* Yes you have choices . . . after you UNDERSTAND the . . . composition. But
> first . . . you are lucky to be standing on that intersection. THEN you can make
> your choices. . . . If you don't . . . find that intersection. . . . Choices come later.
> *KM:* Sometimes people . . . start from that intersection, and sometimes people
> have to find that intersection.
> *SB:* AH . . . Yes! . . . You are connecting the dots. If you are starting from that
> intersection, YOU DO HAVE CHOICES.

Musical Mobility beyond Global Cities

Interest in music and mobility has grown exponentially since the 1980s. In
addition to giving more prominence to how performers navigate transnational pathways (Kapchan 2007; Silverman 2012), music scholarship has
gradually moved past the polarizing world-music debates of the 1990s, debates that seemed to channel discourse in one of two directions: toward,
on one hand, glass-half-empty approaches emphasizing global systemic
constraints on local musical life; and on the other, glass-half-full stances
privileging cultural flows, hybridity, and local agency. Indeed, much work
since the early 2000s has focused on mediating between top-down and
bottom-up positions (Stokes 2004, 50). Transnational forces have been localized, and musical practices have been more compellingly situated as
contingent on broader conditions of encounter with ideology and political economy (White 2012, 7). Missing from most literature on music and
transnationalism, however, is recognition of the urban common ground
these perspectives share: cities.

Ethnomusicologists have only recently begun examining the many
ways urban, semi-urban, and interurban sites have been catalytic for creative innovation and musical entrepreneurship (Nettl 1978). As Bruno

Nettl suggests in his reflexive chapter for this volume, the idea of urban ethnomusicology was a response to a pervasive disavowal of urbanness in research on music cultures of presumably sedentary village/rural locations. The irony, of course, was that most ethnographic research on music was already a product of urban ethnomusicology, even if fields were primarily framed as rural. Had mobility rather than stasis been taken as the rule and not the exception, earlier research would have more readily recognized cities in the countryside and vice versa. Nettl intimates that only when music studies started embracing the premise of cultural diversity over homogeneity did scholarship begin approaching classic anthropological tropes like the "village" and "tribe" from the perspective of "miniature cities."

The paradigm shift that made this possible, in Nettl's view, was a turn toward privileging interrelations, to which I would add power and mobility. The intersection of mobilities, power relations, and urban mediation not only contributed to making movement in and between cities the rule, but it also opened promising lines of inquiry with the potential for integrating top-down awareness of global structuring economic and political forces with bottom-up understanding of local creative interactions and livelihoods.

Returning to the opening epigraph, I submit that Anna Tsing's work on the convergence of environmental activism and Indigenous rights movements in Indonesia invites us to consider focusing on global connections in the friction of everyday musical livelihoods (Tsing 2005). Her heuristic category of friction is a useful metaphor in research on musical labor because it foregrounds relations characterized by motion and varying degrees of mutual resistance or struggle. When a given set of actors is unequally positioned, which is almost always the case, friction can be understood as productive resistance to one group's or actor's imposition of interests over another's, or as Eric Wolf cogently put it: "The enactment of power always creates friction—disgruntlement, foot dragging, escapism, sabotage, protest, or outright resistance" (Wolf 1990, 590). This would be the friction we observe at play in the kinds of adversity that many working musicians face every day, including exploitative labor relations, systematic devaluation of work, social stigmas, and the absence of income stability.

Tsing's concept also shows how degrees of friction are a necessary precondition for all movement and social action, and that these interactions or interrelations are simultaneously agentive as well as restrictive. The friction that energized Sandip's and John's intercultural cooperation in the field of Indian music appreciation is one case in point. Friction, generated through diverse encounters between people, can hold a performer back or propel her forward. It can be both debilitating and empowering, depending on the particular set of interactions that emerge from "awkward, unequal, unstable, and creative qualities of interconnection across difference" (Tsing 2005, 4). Tsing provides the most compelling conceptual synthesis yet for bringing mobility, power relations, and cities together in research on the local and transurban dynamics of musical labor.

In this chapter I draw on the case of one Indian Chicago-based musician, Burman, to show how thinking through the prism of mobilities and musical entrepreneurship alters the way we conceptualize musicians as agents of urban transformation. Departing from narratives that emphasize metropolitan centers as destinations for migrant workers (Turino 2000; Sassen 2001), I trace the ways Sandip approaches the city as a space of mobility, a constellation of transit sites rather than a final destination. The global city represents for him intersecting mobility systems that bring him to where the work is, which is often far from metropolitan centers. Chicago in this case is not the "City That Works" as a destination in itself, but rather the city that works as a transportation hub moving him swiftly and efficiently to gigs anywhere in the world, from small cities in Kansas, Oklahoma, and Manitoba, to urban and semi-urban places in Sweden, Singapore, and New Zealand. By examining the entrepreneurial friction and musical strategies that characterize the work of musicians and tour managers like Burman and Gardner, we deepen our understanding of how musical cosmopolitanism from below finds avenues for transcending the local and surviving the global in Indian music.

References

Aguiar, Marian. 2011. *Tracking Modernity: India's Railway and the Culture of Mobility*. Minneapolis: University of Minnesota Press.

Bakhle, Janaki. 2005. *Nationalism in the Making of an Indian Classical Tradition: Two Men and Music*. New York: Oxford University Press.

Bohlman, Philip V. 1996. "Pilgrimage, Politics, and the Musical Remapping of the New Europe." *Ethnomusicology* 40 (3): 375–412.

Bohlman, Philip V., Sebastian Klotz, and Lars-Christian Koch. 2007. "Tales of Three Cities—Berlin, Chicago, and Kolkata at the Metropolitan Musical Crossroads." In *Cultural Diversity in the Urban Area: Explorations in Urban Ethnomusicology*, edited by Ursula Hemetek and Adelaida Reyes, 15–25. Vienna: Institut für Volksmusikforschung und Ethnomusikologie.

Burman, Sandip. 2011. "Sandip Burman—Kennedy Center—Tabla Tarang—2005-03-13 (part 1)." YouTube video, posted by "tablathusiast," March 9, 2011. https://youtu.be/NSlSFOxePFw.

Cottrell, Stephen. 2007. "Local Bimusicality among London's Freelance Musicians." *Ethnomusicology* 51 (1): 85–105.

Farrell, Gerry. 1997. *Indian Music and the West*. Oxford: Oxford University Press.

Hardt, Michael, and Antonio Negri. 2004. *Multitude: War and Democracy in the Age of Empire*. New York: Penguin.

Hochschild, Arlie Russell. 1983. *The Managed Heart: Commercialization of Human Feeling*. Berkeley: University of California Press.

Kapchan, Deborah. 2007. *Traveling Spirit Masters: Moroccan Gnawa Trance and Music in the Global Marketplace*. Middletown, CN: Wesleyan University Press.

Kippen, Jim. 1988. *The Tabla of Lucknow: A Cultural Analysis of a Musical Tradition*. Cambridge: Cambridge University Press.

Kraus, Daniel. 2017. "Daniel Kraus: The Work Series." Accessed July 26. http://movies.workseries.com.

Lindberg, Richard. 1997. *Passport's Guide to Ethnic Chicago*. Lincolnwood, IL: Passport Books.

Nettl, Bruno. 1978. "Introduction." In *Eight Urban Musical Cultures: Tradition and Change*, edited by Nettl, 3–18. Urbana: University of Illinois Press.

Neuman, Daniel M. 1978a. "Gharanas: The Rise of Musical "Houses" in Delhi and Neighboring Cities." In *Eight Urban Musical Cultures: Tradition and Change*, edited by Bruno Nettl, 186–222. Urbana: University of Illinois Press.

———. 1978b. "Journey to the West." *Contributions to Asian Studies* 12: 40–52.

———. 1984. "The Ecology of Indian Music in North America." *Bansuri* 1: 9–15.

———. (1980) 1990. *The Life of Music in North India: The Organization of an Artistic Tradition*. Chicago: University of Chicago Press.

Qureshi, Regula. 1997. "The Indian Sarangi: Sound of Affect, Site of Contest." *Yearbook for Traditional Music* 29: 1–38.

———. 2007. *Master Musicians of India: Hereditary Sarangi Players Speak*. New York: Routledge.

Rangaswamy, Padma. 1995. "Asian Indians in Chicago: Growth and Change in a Model Minority." In *Ethnic Chicago: A Multicultural Portrait*, edited by Melvin G. Holli and Peter d'A. Jones, 438–62. Grand Rapids, MI: Eerdmans.

Reck, David. 1978. "The Neon Electric Saraswati." *Contributions to Asian Studies* 12: 29–39.

Sassen, Saskia. 2001. *The Global City*. Princeton, NJ: Princeton University Press.

Silverman, Carol. 2012. *Romani Routes: Cultural Politics and Balkan Music in Diaspora*. New York: Oxford University Press.

Slawek, Stephen M. 1991. "Ravi Shankar as Mediator between a Traditional Music and Modernity." In *Ethnomusicology and Modern Music History*, edited by Stephen Blum, Philip V. Bohlman, and Daniel M. Neuman, 161–80. Urbana: University of Illinois Press.

Stokes, Martin. 2004. "Music and the Global Order." *Annual Review of Anthropology* 33: 47–72.

Subramanian, Lakshmi. 2006. "Musical Aesthetics: 'Accompanist' as 'Star' Performer." *Economic and Political Weekly* 41 (14): 1307–9.

Tsing, Anna Lowenhaupt. 2005. *Friction: An Ethnography of Global Connection*. Princeton, NJ: Princeton University Press.

Turino, Thomas. 2000. *Nationalists, Cosmopolitans, and Popular Music in Zimbabwe*. Chicago: University of Chicago Press.

Urry, John. 2007. *Mobilities*. Cambridge: Polity Press.

Wade, Bonnie C. 1978. "Indian Classical Music in North America: Cultural Give and Take." *Contributions to Asian Studies* 12: 119–40.

———. 2001. "Paluskar, Vishnu Digambar." In *The New Grove Dictionary of Music and Musicians*, edited by Stanley Sadie, vol. 19, 19–20. London: Macmillan.

White, Bob W. 2012. "Introduction: Rethinking Globalization through Music." In *Music and Globalization: Critical Encounters*, edited by White, 1–14. Bloomington: Indiana University Press.

Wolf, Eric R. 1990. "Distinguished Lecture: Facing Power—Old Insights, New Questions." *American Anthropologist* 92 (3): 586–96.

Photo Essay: Soundscapes and Streetscapes—Devon Avenue, Chicago

Philip V. Bohlman and Lars-Christian Koch

> She'd observed the world, she told him, all of life, from this balcony.
> Political processions, government parades, visiting dignitaries.
> The momentous stream of vehicles that started each day at dawn.
> The city's poets and writers passing by after death, their corpses
> concealed by flowers. Pedestrians wading knee-deep through the
> streets, during the monsoon. In autumn came the effigies of Durga,
> and in winter Saraswati. Their majestic clay forms were welcomed
> into the city as dhak were beaten, as trumpets played. They were
> ushered in on the backs of trucks, then carried away at the end
> of the holidays to be immersed in the river.
> —Jhumpa Lahiri, *The Lowland*

Music lives on the streets of the city. The street breathes sound into passing processions and parades, into the passage of lives no less than into the rites of passage. Music turns the city street into a site for ritual and for the colportage of history's artifacts, in Chicago no less than North Kolkata in the epigraph above. Music moves along the streets of the city, defining its neighborhoods while bounding and intersecting its neighborhoods (cf. Sampson 2011; Chaudhuri 2013).

In the photo essay that follows we gather images from the soundscape of the street in northern Chicago that has been symbolic, even synonymous, with the South Asian diaspora in Chicago: Devon Avenue. Devon, as it is simply known to the city dwellers of Chicago, South Asian or not, is an urban neighborhood that stretches for little more than a kilometer west of Lake Michigan. It is a single street proclaiming allegiance to post-independence nations, India, Pakistan, and Bangladesh, but spawning a latticework of cross streets, which allow for regional and linguistic difference, Bengali fish shops or Punjabi travel agents (for further discussion of the urban geography of Devon, see Bohlman, Klotz, and Koch 2007). Devon is a site of urban pilgrimage, the weekly shopping trips to stock up on rice and music videos, even tabla lessons or religious instruction. It is on Devon, moreover, that pilgrimage begins, *hajj* to Mecca, or the annual trip to see family in Bengaluru. Devon is a site of transit and movement. Its sense of place is one of ceaseless urban transformation.

Music, too, enters the street ceaselessly, sounded and seen, creating a sonic ecology that is at once local and global. The sounds of traffic in Kolkata are different from those on Devon, but they are equally omnipresent, the squawking horns of the autorickshaws in Kolkata traded for the deep bass of *desi* hip-hop in the passing autos of Devon Avenue itself—or "Gandhi Marg," as its also known. No less prevalent are the micro-worlds of sound, the vegetable saleswoman or the *panwallah* in the Indian city, the South-Asianized muzak in Devon's restaurants and cellphone shops, or a "colorful musical evening" with Bollywood hits or meditation in a storefront temple dedicated to the clephant-headed god, Ganesh. The streetscape is realized as a soundscape in many different ways, but the photographs that follow lead us to propose that there are four ways in which the sonic ecology of the urban street affords agency to those who transform the street with their presence: sound; sight; mobility; memory.

Sound. We have already observed that sound is everywhere on Devon. The sound of Devon is at once very South Asian and very American. There are countless shops along the street that allow one to affirm life in the South Asian diaspora, *sari* shops, luggage shops, food stores large and small, CD and bookshops, the ubiquitous cellphone shops, meditation centers. The bride who needs guidance for her *desi* wedding finds it here; the student wishing lessons for qur'anic recitation has choices from many audio guides. Each of these shops sounds South Asia in its own way, and they provide the individual visitor multiple opportunities to personalize her or his own sonic world, in other words, to bring the soundscape of Devon home.

Sight. The South Asian communities of Chicago and the American Midwest that regularly visit Devon contribute to the ways in which it is a site for the colportage and consumption of South Asian music. Posters announcing concerts or festivals with special guest musicians fill many windows. The sounds of South Asia are constantly on display, not simply symbolically, but rather as a means of leading one to the source of sound, presenting potential listeners with the choices that make it possible to join others in the sonic connection of past to present. The visual onslaught and the juxtaposition of images are only slightly less cacophonous on Devon than in Kolkata. The sights of sound fit together because they do not really fit together. They articulate the soundscape because they form the streetscape.

Mobility. It is the rare denizen of Devon who actually lives on the street or along its side streets. One "goes to Devon," according to the Chicago catchword, to do something, not randomly or a single time, but as part of a chain of action that gives texture to the everyday and the annual cycle. To prepare for *Diwali* or *Ramadan* one goes to Devon. To buy CDs and karaoke kits one goes to Devon. To meet friends for a birthday celebration one goes to Devon. There are many, also, who go to Devon to work. Their livelihood depends on the many who pass through the neighborhood to buy the smallest trinket or to order food in bulk to stock the reserves of a restaurant in one of the distant suburbs, where most South Asians in Chicago live in the early twenty-first century. Because of this mobility the street's soundscape is always changing. New immigrants from Gujarat or Andhra Pradesh bring their musical tastes with them, and they expect there will be CDs in Gujarati and Telugu. Seldom are they disappointed.

Memory. As an urban space Devon creates a template that allows those who move through it to enact the past. It is not by chance that Devon, when experienced intimately and up-close, looks like an Indian or Pakistani city. The sense of the familiar is intentional. The memories that are overlaid to create the streetscape, however, form numerous layers that require archeological excavation. Again, it is music that opens the *lieux de mémoire* of Devon. The street announces the many ways and places—the concerts, festivals, and holidays—that allow individuals to choose which memories will become theirs through performance. Musical memory means that desi culture will be writ small, not large, rendered intimate, sounding the life of the present through the remembrance of things past.

The photo essay that follows unfolds as one might experience the soundscape of South Asian Chicago by going to Devon. On September 19, 2013 and again on January 22, 2017, we followed an ethnographic path that traces the political geography of the street itself, moving from east to west, from those city blocks that are more Muslim (Pakistani and Bangladeshi) to those that are more Hindu (in particular, South Indian) (see Bohlman, Klotz, and Koch 2007). The photo essay concludes in moments of the ethnographic present, with an internet announcement for the 2016 Indian Independence Day celebration in Chicago and the invitation from a Chicago Indian newspaper, *Desi Talk* (September 28, 2017), to the city's celebration of the 2017 Diwali festival. The borders between east and west—or north and south in South Asia—are blurred, just as Chicago streets resound with the music of South Asia. The constant passage and transformation that makes the streetscape ensures that Devon and Chicago's streetscapes are places in which culture and music are shared and exchanged, opening a soundscape encountered by many rather than few, those who would make South Asia their own in the city of Chicago.

References

Bohlman, Philip V., Sebastian Klotz, and Lars-Christian Koch. 2007. "Tales of Three Cities—Berlin, Chicago, and Kolkata at the Metropolitan Musical Crossroads." In *Cultural Diversity in the Urban Area: Explorations in Urban Ethnomusicology*, edited by Ursula Hemetek and Adelaida Reyes, 15–25. Vienna: Institut für Volksmusikforschung und Ethnomusikologie.

Chaudhuri, Amit. 2013. *Calcutta: Two Years in the City*. New York: Alfred A. Knopf.

Lahiri, Jhumpa. 2013. *The Lowland*. New York: Alfred A. Knopf.

Sampson, Robert J. 2011. *Great American City: Chicago and the Enduring Neighborhood Effect*. Chicago: University of Chicago Press.

Figure 64. New Devon video shop.

Figure 65. Belly dance accessories.

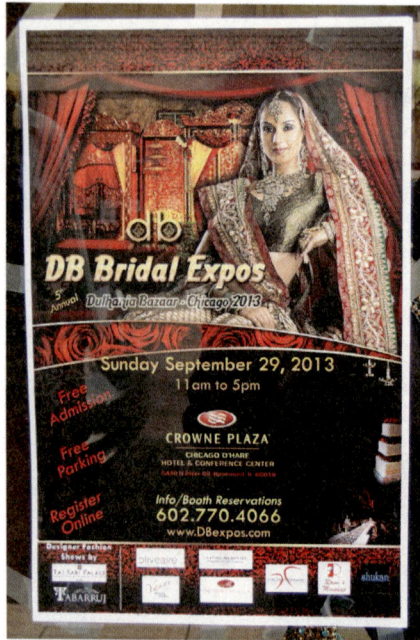

Figure 66. DB Bridal Expos.

Figure 67. Urban India.

Figure 68. Fish Corner.

Figure 69. Chicago Partnership Walk/Run.

Figure 70. Chicago Indian Icon.

Figure 71. Musical instrument and DVD shop.

Figure 72. Gandhi Marg/Devon Avenue street signs.

Figure 73. Dr. Cell cellphone shop.

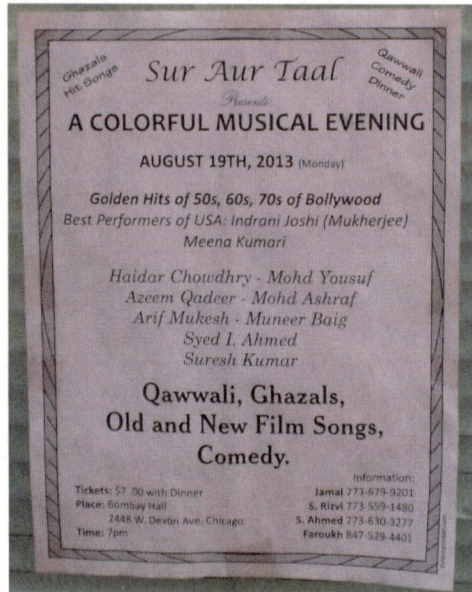

Figure 74. Colorful musical evening.

Figure 75. Ganesh Temple and Meditation Center.

Figure 76. The Everest Taj Mahal Restaurant.

Figure 77. Shah Jahal Grocery.

Figure 78. India's A Glo Annual Independence Day Party 2016.

Figure 79. Chicago Diwali Mela 2017. Courtesy of Bhailal Patel, *Desi Talk Chicago.*

Afterword: The Study of Urban Music from Trans-Cultural Perspective

Sebastian Klotz

The production, distribution, and consumption of music in a city do not simply happen. They are embedded in a network of social, economic, and affective relations, and they give these relations a powerful form of expression. Music can evoke urban imagination and materiality in semantically complex ways. Although it might be authentic or immediately suggestive and direct, music is part of mediating processes. In transnational soundscapes, the mediatedness of music is even more complex. Meaning cannot be found on the objective plane alone, but rather in strategies of appropriation, trivialization, and commodification that are all transnationally marked. Individuals who live in transcultural contexts actively engage music and auditory materials from an informed and reflective position, for their lives and experiences have been marked by transculturalism. The potential perspectives for appropriation and the construction of meaning proliferate in hitherto unknown ways (Gaupp 2012, 157).

While the modern metropolis offered clearly marked functional spheres and occasions of music making, the postmodern und postcolonial city are complex sites of intensive socio-technical processes that make it hard to determine where music is. Drawing upon critical urban studies that shift the focus from objects and forms to processes and actions, the contributors to this book argue for the necessity of looking at the *musical situations* of the metropolis as a means of access to urban transformations encapsulated in those situations. This shift is based on the premise that music is a powerful tool of scene-building, an identity marker, a producer of spaces, and a medium of social synchronization, as well as of segregation.

The TransCoop project *Music as Medium of Urban Transformation*,[1] the project that gave birth to this book, went even one step farther: It located musical observations from one metropolis, either historical or current, in comparative perspective to understand how actors in different cities deal with traditions, media technologies, the effects of globalization, and the economy of transnational soundscapes. The project's perspective, first tested during TransCoop field research in Berlin, Chicago, and Kolkata, confronted a formidable methodological challenge. Cities cultivate different traditions, institutions, funding schemes, and cultural values, which can be grasped in the diversity of musical situations and urbanity. One of our concerns was to understand how music emerges as an immanent site of this pluralism. Auditory practices and experiences together structure urban realities and are the most mobile and adaptive forms of cultural expression, of subject positioning, and of temporal relationalities[2] in urban environments.

The research studies gathered in this volume serve as an important forum to debate findings from this work-in-progress, encouraging input from other cities, disciplinary approaches, and musical experiences. The contributors to the volume examine music not as a social or cultural attribute, but rather as a powerful organizing force that structures social action and gains urgency in the city.[3] Music and auditory cultures emerge

---

1 Funded by the Alexander von Humboldt-Stiftung, Bonn, and by the University of Chicago, 2008–13, The research partners in this project were Philip V. Bohlman, Sebastian Klotz, and Lars-Christian Koch.

2 The relational nature of the auditory experience has been emphasized in new studies on the ecology of perception in auditory cultures (cf. Bull and Back 2003). For a sociological approach to popular music as a medium of urban negotiation, which draws on a wide range of cultural, urban, and auditory studies, see Klotz 2006.

3 For an evaluation of sound and its interactions in urban spaces, see Kleilein et al. 2009. For a discussion of the popular-music imaginary and its interplay with the urban, see Friedrich 2010.

as *sites of negotiation* for urban identities that anticipate change and analyze urban transformations. Auditory cultures, thus, can be regarded as catalysts that signal social and cultural transformations for which urban anthropologists and social scientists seek to develop clear categories. Musical and sonic practices affect the image of the metropolis in many ways. Music is not only a key form for the self-description and self-generation of societies (Wicke 2001, 59), but also perhaps for co-modeling and implementing urban realities.

Any exploration of the city needs to sort out the actual subject of fieldwork. In the case of musical practices, the actual topic is not easy to pin down, for there are too many angles of observation and music radiates into a plethora of contexts. If the *subjective* motivations and experiences of actors directly involved are accessed, qualitative research will yield invaluable insights into the constructedness of social realities and the role of music. A perspective from cultural criticism might be employed when considering the *conditions of the musical appropriation* of urban experiences, or when studying the social and ideological textures of musical situations in the city. The *affective structures* created across urban landscapes could be studied along with the scientific study of affect, which stresses the importance of mood, atmosphere, and affective regulation, all highly implicated in music and auditory practices. While pondering these methodological issues, musical practices emerge as part of complex sociotechnical processes and ways of life in which mere musical components cannot be itemized. In the face of music's ubiquity we live in the era of *audio-governmentality*, in which the audio is already embedded in social practices, in structures of power, and in schemes of production.[4] These embedded relations are bound to have consequences for an emerging musicology of the metropolis.

The role of music in the city has been primarily assessed in terms of a *reflection* of urban life. By combining empirical, historical, and comparative perspectives, the essays gathered here develop a methodological framework in which urban auditory cultures can be accessed as an *ac-*

---

4   Terre Thaemlitz coined this term in response to Michel Foucault's concept of *governementalité*. Tom Holert further introduced it into current debate (Holert 2009).

tive means of social agency. Our focus has not only been hermeneutical, but also constructivist: We aim to discover how city-dwellers *use music to stage the metropolis* in order to flesh out their daily routines and their cultural, collective, and personal aspirations, and to come to terms with fast-paced, dense inner-city life.[5] The book weaves together complementary and alternative perspectives on urban transformations from the fields of urban sociology, urban anthropology, cultural studies, and theater studies, and from artists and urban musicians. Working in these different fields the contributors embrace case studies, empirical reports, conceptual research, methodological remarks, and other academic accounts of musical experiences to establish a research platform that implements this topic within an extensive institutional framework.

As this book emerged from the project on which it was built, we took as our initial hypothesis a belief that musical and listening practices could be regarded as catalysts that signal social and cultural transformations. Following the inspiring work of Jacques Attali (1985), Tia DeNora (2000), and John Shepherd and Peter Wicke (1997), the contributors to this volume locate music studies at the heart of the social sciences and regard music research as a major tool of social inquiry. Attali suggests that one should approach societies via the music they make and the lines they draw between accepted music and censored noise. He therefore reverses the more common approach, which first analyzes institutions and then turns to music as a medium that simply reflects cultural processes. All these observations and insights have contributed to the analytical perspectives in the present volume. Among our key questions have been the following:

- Is the metropolis still a *laboratory of modernity*? This concept implies depth, complexity, and demarcation of the public and private, and the coherence of interlocking functions. Or is it a socio-technical space

---

5   Preliminary presentations from the project took place at the following international symposia: "Cultural Diversity in the Urban Area: Explorations in Urban Ethnomusicology," UNESCO working group, Vienna 2006 (Bohlman, Klotz, and Koch 2007); "Sound Works: Musicians and Media in South Asian Cities," University of Chicago, 2009; "Hearing Modern History: Auditory Cultures in the 19th and 20th Century," Ninth Blankensee Colloquium, Wissenschaftskolleg zu Berlin 2010.

marked by spaces that break off, temporary alliances, provisional atmospheres, and tactical networking? Or do both paradigms apply?

- Which institutions, discourses, and practices shape a visible identity or identities in a city? Which social and cultural transformations are anticipated or play out in musical and listening practices?
- Can Berlin's re-metropolization be grasped in musical terms? Does Chicago fashion itself as a city of neighborhoods through musical expression? Is music perhaps a regulatory factor in Kolkata's permanent struggle to manage its (potentially violent) population density? Which insights can we gain comparatively from other cities?
- How do musical practices and strategies of consumption affect the nexus between the local and the global? Are places and situations of music making and music consumption still relevant criteria for the social actors and for academic analysis?
- How can these transformations be analyzed in the face of media technologies that circulate images, sounds, and musical styles in a way that betrays local phenomena, while at the same time paradoxically insisting on locality?
- Which levels of mediation have to be taken into account when dealing with musical practices?
- What are the specific benefits of a comparative or parallel-city perspective?
- To what extent do artists evoke new readings of or listenings to the metropolis? To what extent do auditory and musical practices affect the perception of the metropolis?
- How can the role of music in the city be introduced into the agenda of politicians and community leaders in order to achieve a sustained development in dense inner-city areas?
- Can we get a better picture of urbanity by studying musical practices and technologies of the self and of the collective?

The contributors to this volume firmly believe that the complex sociodynamics of current metropolitan auditory and musical cultures in Berlin, Chicago, and Kolkata, and in other cities, calls for a reassessment of research procedures and of existing cross-disciplinary cooperation. Comparative approaches form a relatively recent topic in the sociology of cities (Löw 2008, 18; for India, including Kolkata, see, e.g., Ahuja and Brosius 2006). On one hand, it is not always clear how the city enters into such comparisons (Löw 2008, 39). On the other, comparisons can level differences between cities instead of exemplifying their peculiar logic and emotional structure (ibid., 19). Urban sociologies might themselves become transnationalized to include more processes of glocalization that transcend the jurisdiction and economic impact of a single city. The research agenda of an advanced urban sociology might itself be articulated as a transnational agenda, thereby implying a translocal *extension* of its guiding research question (Eckardt 2004, 110–11). One could paraphrase the project that led to the present book as an attempt to *extend* the research question for the domain of urban musical cultures in which theory-driven and translocal comparative projects emerged during the past decade.[6]

The comparative perspective yields discoveries that point toward area-specific self-images and toward the complex filtering effects of cities: Kolkata's dense and cacophonous auditory intercourse in the public sphere and its high-profile classical-music tradition contrast with the sounds in Chicago that distinguish its various neighborhoods, which in turn are connected by parades that create an integrative auditory image for the city. Berlin, in contrast, prides itself for its highly diversified electronic-music culture, produced by mobile DJ decks and celebrated in makeshift clubs in sparsely populated inner-city spaces.[7] The electronic music scene has become part of an event culture that represents a large portion of Berlin's tourism industry. Through comparative studies we also recognize the ways specific musical styles and social settings might easily connect to similar scenes in distant cities, seemingly requiring little integration into their original urban network. Tabla and sitar players travel between

---

6   The 2008 International Congress of Gesellschaft für Musikforschung in Leipzig took the traditions and perspectives of urban musical cultures as its main theme, bringing together a variety of transcultural perspectives (see the essays in Klotz 2012).

7   In the course of the past decade there has been a growing number of studies of music and the formation of urban culture in Berlin. Among the earliest studies in this period are Scharenberg and Bader 2005, and Beins et al. 2011; among the more recent studies are Heinen 2013, and Rüther 2014.

and among the three cities and reach out to dedicated audiences as easily as the DJs producing EDM, who have little trouble adapting to the exact technical and social setting wherever they are.

Because particular emphasis was given to the role of music in urban *transformations*, it soon became clear that, despite the pervasive discourse of globalization and its offspring, cities provided very specific conditions for music cultures. It became obvious that there were few previous comparative paradigms in trans-urban or global economic studies to connect the financial, political, and infrastructural realities of Berlin, Chicago, and Kolkata.[8] We therefore chose a hands-on approach in which we condensed observations and findings from various research arenas. We found it particularly valuable to sketch some city-specific transformational processes that provided a grid for our comparative fieldwork and hypotheses.

Chicago is recognized by most as a powerful global city. Berlin is deemed culturally influential on a global scale, but economically weak, even when compared with other German cities. Kolkata boasts an elaborate discourse of self-neglect, of the misunderstood city, and of the city that failed in terms of urbanization. Its multilayered, asynchronic modernity, marked by a lack of industrial investment and a permanent struggle to implement urban governance, are dramatically visible and belie any single vision of city development. Kolkata displays no clear line between private and public spaces, between official and unofficial functions. The management of proximity is more important than the management of individual lifestyles and the expression of collective aspirations as in a Western metropolis.

Urban transformation in Berlin is marked by a decline of industrial labor, the rise of service industries, the growing impact of the creative class, a re-metropolization of inner-city areas, the collapse of the multicul-

---

8 It was difficult, for instance, to find information on the music industries of Kolkata and Chicago that would match the parameters culled from the Berlin Music Commission. According to this institution, there are over 1,400 companies with more than 14,000 employees in music-related business and creative industries in the Berlin area, together generating about 700 Million Euros annually; see Berlin Music Commission 2017.

tural city, the spread of gentrification, and segregation.[9] Since 1990, Berlin has witnessed a population growth in trendy urban neighborhoods of up to 70%.

Chicago has responded to and rebounded from the global financial crisis of 2008 in ways both similar to and different from other American cities. From a rate of ca. 9% at the time of the crisis unemployment has dropped significantly to as low as 4.2% in April 2017, approximating the national average, but remaining much higher in minority neighborhoods, especially those on the south and west sides of the city with large African American populations. Crime, too, has diminished since 2008, while gang violence remains unacceptably high in minority neighborhoods. Large projects such as the O'Hare Modernization Program ($1.17 billion) offered signs of economic growth, while 2016 plans to build the national library and museum to honor President Barack Obama in Jackson Park on the city's south side consciously aim to produce new employment opportunities and transform several neighborhoods, economically and culturally.

In Kolkata, regulating street hawking, controlling the multiplicity of governance functions, and attempting to secure standards of accountability among government institutions have turned out to be vital. The struggle to secure basic urban standards, no less than a negotiation of urbanity itself, has been crucial. The failure to attract substantial industrial investors and the lack of multimodal transport facilities further inhibited the management of a potentially violent density and threatened the critical balance of the rural/urban continuum.

Although these processes may seem to be far-removed from the musical concerns of the present volume, they immediately translate into city-specific frames and sites for inquiry. Among the city-specific frames of field research, the following are especially important. Berlin features highly separate musical scenes, the "invisible" musics of its subculture, the considerable role of popular-music criticism, and discourses about temporary places and strategies for musical practices in the city (see, e.g., Heinen 2013; Rüther 2014). One of the best ways to approach Chicago

---

9   For a sociomusicological study that highlights gentrification and its consequences for music in the Berlin district of Neukölln, see Heinen 2013.

is through the soundscapes and narratives related to specific streets and neighborhoods. In Kolkata, the interplay of new technologies and new music scenes with the proud heritage of classical Bengali music and the rural/urban interaction of metropolitan Kolkata nourishes urban transformations. Equally important has been the data collection for musical events in Kolkata, as well as ethnographic study of the wedding band musicians on Mahatma Gandhi Road (see Adhikary and Bohlman in this volume).

The comparison of the three cities also reveals some musical interrelations among them, ranging from Daniel Barenboim's prestigious positions as principal conductor of the Chicago Symphony Orchestra and of the Staatsoper unter den Linden in Berlin to the prominence of Indian classical music in the Chicago and Berlin world-music concert scenes, to the collaborations among EDM artists in Berlin's and Chicago's DJ communities. It was no mere coincidence that the first book publication on India's DJ and electronic-music scene was released during the TransCoop research in Kolkata (Puneet 2010; see also Rapp 2009). Against this background we understand better why the Berliners who ran Bar25 considered moving to Kolkata once it became clear they would lose their operating license due to real-estate development along the Spree River (see Rippert in this volume).

The research projects gathered in this book reveal unexpected parallels and inner alliances among the cities. The improvisational and existential dimensions of everday life in Kolkata share similarities with Berlin's subcultural habitus, and Berlin's financial weakness is mirrored in Kolkata's economic weakness and financial turnover. The demise of municipal and governmental control in Kolkata demonstrates similarities with Berlin's self-proclaimed surrender or intended invisibility of political functions. That Berlin's citizens and visitors themselves should embrace the city and make it theirs is evident in the slogan, "Be Berlin!"

The alignment of Berlin with Kolkata, on one hand, and with Chicago, on the other, is not an ephemeral or tentative triangulation, but rather is confirmed once one adopts a managerial and solely economic perspective on the performance of major cities. According to a 2013 report, Berlin and Kolkata failed to be counted among the seventy-seven most successful financial hubs worldwide. The same report also analyzed the global performance of cities in the arts sector, where, paradoxically when compared to its financial status, Berlin featured most prominently.[10] The Asian cities turned out to be both financial and arts centers, albeit Kolkata was not included. While Kolkata and Berlin perform poorly on the financial side, they have earned a reputation in the arts, and, in the case of Berlin, in the creative industries. Berlin's reputation among the young and creative is now used to attract investors, despite the fear that long-term global investment might jeopardize its subcultural capital and level the differences upon which Berlin has prided itself since the 1980s.[11]

There is emerging scholarship on sound-based socialities and forms of behavior in transcultural metropolitan contexts that looks beyond generic and stylistic boundaries.[12] For Berlin, Chicago, and Kolkata, nonetheless, such scholarship demonstrates different strategies and a different degree of musical self-documentation. In order to ask informed questions and to structure the research field,[13] the impact of the urban condition on musical practices must also be taken into consideration. A systematic charting of this interplay along the poetics, the production, distribution, perception, and appropriation of music must bear in mind the highly technologically and socially mediated character of all these dimensions. Causal explanations, thus, might give way to tactical clusters, to the observation of differences, and to the pluralizing agency of musical practices.

Because the metropolis comprises heavily condensed, heterogeneous, and dynamic socio-technical processes, such features reveal themselves in the musical practices that are relevant to the metropolis and its inhabi-

---

10 See Skórska and Kloosterman 2012; Girgert 2013 directed my attention to this report.

11 Only recently has public spending for the arts been regarded as a context for attracting investors and enhancing the appeal of a metropolis (cf. Bernau 2013; Büttner and Janeba 2013). When cities find themselves in a global competition, glocalization that strengthens local traditions comes into play.

12 A pioneering project for club culture as youth culture is Vogt 2005. In this study Sabine Vogt ventures into the lived-in worlds of club fans and protagonists of the scene, using elaborate qualitative research; see also Garcia 2011.

13 One of the few theory-directed surveys on Berlin's popular-culture industry can be found in the *PopScriptum* special issue of *Sounds like Berlin*, an online publication from Forschungszentrum Populäre Musik, Humboldt University of Berlin (see Binas 2000).

tants, and consequently they affect the methodological toolbox. If music is a medium for social self-description, it carries analytical contingency that makes it, in a radical reading, co-extensive with academic research and additional research modalities, stretching from hip-hop in the *banlieux* of Paris to *baile funk* in Brazilian favelas[14] to the Bengali heavy-metal underground scene witnessing "the sound of a cultural history reinventing itself."[15] They lead us to new-music compositions, such as Heiner Goebbels's *Surrogate Cities*[16] to the New York homage by the Beastie Boys[17] to Wilco's track "Via Chicago," from the ways Berlin's independent VJ artists flirt with East Berlin's architectural modernism to Peter Fox's "Schwarz zu Blau," which casts an uncanny view on Berlin as an "ugly" city that resists the stereotypes of the "successful" Western metropolis (see Bohlman 2013, 189–206). These different examples of music from and about the city are sociological in the sense of registering differences, of disentangling conflicting subject positions, and of creating unofficial conjunctions in the metropolis. The specific evocation of the city, its streets, sociolects, and neighborhoods situates the musical experience in a specific condition. Music enables negotiation of such situatedness against the backdrop of narratives, experiences, institutions, and other transgressive forces. When musical material comes to address the urban condition explicitly, analysis of the music provides a good vantage point for better understanding musical practices as forms of negotiating the urban condition.

Analysis of explicitly urban contexts on the *philological* level makes possible a hermeneutic interpretation of song lyrics. The visual material, allusions, references, and titles can thus be complemented by an analysis of *auditory dimensions* and their *appropriation*. If cities are *sounding*, how are their sounds and the affordances integrated into the individual and collective technologies of their inhabitants? One example of the global experience of local urban music production would be an online sitar course orig-

---

14 For a reading of *baile funk* within the context of cultural SpaceTime "flections," based on its global circulation via CD sales, see Klotz 2011.
15 From the liner notes by Anjum Katyal on the CD *The Underground Kolkata* 2008.
16 The title of Heiner Goebbels's *Suite for Sampler and Orchestra*, released on CD by ECM in 2000, would surely provide the title for an academic urban project!
17 Cf. their CD *To the 5 Boroughs*, Capitol Records, 2004.

inating in Kolkata, which can be accessed by students around the world. If we are still able only to apply qualitative and quantitative research procedures to the three cities, a more associative mode of triangulation paves the way for consistent theoretical work in the future. Instead of establishing outright *causalities* and of reconstructing *intention*, the contributors to this volume focus on the *conditions* that allow music to configure urban spaces and experiences. This approach serves fully to bring out music's manifold cultural sensorium and its catalytic force vis-à-vis urban transformation.

The future challenge for comparative research such as that represented in the present volume is to achieve a careful calibration between selectivity and representativeness, between causality and mediatedness, between specificity and totality. With such approaches one could try to explore the "organizational metrics" and "peculiar logics" of cities, in which territorializing and de-territorializing processes intersect (Löw 2008, 131). While calibrations of this order present themselves in different ways depending on the topic, they point toward a fundamentally new profile of academic research no longer able to speak from a privileged viewpoint. This directly affects the selection of the phenomena and approaches taken. No single cultural expression, actor, or institution can claim a single or authoritative position, surely also none emanating from the academy. We cannot speak for the diverse actors and experiences in cities, but we can approach phenomena as meaningful as long as they establish access to a communicative relation, historical narrative, or perception of urban reality not yet considered. In this book the contributors have taken an explicit stance to this problem. They have opted for an eclectic mix of methods and viewpoints, taking into consideration that music and auditory practices, through their socialization, are themselves heterogeneous, complex, ever-changing, and multivalent, thus emblematic of the metropolis. In considering early methodological options, we eschew the big-science perspective of globalization studies that perpetuate the managerial, directional, bureaucratic, financial, and big-actor attitudes toward cities.[18] Big

---

18 See Rode et al. 2008 for a comparative survey that focuses on Mumbai, New Dehli, Kolkata, Bangalore, London, New York City, Berlin, and Johannesburg, and provides important and useful insights. The *city-making* examined in the "Urban Age India"

science commodifies the city, using a discourse similar to *nation-building*. A more productive stance asks, What makes a space urban (Geisler and Patel 2009)? It seeks, moreover, to understand how urbanity is modified, stabilized, and questioned by understanding musical practices.

Despite criticism of established global-city narratives, they have paradoxically yielded insights or viewpoints that affect the concerns of the present volume. By its very nature the global finance industry must rate metropolitan hubs for their performance and functional potential. The global finance industry has thus long begun to apply comparative perspectives, and, through its dialogue with social scientists and urban sociologists, has addressed the complexity of trans-urban processes in ways relevant to the present project. The motto of the "Endless City" conference, which addressed processes in New York, Shanghai, London, Mexico City, Johannesburg, and Berlin, acknowledged the impossibility of defining where global and metropolitan cities begin or end, while critiquing the never-ending productivity of new social, economic, and cultural forms (Burdett and Sudjic 2007). The methodological challenges that emerged in the present volume are intimately entangled with such endlessness and with the immanent pluralism of urban processes, structures, and situations (Heeg and Denzel 2011). Berlin has managed to secure itself a place in this global-city perspective despite its financial weakness. It also joins New York City and Mumbai in a trio examined in a Guggenheim-supported research project (see Guggenheim 2017) that features makeshift event sites (BMW Guggenheim Lab) in the three cities to engender discussion on a variety of themes with local communities. The Berlin phase of the Guggenheim project was met with fierce resistance, confirming Berlin's skepticism about big money and projects implemented by actors using Berlin as a playground to articulate global interests, in this case the luxury-car manufacturer BMW, which underwrote the project. A prominent actor in the global culture industry, Daniel Barenboim, was a member of the advisory committee, a fact that confirms how hard it is to draw lines and develop

---

program, however, adopts a governmental perspective and does not project models of participatory intervention beyond those that take infrastructure and discursive constructs for granted. Data are available at Urban Age 2017.

a critical point of view. In this volume we believe it is critical to aim for a rich, non-reductive contextualization of musical practices as forms of social practice that both take place within the city and transgress it through trans-cultural and technological processes. In contrast to the managerial approach that seeks to impose order on the city, we argue for strengthening positions that consider music and musical practices as important for city-making itself.

Engaging the social and aesthetic forms of the metropolis requires many and complex methods, ranging from grounded theory to analysis of the actor's perspectives and lived-in worlds in scholarly monographs and artistic intervention and, finally, to substantial conceptual work about the urban paradigm and its transformations to the conditions of the endless city. With this volume we have taken the first steps toward developing approaches for a fuller understanding of such transformations and their impact on music and the city. As we join with scholars worldwide in such an approach, we look optimistically toward the potential and challenge of forging new, comparative tools to engage with the cultural labor that creates the metropolis, for which music plays such a fundamental role.

References

Ahuja, Ravi, and Christiane Brosius, eds. 2006. *Mumbai—Delhi—Kolkata: Annäherungen an die Megastädte Indiens.* Heidelberg: Draupadi.

Attali, Jacques. 1985. *Noise: The Political Economy of Music.* Translated by Brian Massumi. Minneapolis: University of Minnesota Press.

Beins, Burkhard, Christian Kesten, Gisela Nauck, and Andrea Neumann, eds. 2011. *echtzeitmusik berlin: selbstbestimmung einer szene/Self-Defining a Scene.* Hofheim: Wolke.

Berlin Music Commission. 2017. http://www.berlin-music-commission.de/178-0-Music-Industry-Facts.html (most recent access, 8 March 2017).

Bernau, Patrick. 2013. "Zu viele Opern in Deutschland." *Frankfurter Allgemeine Sonntagszeitung,* September 1.

Binas, Susanne, ed. 2000. *PopScriptum.* Vol. 5, *Sounds like Berlin.* Accessed July 26, 2017. http://www2.hu-berlin.de/fpm/popscrip/themen/pst05/pst05_02_04.html.

Bohlman, Philip V. 2013. *Revival and Reconciliation: Sacred Music in the Making of European Modernity.* Lanham, MD: Scarecrow.

Bohlman, Philip V., Sebastian Klotz, and Lars-Christian Koch. 2007. "Tales of Three Cities—Berlin, Chicago, and Kolkata at the Metropolitan Musical Crossroads." In *Cultural Diversity in the Urban Area: Explorations in Urban Ethnomusicology,* edited by Ursula Hemetek and Adelaida Reyes, 27–50. Vienna: Institut für Volksmusik-forschung und Ethnomusikologie.

Bull, Michael, and Les Back, eds. 2003. *The Auditory Culture Reader*. Oxford: Berg.

Burdett, Ricky, and Deyan Sudjic, eds. 2007. *The Endless City*. London: Phaidon.

Büttner, Thiess, and Eckhard Janeba. 2013. "City Competition for the Creative Class." In *CESifo Working Paper Series* 4417, Category 1: Public Finance (October).

DeNora, Tia. 2000. *Music in Everyday Life*. Cambridge: Cambridge University Press.

Eckardt, Frank. 2004. *Soziologie der Städte*. Bielefeld: transcript.

Friedrich, Malte. 2010. *Urbane Klänge: Popmusik und Imagination der Stadt*. Bielefeld: transcript.

Garcia, Luis-Manuel. 2011. "'Can You Feel It, Too?': Intimacy and Affect at Electronic Dance Music Events in Paris, Chicago, and Berlin." PhD diss., University of Chicago.

Gaupp, Lisa. 2012. "Musik in transkulturellen Kontexten: Eine kulturpolitische Analyse der Stadt Hamburg." In *Musik als Agens urbaner Lebenswelten: Musiksoziologische, musikethnologische und organologische Perspektiven*. Vol. 2, *Musik—Stadt: Traditionen und Perspektiven urbaner Musikkulturen*, edited by Sebastian Klotz, 148–57. Leipzig: Gudrun Schröder.

Geisler, Ulla, and Aland Patel, eds. 2009. *What Makes India Urban? Challenges towards Mobility, Infrastructure, Energy, and Perceptual Change*. Exhibition Catalogue, Galerie Aedes East. Berlin: Aedes a. P.

Girgert, Werner. 2013. "Städtevergleich: Die Künste und das Kapital." *Berliner Zeitung*, January 1.

Guggenheim. 2017. "BMW Guggenheim Lab." Accessed July 26. https://www.guggenheim. org/bmw-guggenheim-lab.

Heeg, Günther, and Markus Denzel. 2011. "Einleitung: Globalizing Areas, kulturelle Flexionen und die Herausforderung der Geisteswissenschaften." In *Globalizing Areas, kulturelle Flexionen und die Herausforderung der Geisteswissenschaften*, edited by Heeg and Denzel, 7–14. Stuttgart: Franz Steiner.

Heinen, Christina M. 2013. *"Tief in Neukölln": Soundkulturen zwischen Improvisation und Gentrifizierung in einem Berliner Bezirk*. Bielefeld: transcript.

Holert, Tom. 2009. "Digitale Ich-Maschine." Last modified January 22, 2009, accessed July 26, 2017. http://jungle-world.com/artikel/2009/04/32482.html.

Kleilein, Doris, Anne Kockelkorn, Gesine Pagels, and Carsten Stabenow, eds. 2008. *Tuned City: Zwischen Klang- und Raumspekulation/Between Sound and Space Speculation*. Idstein: Kookbooks.

Klotz, Sebastian. 2006. "Negotiate, Review the Situation: Musik und Urbanismus." In *Soziale Horizonte von Musik: Ein kommentiertes Lesebuch zur Musiksoziologie*, edited by Christian Kaden and Karsten Mackensen, 324–46. Kassel: Bärenreiter.

———. 2011. "'Pavarotti do brasil': Musikanthropologische Lektüren von *baile funk* im Zeichen kultureller Flexionen." In *Globalizing Areas, kulturelle Flexionen und die Herausforderung der Geisteswissenschaften*, edited by Günther Heeg and Markus A. Denzel, 135–48. Stuttgart: Franz Steiner.

Sebastian Klotz

———, ed. 2012. *Musik als Agens urbaner Lebenswelten: Musiksoziologische, musikethnologische und organologische Perspektiven.* Vol. 2, *Musik—Stadt: Traditionen und Perspektiven urbaner Musikkulturen.* Leipzig: Gudrun Schröder.

Löw, Martina. 2008. *Soziologie der Städte.* Frankfurt a. M.: Suhrkamp.

Puneet, Simar, ed. 2010. *HUB: Indian Electronica 2010.* New Delhi: Goethe Institute/Max Mueller Bhavan.

Rapp, Tobias. 2009. *Lost and Sound: Berlin, Techno und der Easyjetset.* Frankfurt a. M.: Suhrkamp.

Rode, Philipp, Julie Wagner, Richard Brown, Rit Chandra, and Jayaraj Sundaresan. 2008. *Integrated City Making—Governance, Planning, and Transport.* London: Urban Age Programme, London School of Economics and Political Science.

Rüther, Tobias. 2014. *Heroes: David Bowie and Berlin.* Translated by Anthony Matthews. London: Reaktion Books.

Scharenberg, Albert, and Ingo Bader, eds. 2005. *Der Sound der Stadt: Musikindustrie und Subkultur in Berlin.* Münster: Westfälisches Dampfboot.

Shepherd, John, and Peter Wicke. 1997. *Music and Cultural Theory.* Cambridge: Polity.

Skórska, Monika J., and Robert C. Kloosterman. 2012. "Performing on the Global Stage: Exploring the Relationship between Finance and Arts in Global Cities." *GaWC Research Bulletin* 412, last modified October 1, 2012, accessed July 26, 2017. http://www.lboro.ac.uk/gawc/rb/rb412.html.

The Underground Kolkata. 2008. *The Underground Kolkata: The Best of What's Next.* Vol. 1. Saregama Soul of India B01A7U58I6, compact disc.

Urban Age. 2017. "Urban Age." Accessed July 26. https://www.urban-age.net.

Vogt, Sabine. 2005. *Clubräume—Freiräume: Musikalische Lebensentwürfe Jugendlicher in den Jugendkulturen Berlins.* Kassel: Bärenreiter.

Wicke, Peter. 2001. "Sound-Technologien und Körper-Metamorphosen: Das Populäre in der Musik des 20. Jahrhunderts." In *Handbuch der Musik im 20. Jahrhunderts.* Vol. 8, *Rock- und Popmusik,* edited by Peter Wicke and Monika Bloss, 11–60. Laaber: Laaber.

Contributors

Abhishek Adhikary is a music scholar and sitarist, whose lineage emphasizes spirituality and dexterity, thereby connecting him to the Senee Maihar Gharānā. His lineage starts with Pandit Haricharandas Swami of Varanasi and extends to vocal and instrumental traditions in Kolkata. He studied at the Rabindra Bharati University of Kolkata, taking both his bachelor's and master's degrees before embarking on PhD studies dedicated to the history of the sitar. Among his many awards are a National Scholarship in Sitar from the Indian Ministry of Culture and the title, Sur Mani, from the Sur Sringar Samsad of Mumbai.

Philip V. Bohlman is Ludwig Rosenberger Distinguished Service Professor in Jewish History in the Department of Music at the University of Chicago, and Honorary Professor at the University of Music, Drama and Media in Hanover. His wide-ranging research examines the intersections of music with religion, colonialism, and racism. An active performer, he is Artistic Director of The New Budapest Orpheum Society. His most recent publications include *Song Loves the Masses* (with Johann Gottfried Herder; University of California Press, 2017) and *Wie sängen wir SEINEN Gesang auf dem Boden der Fremde!* (Lit, forthcoming).

One of the leading jazz vibraphonists in the world, **Christopher Dell** has performed widely with different large and small jazz ensembles and taught at various universities in Germany, notably at the University of the Arts in Berlin and at the HafenCity University in Hamburg. His teaching, performance, and publication combine many different approaches to everyday life in urban settings. His intellectual and musical interests converge in his studies of improvisation as a condition of city life, for example in his books, *Tacit Urbanism* (Post Editions, 2009) and *Replaycity* (Jovis, 2011).

Patrick Lal Sanjiv Ghose is a musician and a journalist, actively involved in many different areas of the West Bengal popular music scene. He has written widely about many genres of popular music in India, from folk and traditional repertories, such as the music of the Bauls, to international rock styles. He is especially interested in the intersection of traditional Bengali elements with global pop music. His interest in the sustainability of musical practices in Kolkata and urban India led him to collaborations with Christopher Dell in the project "Kolkata Monodosis."

Rehanna Kheshgi is Assistant Professor of Music at St. Olaf College. She is currently pursuing research on music and politics in the Bodoland tribal sovereignty movement in Assam, India as a 2017–18 Fulbright Scholar. Her research focuses on gender, sexuality, on the body at the intersections of popular, folk, and sacred music, and on dance performance in India, and has received support from the American Institute of Indian Studies, the American Association for University Women, and the Institute of Sacred Music at Yale University, where she was a 2016–17 Postdoctoral Fellow. Her first book is entitled *Sounding Rural Modernities: Gender, Performance, and the Body in Assam, India.*

Sebastian Klotz is Professor of Transcultural Musicology and Historical Anthropology of Music at the Humboldt University of Berlin. He was a researcher at the Istituto Storico Germanico in Rome and a Bosch Fellow at the University of Chicago. He held the professorship in Systematic Musicology at the University of Leipzig and is co-curator of the Lautarchiv at the Humboldt University. His research interests range from fifteenth-century dance to theories of musical action to cultures of musical knowledge. In 2017, he initiated the Erich von Hornbostel Audio Emergence Lab (HAEL) at the Humboldt University. He has published recent research addressing the interplay of music and geography in "Patterns of Consciousness" (*Atodya*, 2014).

Lars-Christian Koch is Head of the Department of Ethnomusicology and the Berlin Phonogram Archive at the Museum of Ethnology in Berlin, Professor for Ethnomusicology at the University of Cologne, and Honorary

Professor for Ethnomusicology at the University of the Arts in Berlin. He has served as Visiting Professor at the University of Vienna and at the University of Chicago. His research focuses on the theory and practice of North Indian raga music, organology with special focus on instrument manufacturing, Buddhist music, popular music and urban culture, historical recordings, and music archaeology. His publications include *Sitar and Surbahar Manufacturing: The Tradition of Kanailal & Brother, Kolkata* (SMB, 2011) and *My Heart Sings: Die Lieder Rabindranath Tagores zwischen Tradition und Moderne* (Lit, 2011).

The urban sociologist, **Rolf Lindner**, is Professor Emeritus at the Humboldt University of Berlin, where he spent most of his career at the Institute for European Ethnology. His research led him to guest professorships and fellowships throughout the world, including Chicago and Vienna. He has consistently drawn upon theory and method in cultural studies and urban studies, applying them to diverse areas, from the understanding of the modern European city and the cultural history of sports. Among his most recent publications are the monographs, *Walks on the Wild Side: Eine Geschichte der Stadtforschung* (Campus, 2004) and *Berlin, absolute Stadt: Eine kleine Anthropologie der großen Stadt* (Kadmos, 2016).

Kaley Mason is Assistant Professor of Music at Lewis and Clark College in Portland, Oregon. His research is broadly concerned with the interplay of creative agency and material constraints in contemporary musical experience. This is the focus of his first book, *The Labor of Music: South Indian Performers and Cultural Mobility* (OUP, forthcoming). His current India-centered project tracks the relations between art and activism in song, from the music of political theater and film to alternative rock. He is also interested in how singer-songwriters participate in debates over national belonging and intercultural empathy in the Francophonie.

Bruno Nettl spent most of his career teaching at the University of Illinois, where he is now professor emeritus of music and anthropology. His field experience has been with the Blackfoot people of Montana, the classical music culture of Iran, and Karnatak music. In recent times he has devoted himself to the study of the history of ethnomusicology. His best-known books are *The Study of Ethnomusicology* (3rd ed., 2015); *Heartland Excursions: Ethnomusicological Reflections on Schools of Music* (1995), *The Radif of Persian Music* (rev. ed., 1992); *Nettl's Elephant: On the History of Ethnomusicology* (2010), and *Becoming an Ethnomusicologist* (2013).

Patrick Primavesi has served as Professor of Theater Studies at the University of Leipzig since 2008. His research and teaching on theater has range widely over topics as diverse as the history of theater ca. 1800, forms of theater in the public sphere, theater as a form and force of intervention in modern society, and the pedagogy of new forms of theater for youth. His book publications include *Das andere Fest: Theater und Öffentlichkeit um 1800* (Campus, 2008) and *Kommentar, Übersetzung, Theater in Walter Benjamins frühen Schriften* (Stroemfest, 1998).

Sonja Rippert studied musicology at the University of Leipzig from 2006 to 2010. During her studies she was active as a participant-observer in the German electronic music and dance scene, leading to a thesis on the musical analysis of EDM tracks. In her roles as scholar and participant in the EDM scene she contributed as both insider and outsider to the Alexander von Humboldt TransCoop project. Upon completion of her music studies she returned to her home city of Berlin, where she completed a law degree in 2016. She currently works as a lawyer for a firm specializing in media and intellectual property rights.

Reimar Volker studied music education and performing arts at the University of the Arts in Berlin, thereafter taking his PhD in musicology at the Technical University of Berlin. A saxophonist, he has been active as a performer of jazz, chamber, and orchestral music. After an early career in publishing and as an administrator at the Einstein Forum in Potsdam, he embarked on a career for the Goethe Institute, which led to directorships in Cairo, Kolkata, and Seoul, where he was Head of Cultural Programs for East Asia. He is currently Director of the Goethe Institute in Istanbul.

INDEX

The letters *f* and *n* following a page number denote figures and footnotes.

Berlin Wall, 45, 56, 79
bi-musicality, 233
Blackfoot music, 33–34
blues, 11, 47–48, 91, 221
blogs, 37, 91, 93, 96–97
Bohlman, Philip V., xvii–xix, 7, 10, 13–17, 157–80, 245–48
Bollywood, 65, 94, 212, 220, 244, 246
brass bands, 14–15
Brecht, Bertolt, 70, 126, 136, 147
Burman, Sandip, 219–39

cabaret, 12, 173–74
cafés, 135, 137, 220–21, 233, 236–37
capitalism, 51n, 57, 81, 220, 223, 227, 236; late, 52, 71. *See also* neoliberalism
Cardiff, Janet, 125
Chaudhuri, Amit, 13, 15, 47–49, 66–73
Chicago. *See under* cities
Chicago Musical Instruments, 197–98
Chicago school of sociology, 40–42
Chicago Symphony Orchestra, 263
Christian, Charlie, 197
chronotope, 49–50
cinema. *See* film
cities: Aleppo, 168; Amsterdam, 143; Athens, 83, 143, 173; Bangalore, 165, 266; Basra, 168; Bengaluru, 91, 244; Berlin, 1–2, 4, 6n, 7–8, 11–12, 13, 39, 41, 43–45, 47–75, 79–88, 137–50, 161–63, 171–74, 256, 259–65, 267; Brussels, 141, 143; Buenos Aires, 144–45; Cape Town, 143; Chicago, 1–2, 4, 9–11, 50, 53–54, 64, 64n, 71, 149, 161, 171, 197–98, 205–6, 208–9, 213–14, 217–22, 226–29, 231, 235f, 236, 239, 243–54, 256, 259–65; Cochin (Kochi), 168; Cologne, 39, 162; Copenhagen, 143–44; Delhi, 9, 17, 102, 111, 179, 185n, 208, 211, 213–14, 231; Dhaka, 184n, 187; Dublin, 143; Durgapur, 9, 219, 229–31; Frankfurt, 126n; Groningen, 143; Guwahati, 9, 203, 207–11, 213–14; Hamburg, 39, 169; Heidelberg, 143; Helsinki, 143; Jerusalem, 155–58, 160–62, 165, 170, 173–75, 177; Johannesburg, 266n, 267; Kalamazoo, 197–98; Kolkata (Calcutta), 1–2, 4–12, 13–25, 37, 41–42, 47–48, 50–51, 54–55, 62, 63f, 65–66, 69f, 71, 86–87, 89–103, 107–21, 123–51, 162, 165–72, 175, 179–202, 208, 211, 223, 226, 229–30, 243–54, 256, 259–66; London, 9, 35, 55, 205–6, 208–9, 212–14, 224, 233, 266n, 267; Los Angeles, 231; Lucknow, 225; Mannheim, 143; Mecca, 244; Mexico City, 267; Minneapolis, 143; Moscow, 143; Mumbai (Bombay), 91, 102, 111,

KlangKulturStudien / SoundCultureStudies
Lars-Christian Koch und Raimund Vogels

Philip V. Bohlman
Wie sängen wir Seinen Gesang auf dem Boden der Fremde!
Jüdische Musik des Aschkenas zwischen Tradition und Moderne
Bd. 11, 2018, 400 S., 34,90 €, br., ISBN 978-3-643-13574-2

Ricarda Kopal
Herbert von Karajan
Eine musikethnologische Annäherung an einen „klassischen" Musikstar
Bd. 10, 2015, 244 S., 29,90 €, br., ISBN 978-3-643-12731-0

Lidia Guzy
Marginalised Music
Music, Religion and Politics from Western Odisha/India
Bd. 8, 2013, 264 S., 29,90 €, br., ISBN 978-3-643-90272-6

Raymond Ammann
Sounds of Secrets
Field Notes on Ritual Music and Musical Instruments on the Islands of Vanuatu
vol. 7, 2012, 320 pp., 31,90 €, br., ISBN-CH 978-3-643-80130-2

Diana Brenscheidt gen. Jost
Shiva Onstage
Uday Shankar's Company of Hindu Dancers and Musicians in Europe and the United States, 1931 – 38
Bd. 6, 2011, 320 S., 29,90 €, br., ISBN 978-3-643-90108-8

Lars-Christian Koch
My Heart Sings
Die Lieder Rabindranath Tagores zwischen Tradition und Moderne
Bd. 5, 2012, 520 S., 54,90 €, br., ISBN 978-3-643-10800-5

Nicole Manon Lehmann
Sama und die ‚Schönheit'im Kathak
Nordindischer Tanz und seine ihn konstituierenden Konzepte am Beispiel der Lucknow-gharana
Bd. 4, 2010, 672 S., 49,90 €, br., ISBN 978-3-643-10252-2

Florian Carl
Berlin/Accra
Music, Travel, and the Production of Space
Bd. 3, 2009, 208 S., 29,90 €, br., ISBN 978-3-8258-1905-7

Made Mantle Hood
Triguna
A Hindu-Balinese Philosophy for Gamelan Gong Gede Music
Bd. 2, 2011, 496 S., 49,90 €, br., ISBN 978-3-8258-1230-0

Raimund Vogels
The big Drum was Beaten and the Force Moved East
Islamic Court Music in Northeast Nigeria
Bd. 1, 2018, 360 S., 29,90 €, br., ISBN 3-8258-9698-6

LIT Verlag Berlin – Münster – Wien – Zürich – London
Auslieferung Deutschland / Österreich / Schweiz: siehe Impressumsseite